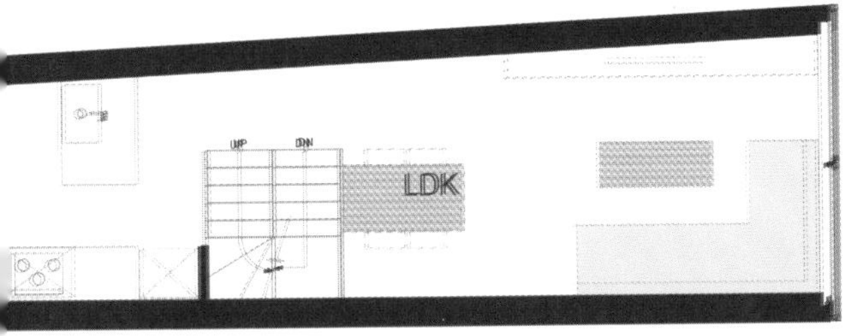
LDK

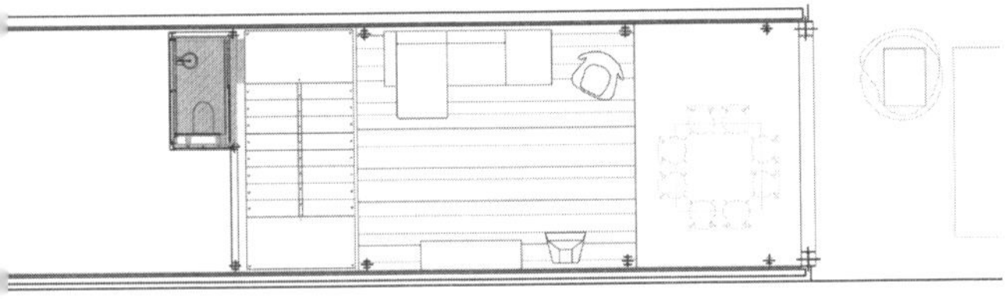

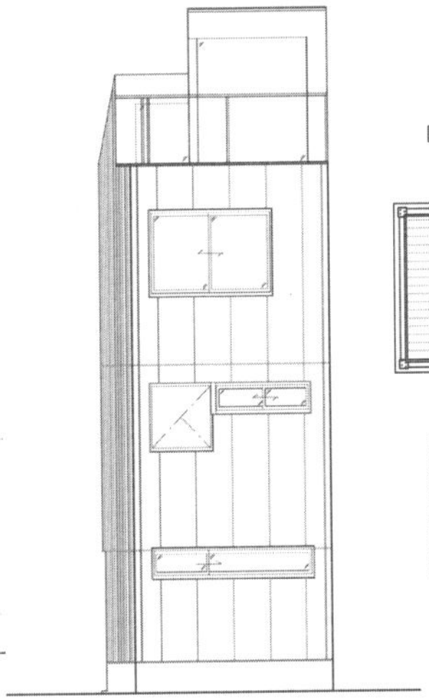

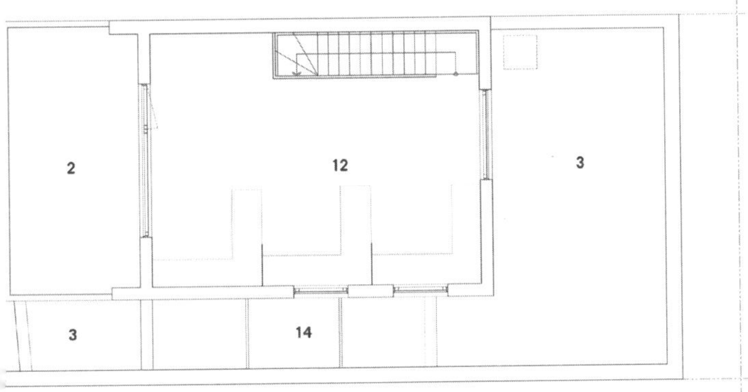
2
12
3
3
14

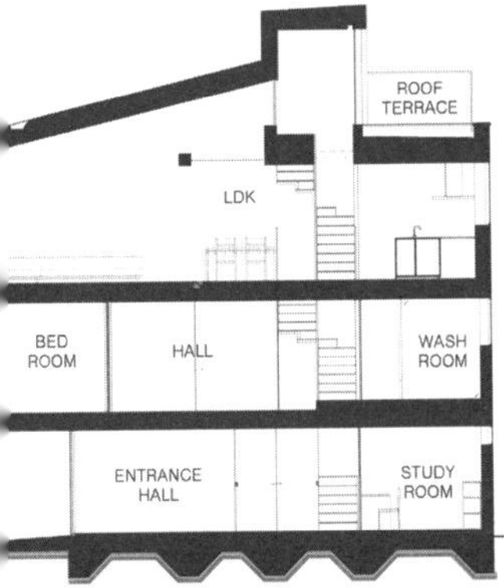
ROOF TERRACE
LDK
BED ROOM
HALL
WASH ROOM
ENTRANCE HALL
STUDY ROOM

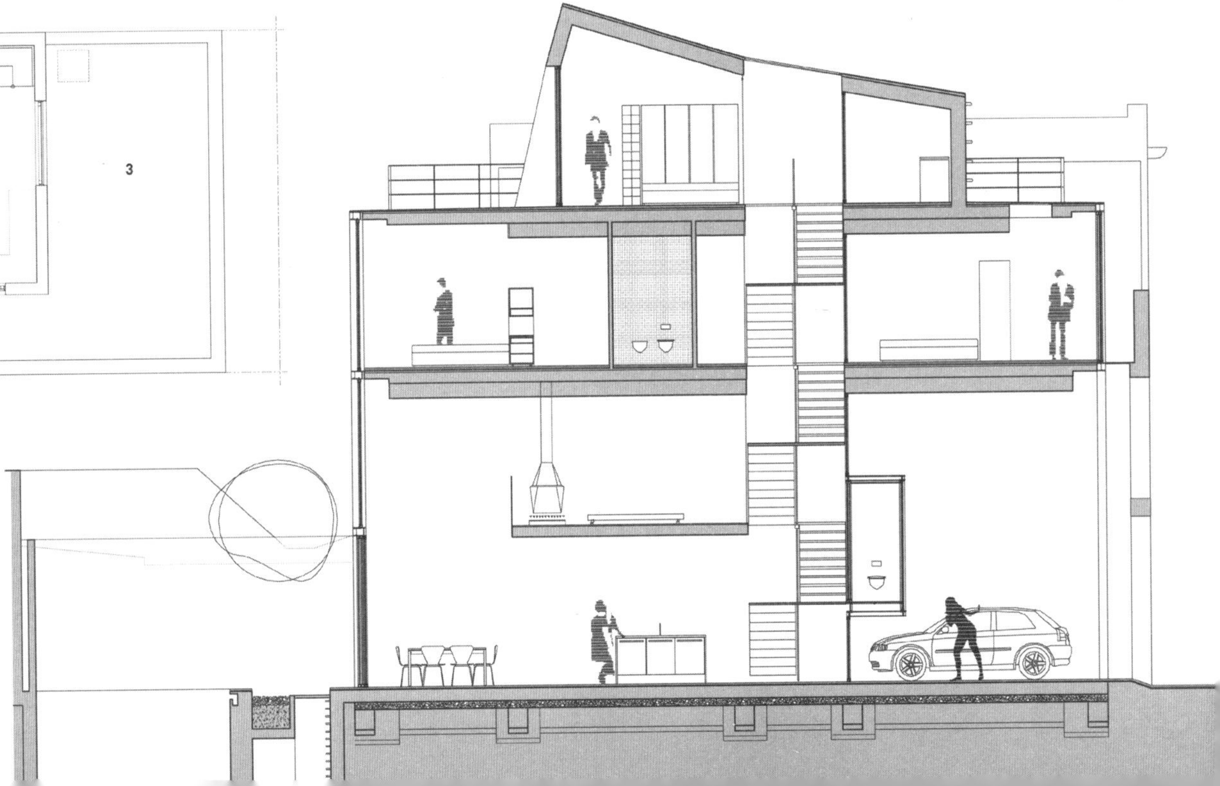

NEW TWONHOUSE PLANS

Editor, concept, and project director
Anna Minguet

Layout
Eva Minguet (equipo editorial Monsa)

Cover design
Eva Minguet

INSTITUTO MONSA DE EDICIONES
Gravina 43 (08930)
Sant Adrià de Besòs
Barcelona (Spain)
Tlf. +34 93 381 00 50
www.monsa.com
monsa@monsa.com

Visit our official online store!
www.monsashop.com

Follow us!
Facebook: @monsashop
Instagram: @monsapublications

ISBN: 978-84-16500-98-7
D.L. B 27097-2018
Printed by Impuls 45

NEW TOWNHOUSE PLANS

monsa

Introduction

New Townhouse Plans contains more than 250 floor and elevation plans, as well as constructive details of 38 housing projects, perfect constructions in tiny pieces of ground of the urban area of the city.

Through these projects, solutions are shown to the construction difficulties that arise in tight plots with incredible results, based on the use of space and light, using curtain walls, facades that open to the street, or on the contrary, lead out to beautiful gardens and interior patios... a dream come true.

New Townhouse Plans contiene más de 250 planos de plantas, secciones, bocetos y alzados, así como detalles constructivos de un total de 38 originales proyectos de viviendas entremedianeras, construcciones perfectas para esos minúsculos y extraños solares del centro urbano de cualquier ciudad.

A través de estos proyectos, se muestran soluciones a las dificultades de construcción que surgen en solares ajustados con unos resultados increibles, basados en el aprovechamiento del espacio y la luz, utilizando muros cortina, fachadas que se abren completamente a la calle, o que por el contrario, se cierran hacia preciosos jardines y patios interiores, así como azoteas convertidas en terrazas, todo un sueño hecho realidad.

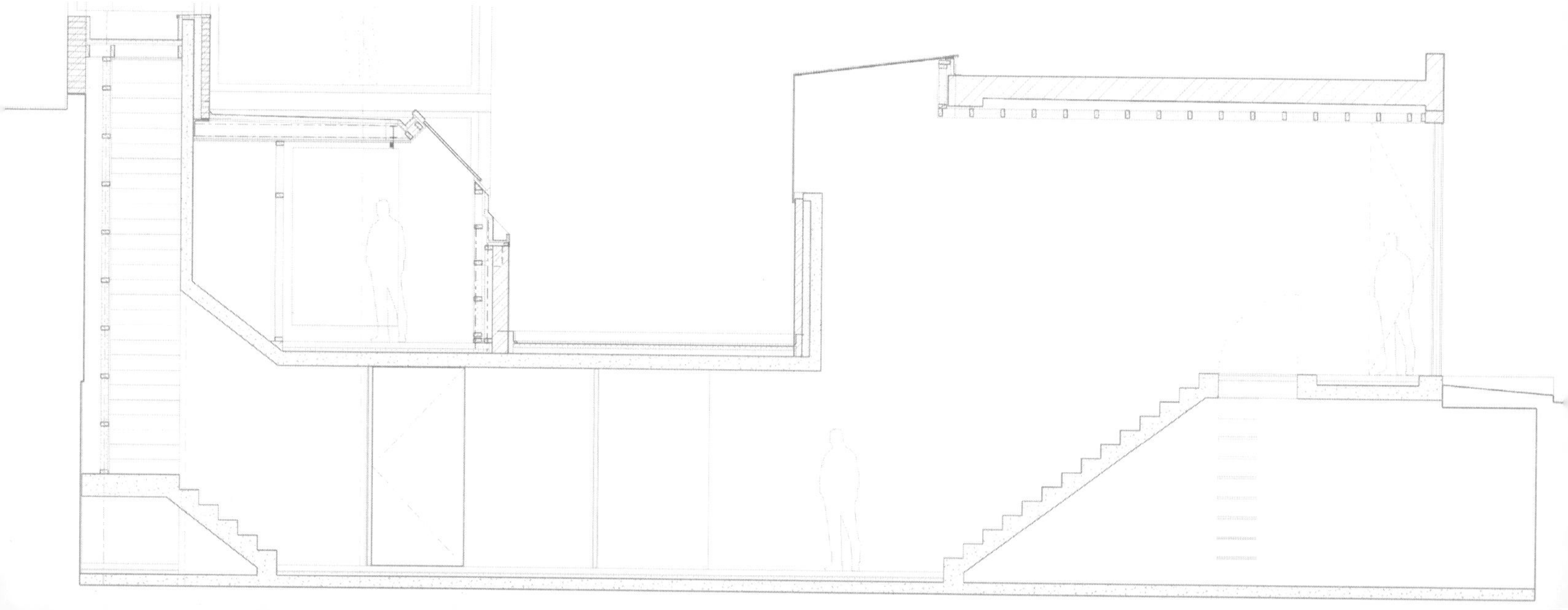

Projects

8 3x9 House
10 Augustrasse 26a
14 Cloe House
18 Love House
20 T House
24 The Anderson House
28 Living Space in Molins de Rei
32 A house Between Party Walls in Lloret
36 Chatou House
38 House in Mosman
40 The Vertical House
44 House in Sant Sadurní
46 Minimum House
48 MR House
52 House T
56 Tsuchida House
60 F House
62 Living Space for Two Artists
66 Duplex on Chattanooga Street
70 Gillipsi Airaghi
74 House in Russian Hill
78 Martin House
82 Alexandra Residence
86 Kohler House
90 Two Duplexes in Campo del Principe
94 Stacked House
98 Bioclimatic Living Space in San Isidro
102 Plastic House
106 50 Pilgrim's Lane
110 Flag House
114 Jyu-Bako
118 House in Uehonmachi
122 Weiss House
126 AYM House
130 Fong House
132 PML House
136 Katendrecht House
138 To Catch a Breeze

3x9 House

a21 studio
Ho Chi Minh City, Vietnam
Photos © Hiroyuki Oki

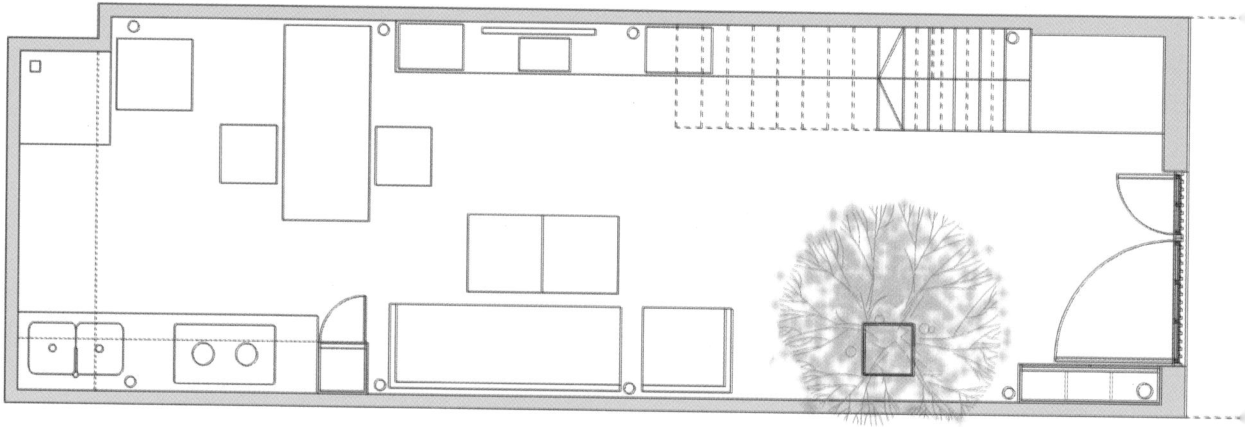

Ground floor plan
Planta baja

Exploded drawing
Vista en despiece

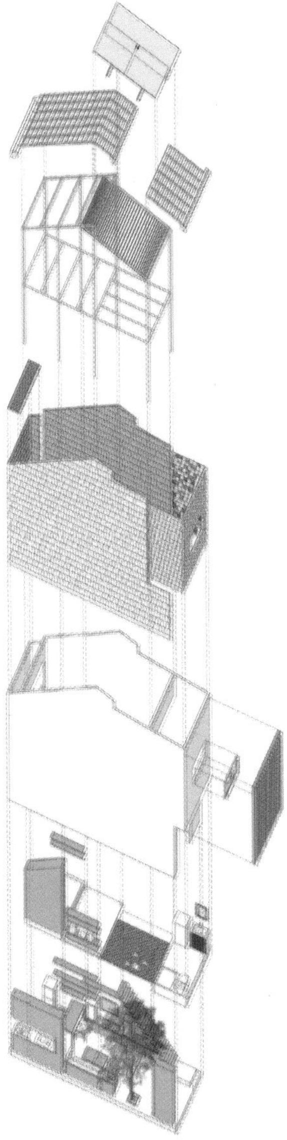

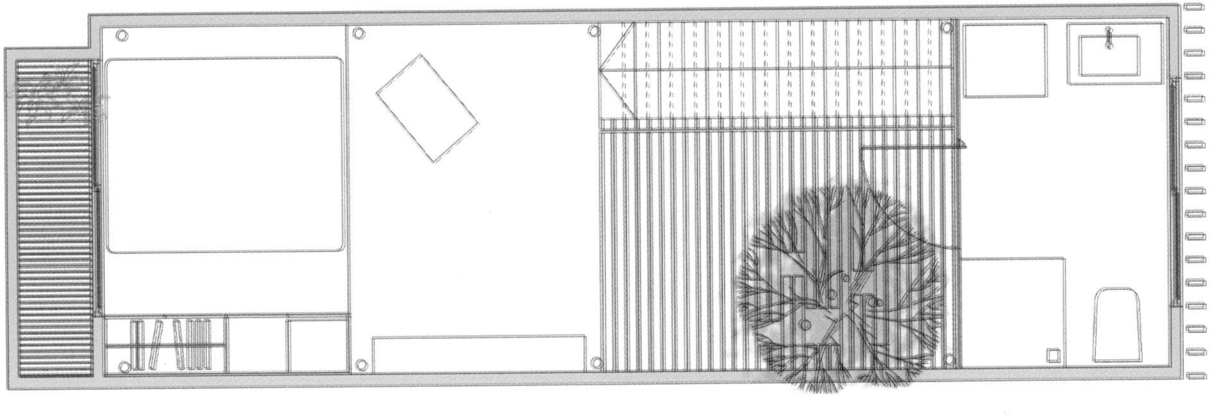

Second floor plan
Planta segunda

Augustrasse 26a

Ebers Architekten
Berlin, Germany
Photos © Linus Lintner

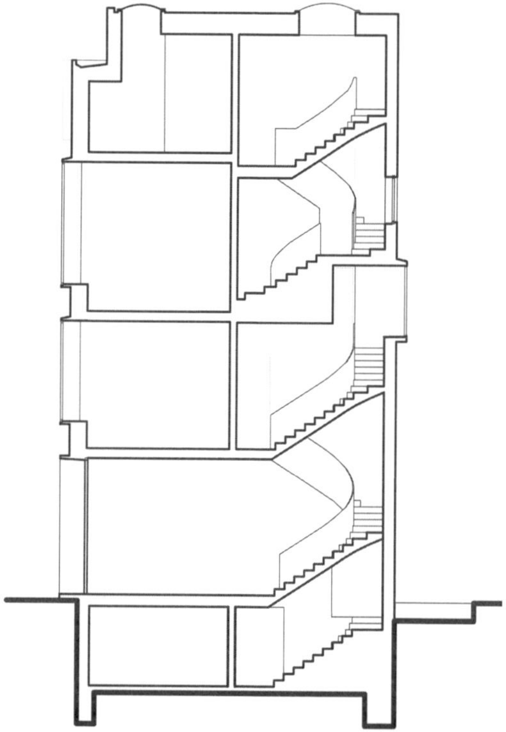

Longitudinal section
Sección longitudinal

Longitudinal section
Sección longitudinal

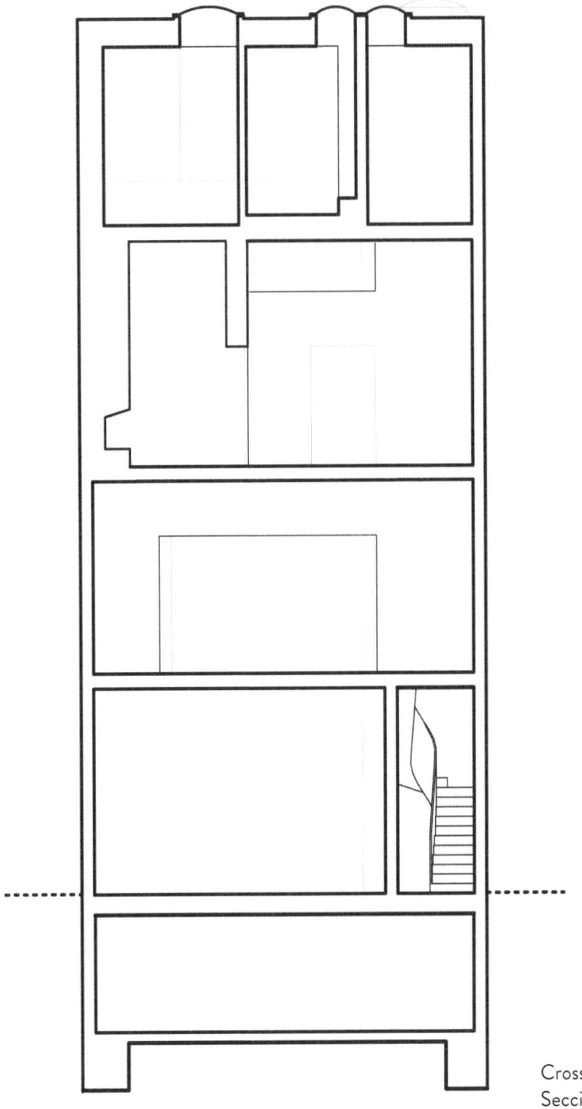

Cross section A
Sección transversal A

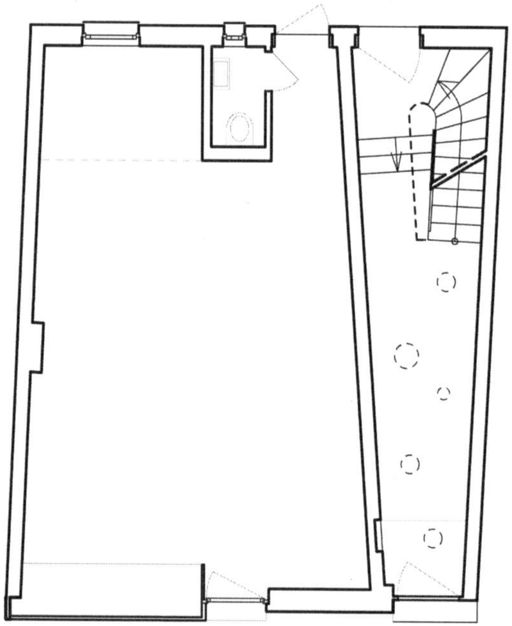

Ground floor plan
Planta baja

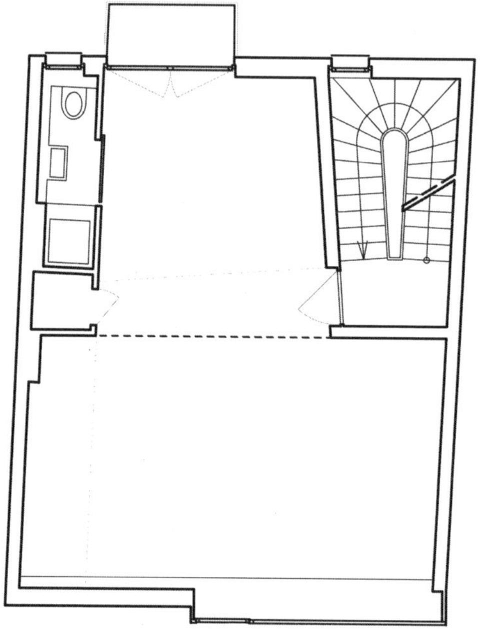

First floor plan
Primera planta

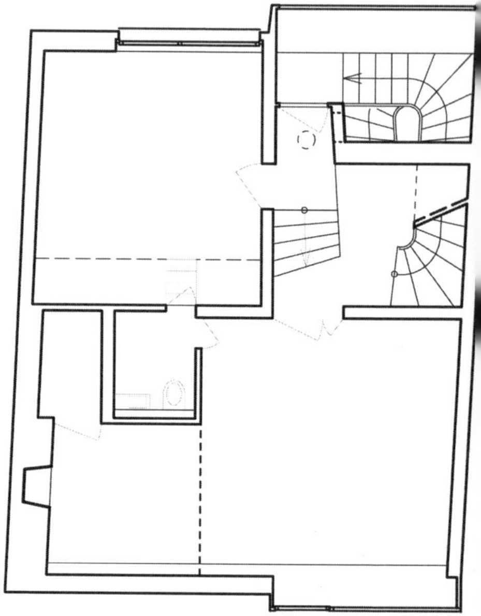

Second floor plan
Segunda planta

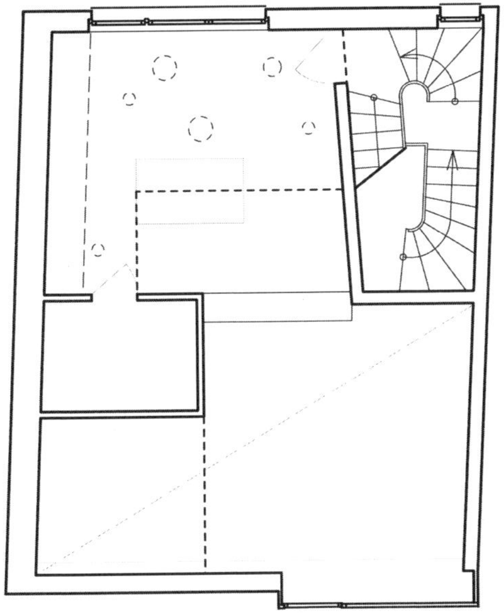

Third floor plan
Tercera planta

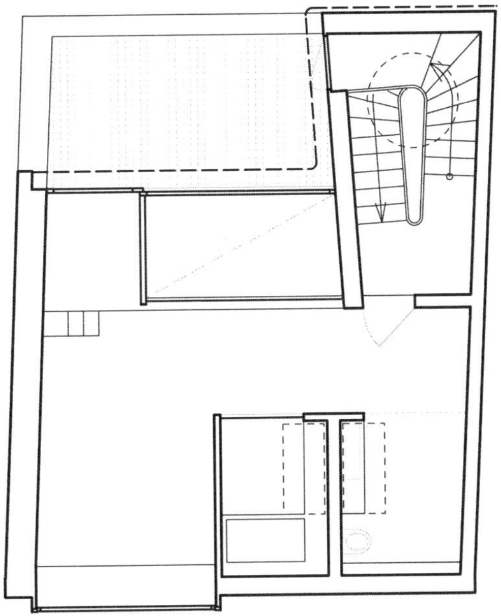

Attic floor plan
Planta del ático

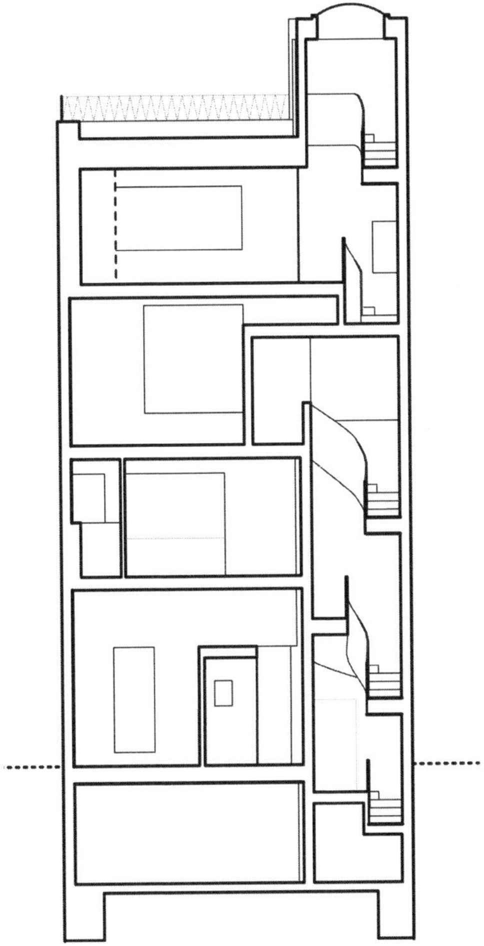

Cross section C
Sección transversal C

Cloe House

Carles Gelpí I Arroyo
Barcelona, Spain
Photos © Eugeni Pons

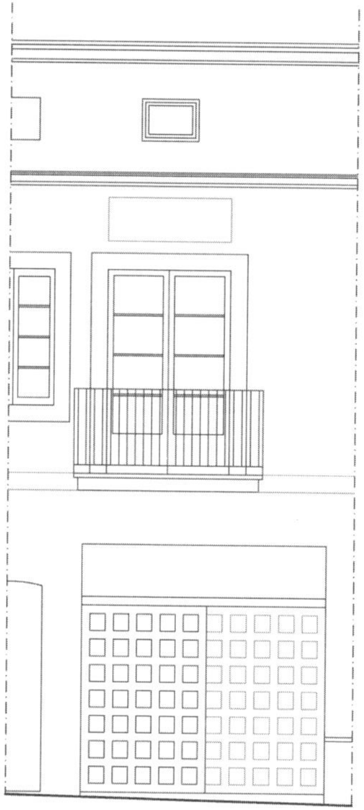

Front elevation
Alzado frontal

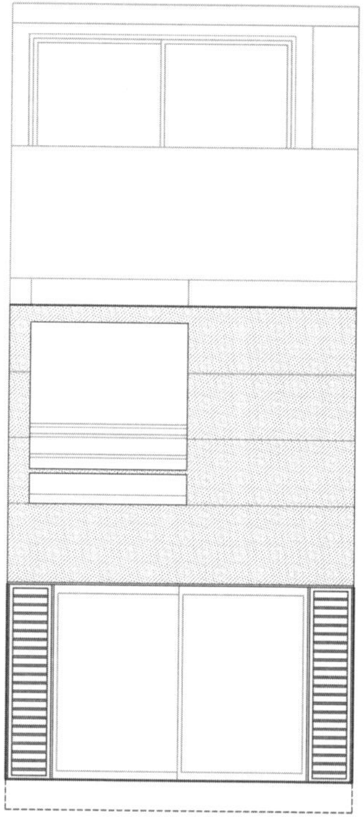

Rear elevation
Alzado posterior

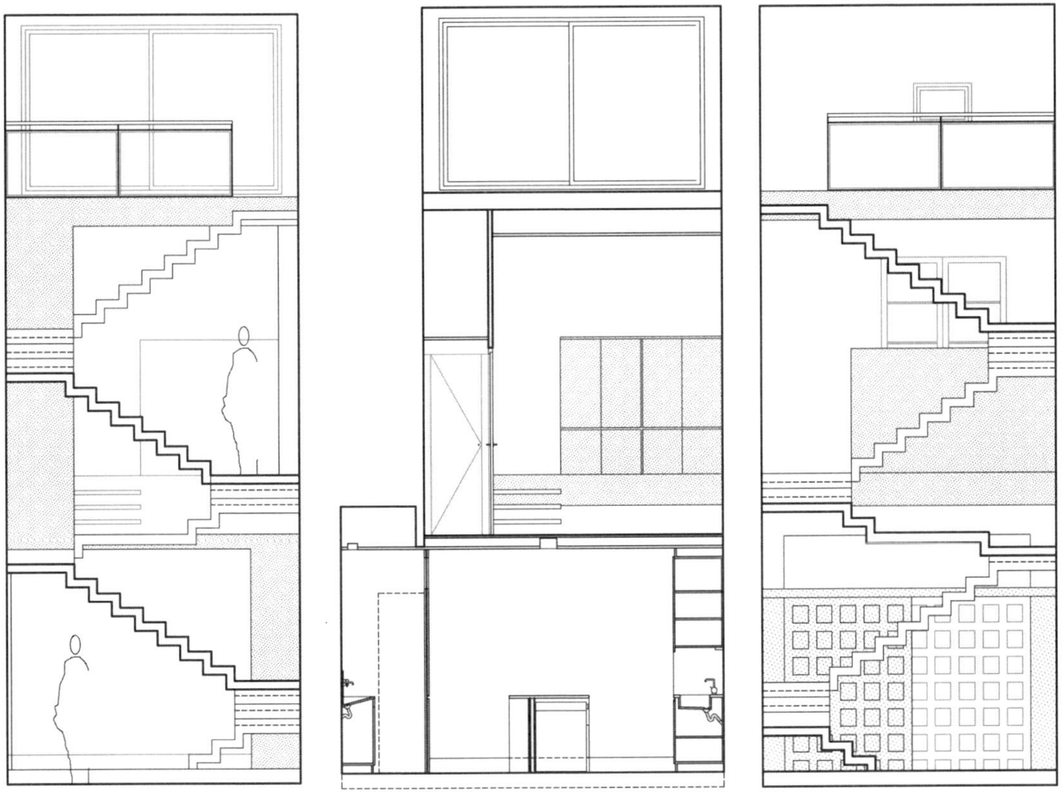

Cross sections
Sección transversal

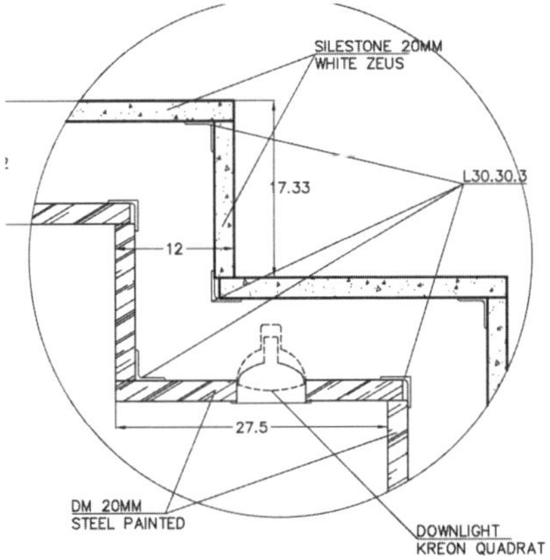

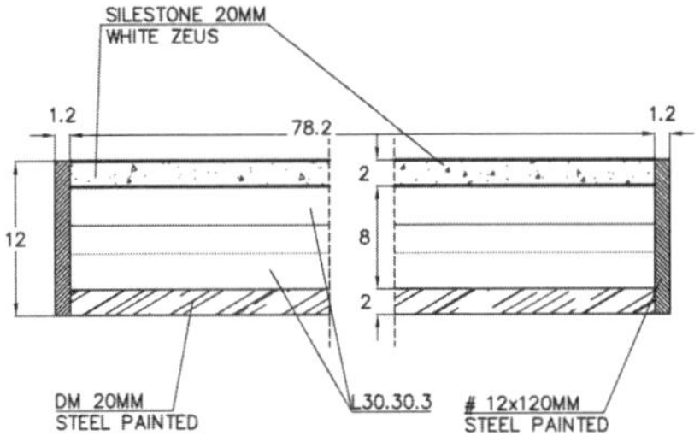

Ladder detail
Detalle de escalera

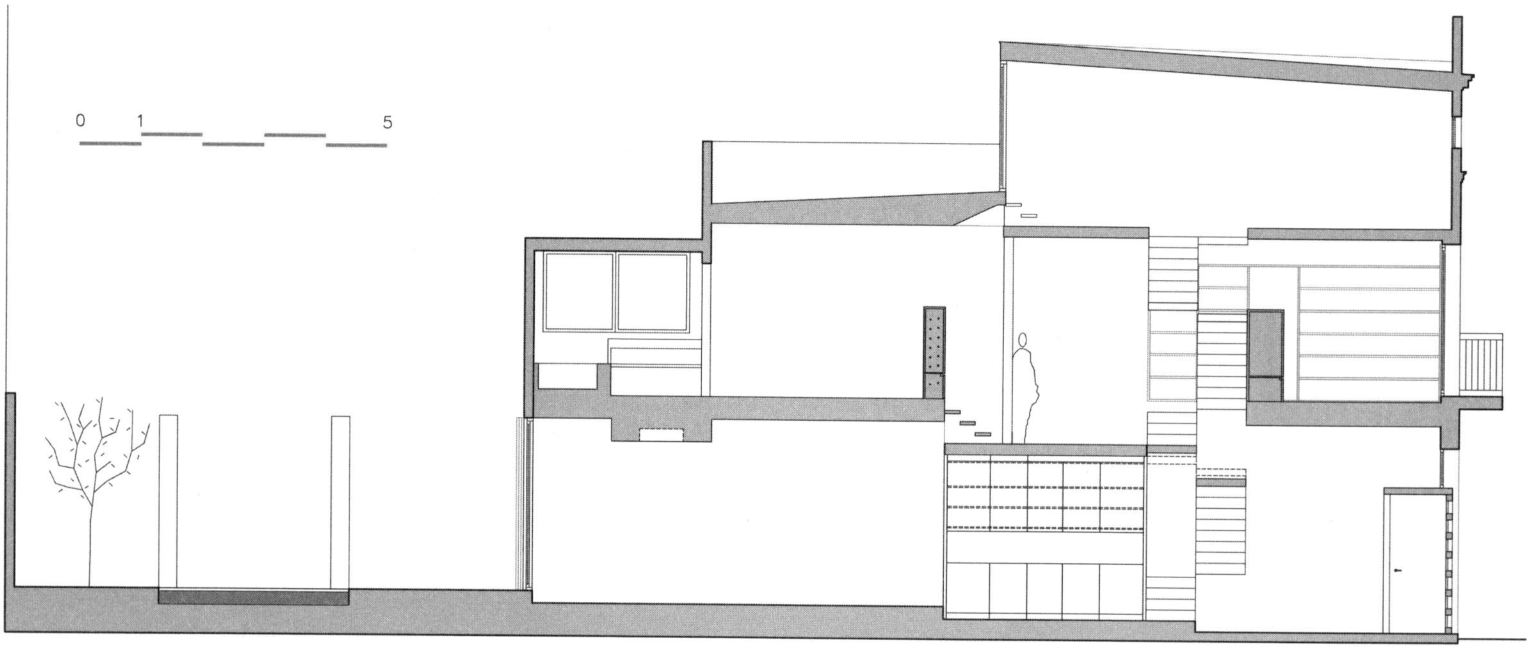

Longitudinal section
Sección longitudinal

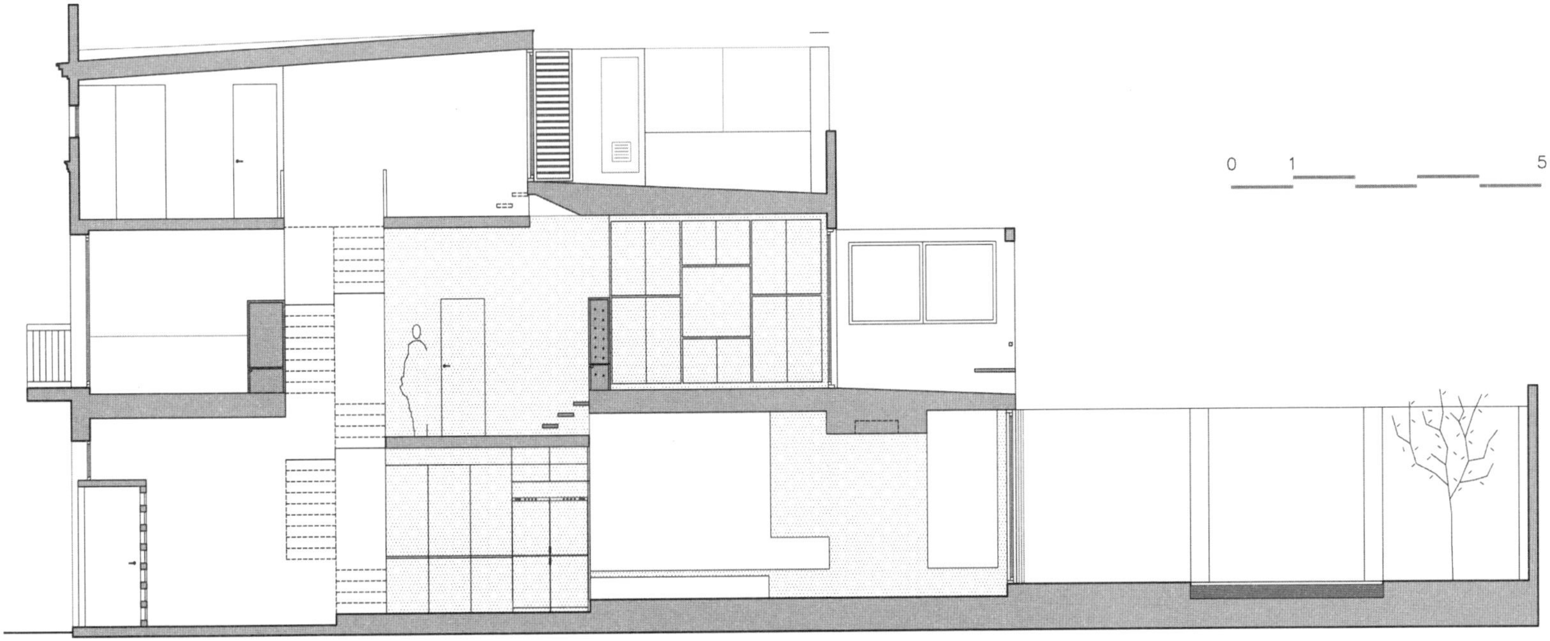

Longitudinal section
Sección longitudinal

Love House

Takeshi Hosaka Architects
Yokohama (Japan)
© Masao Nishikawa, Koji Fujii / Nacása & Partners Inc.

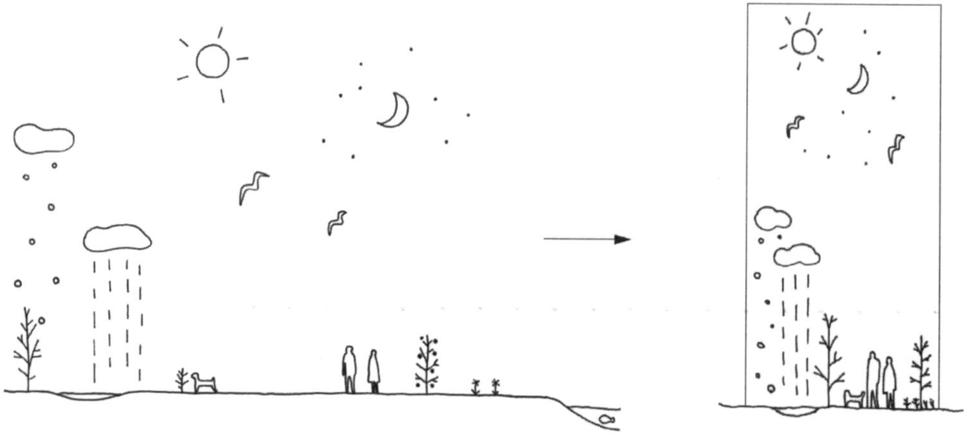

Conceptual development sketch
Boceto del desarrollo conceptual

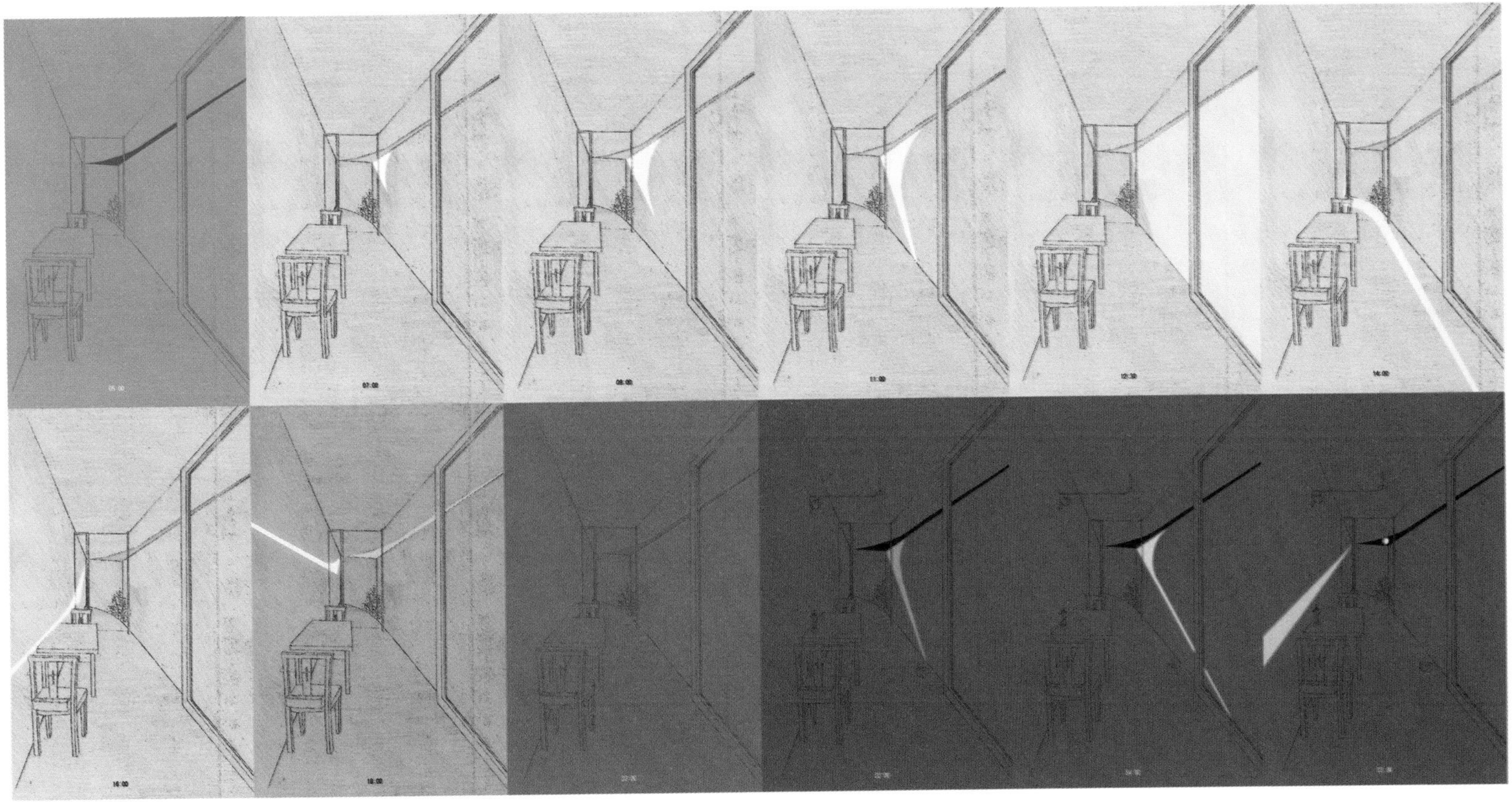

Illumination patterns sketch
Boceto del sistema de iluminación

T House

Stefania Rinaldi / Studio Rinaldi
New York (NY), USA
Photos © Wade Zimmerman

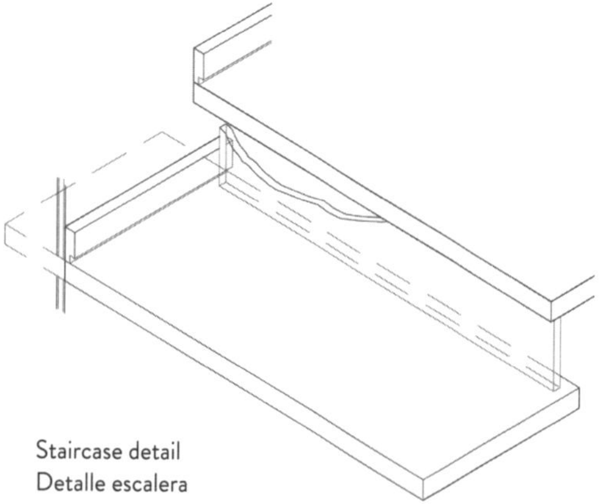

Staircase detail
Detalle escalera

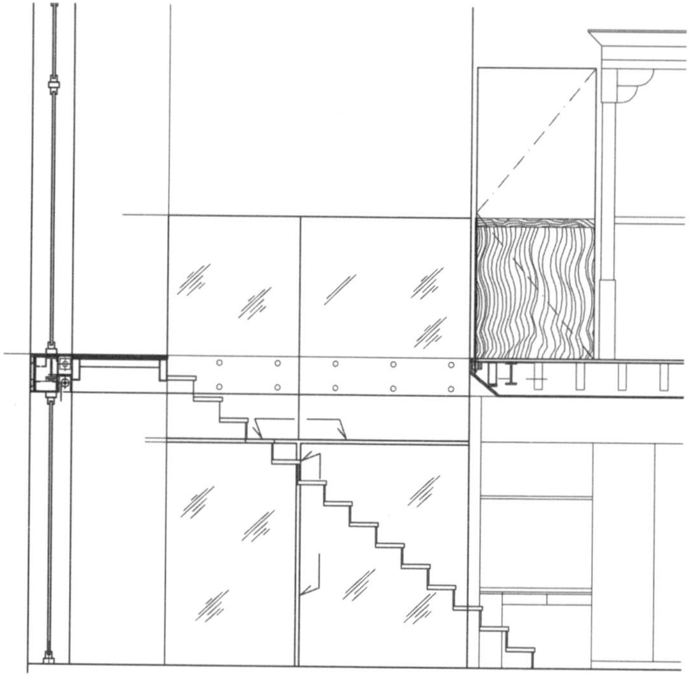

Staircase section
Sección de la escalera

Street elevation
Alzado calle

Rear elevation
Alzado posterior

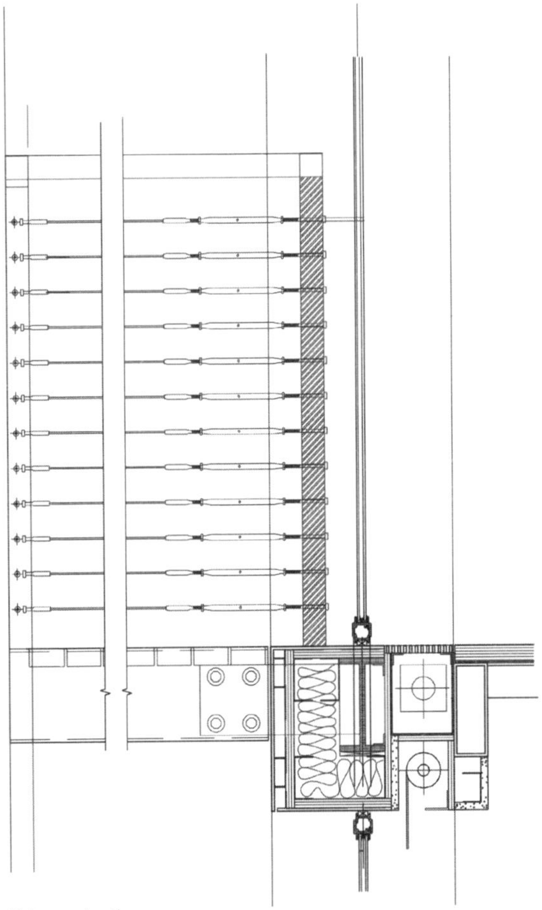

Balcony detail
Detalle del balcón

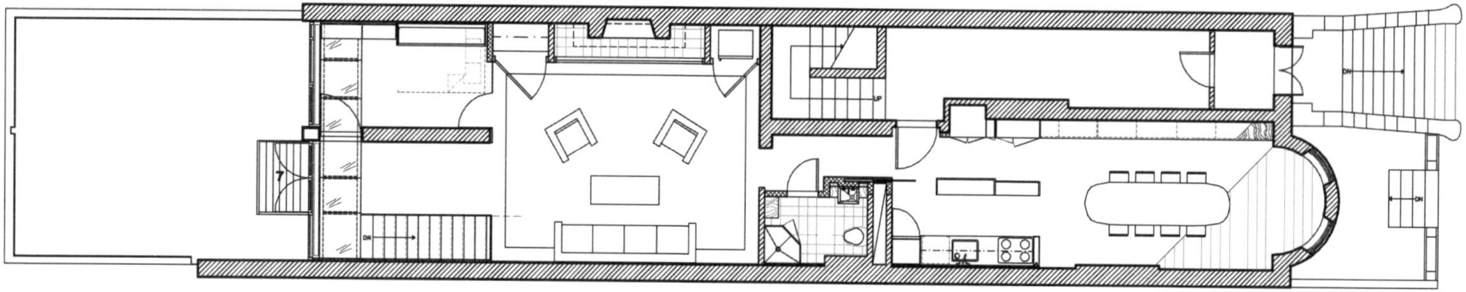

First floor plan
Primera planta

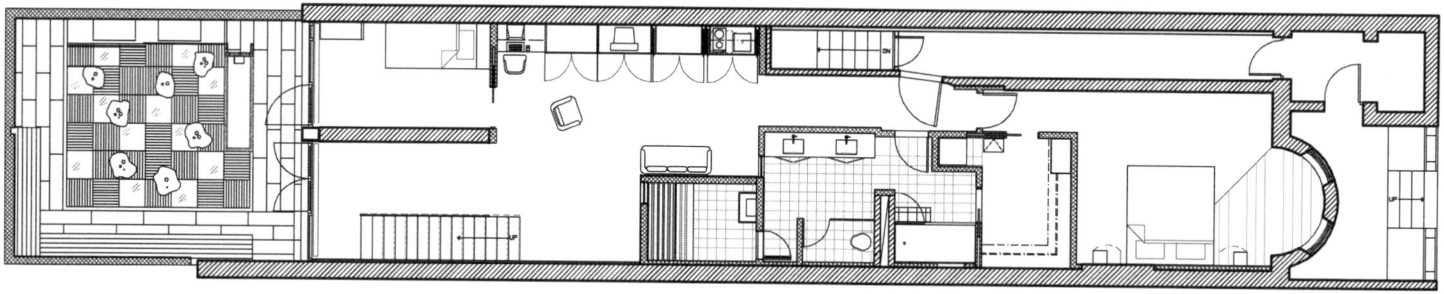

Ground floor plan
Planta baja

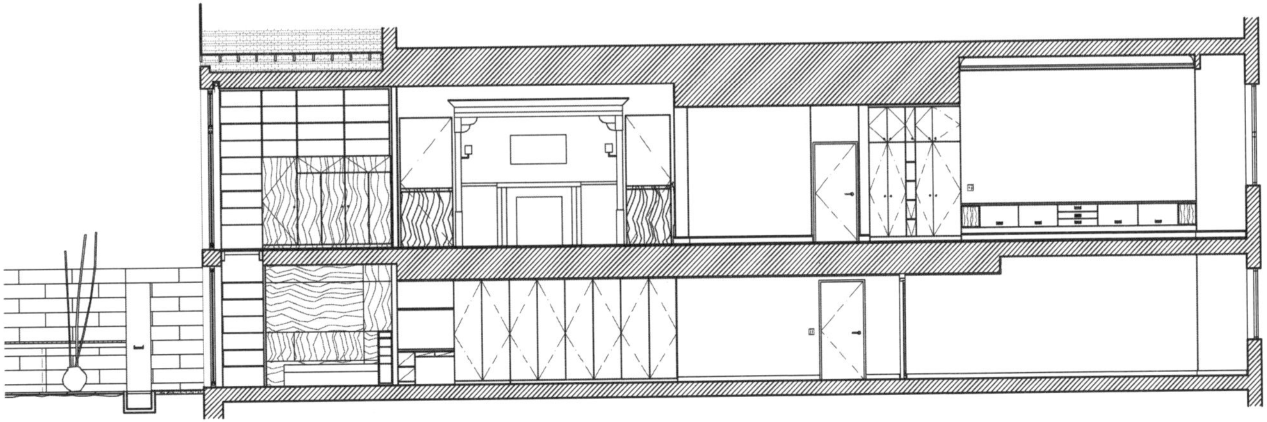

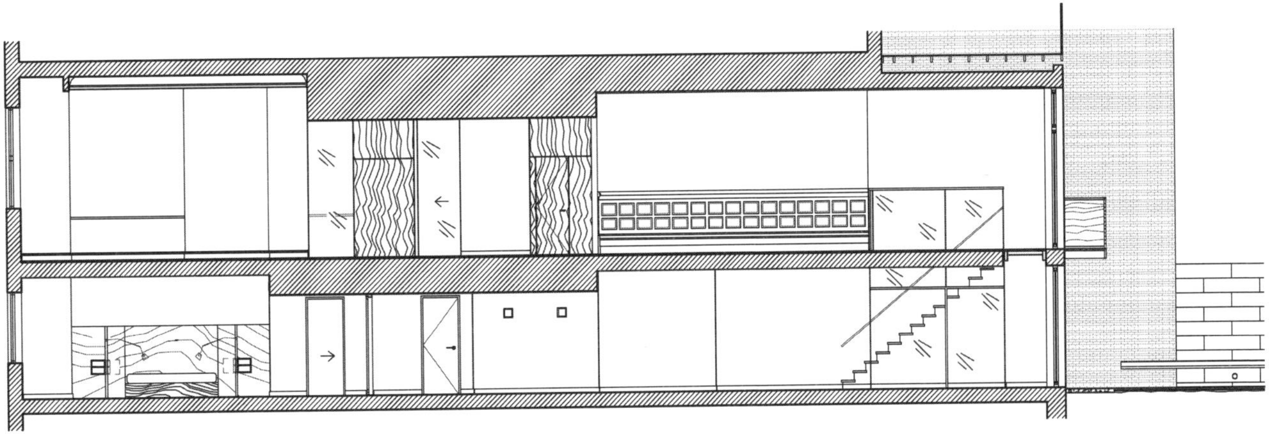

Longitudinal sections
Secciones longitudinales

The Anderson House

Jamie Fobert Architects
London, United Kingdom
Photos © David Grandorge

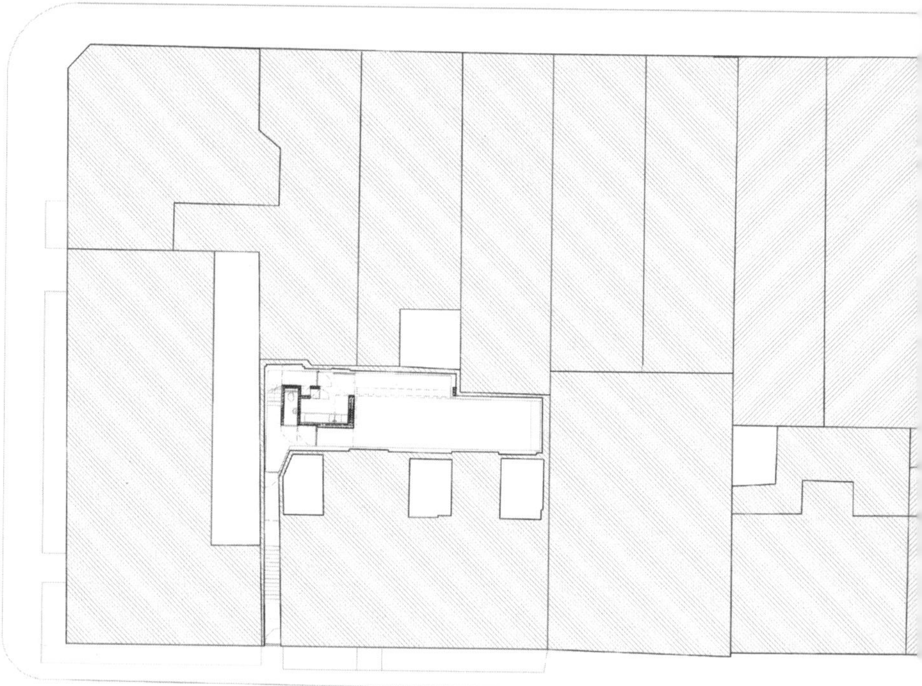

Site plan
Plano de situación

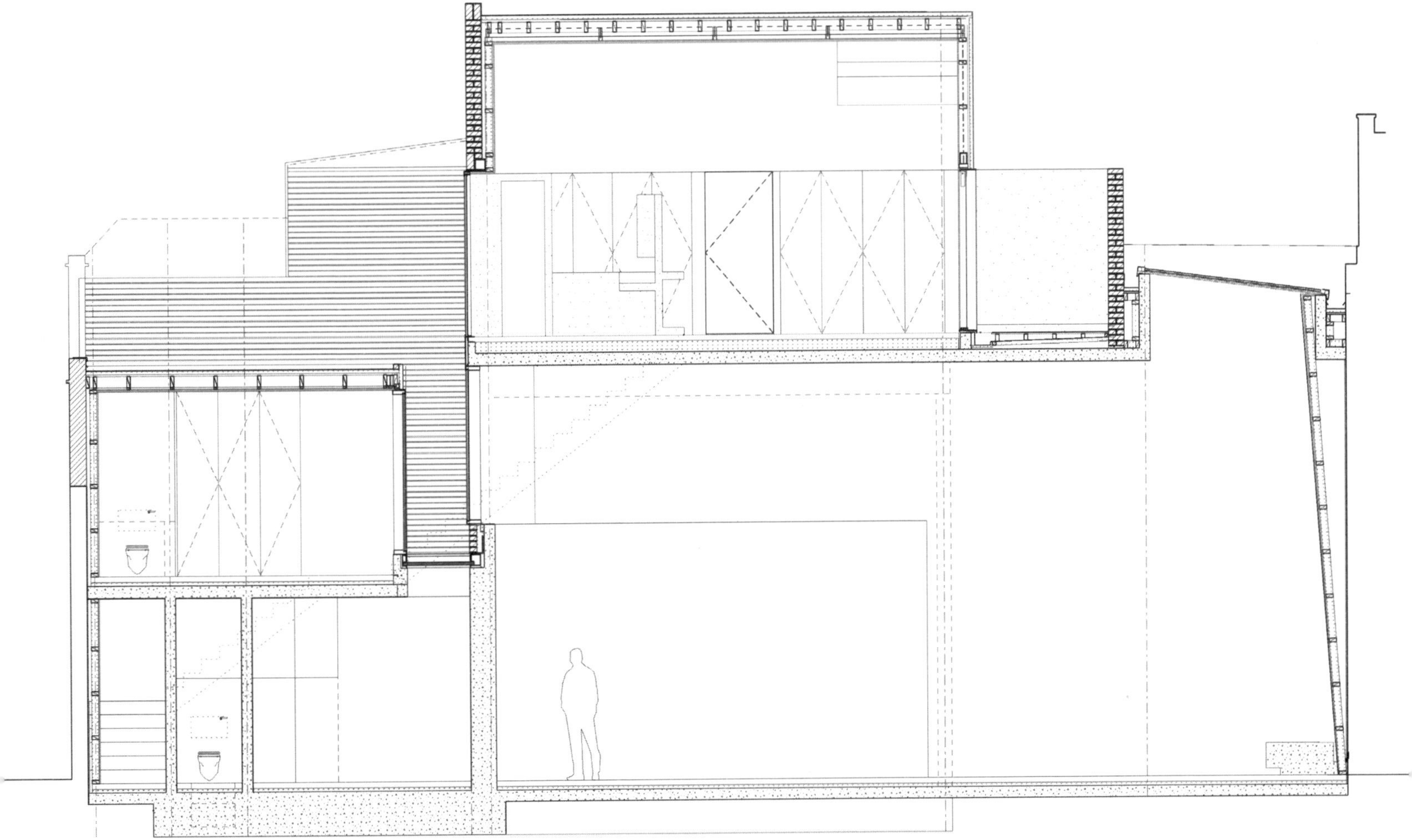

Transversal section
Sección transversal

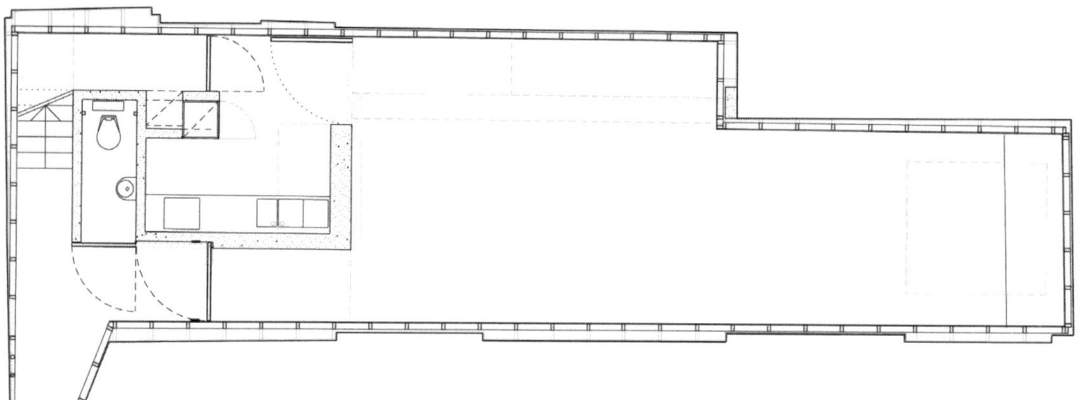

Ground floor plan
Planta baja

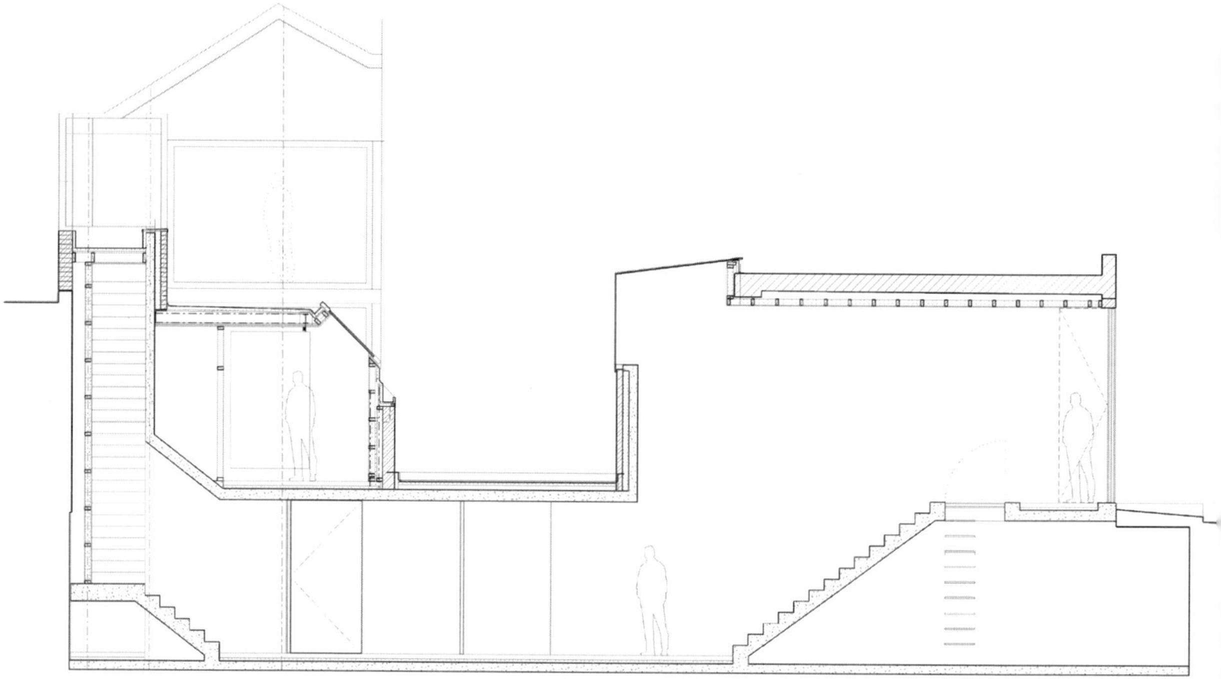

Longitudinal section
Sección longitudinal

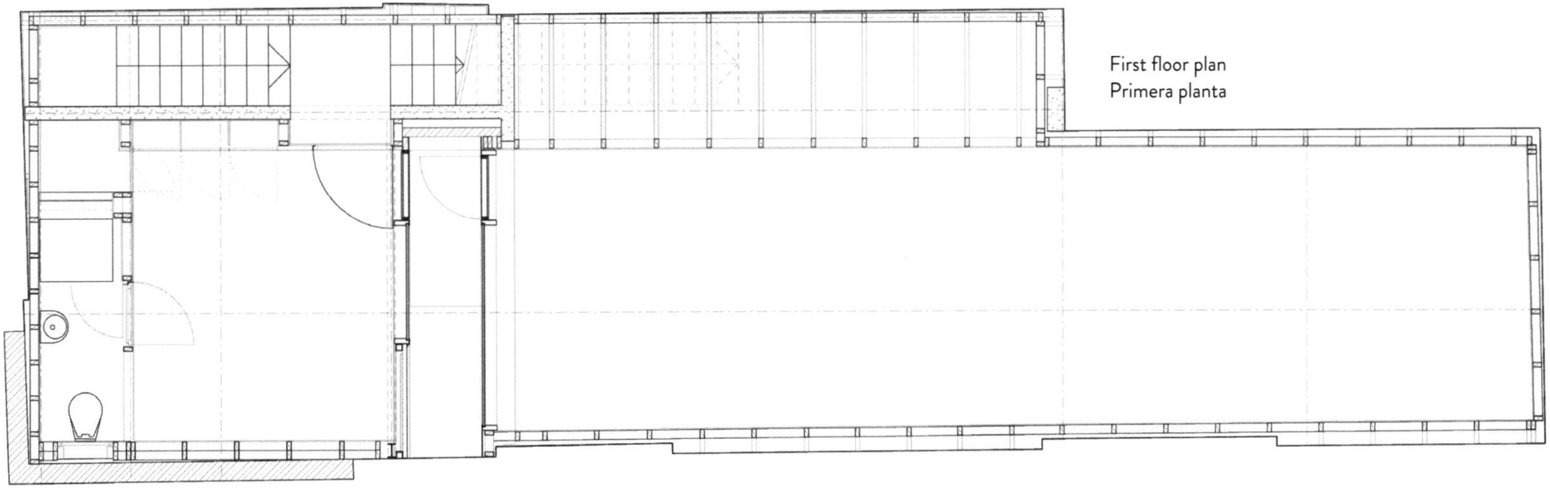

First floor plan
Primera planta

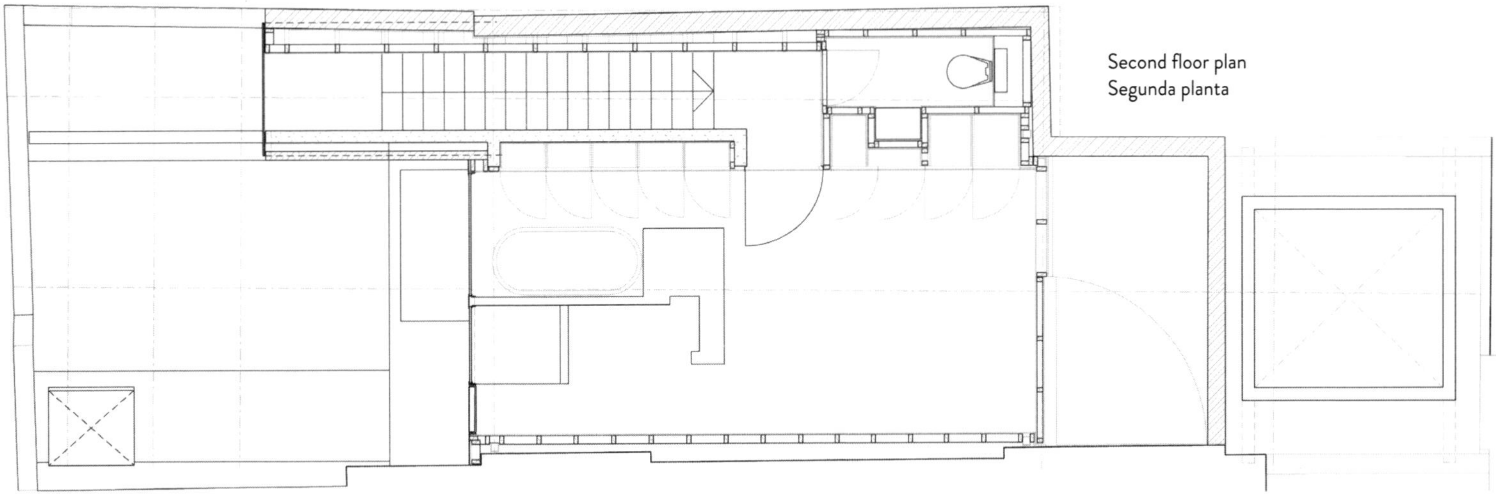

Second floor plan
Segunda planta

Living Space in Molins de Rei

Marc Obradó Cebada + Eli Sadurní Moreta/exe.architecture
Molins de Rei, Spain
Photos © Eugeni Pons

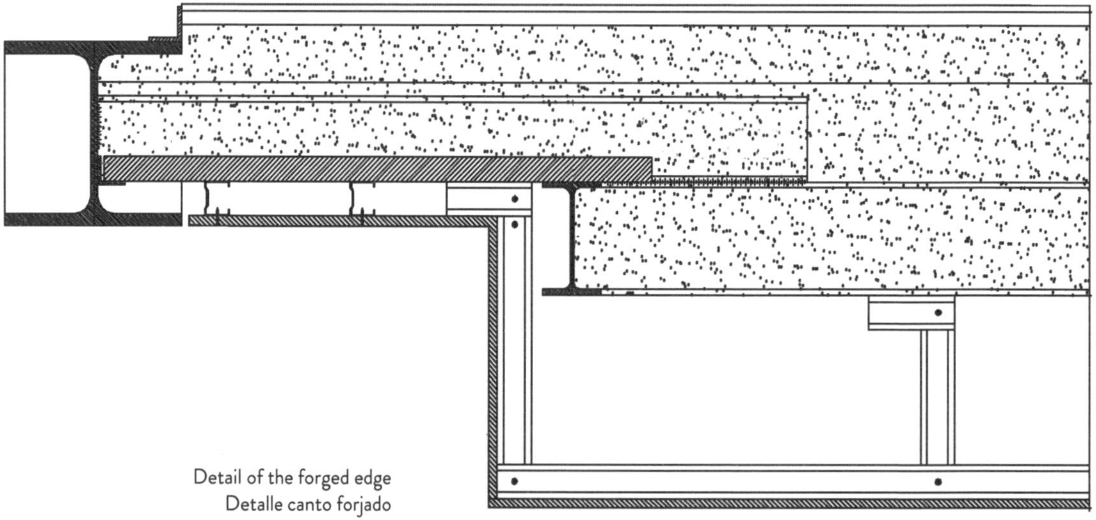

Detail of the forged edge
Detalle canto forjado

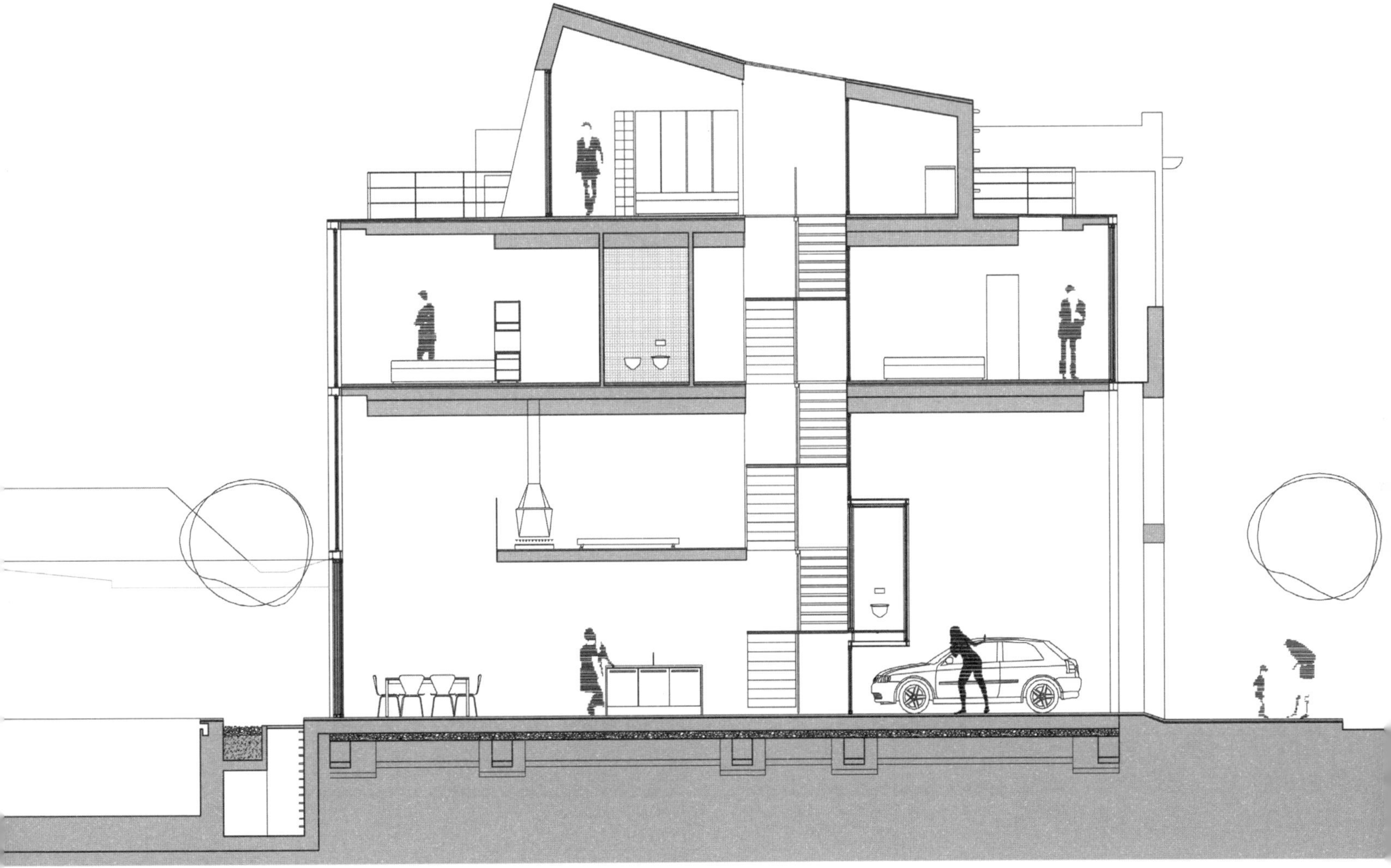

Longitudinal section
Sección longitudinal

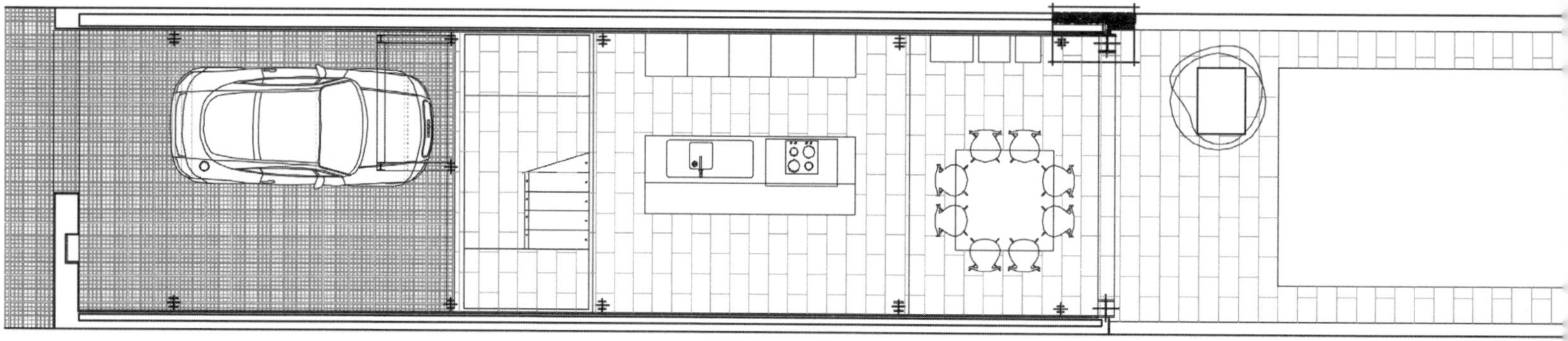

Ground floor plan
Planta baja

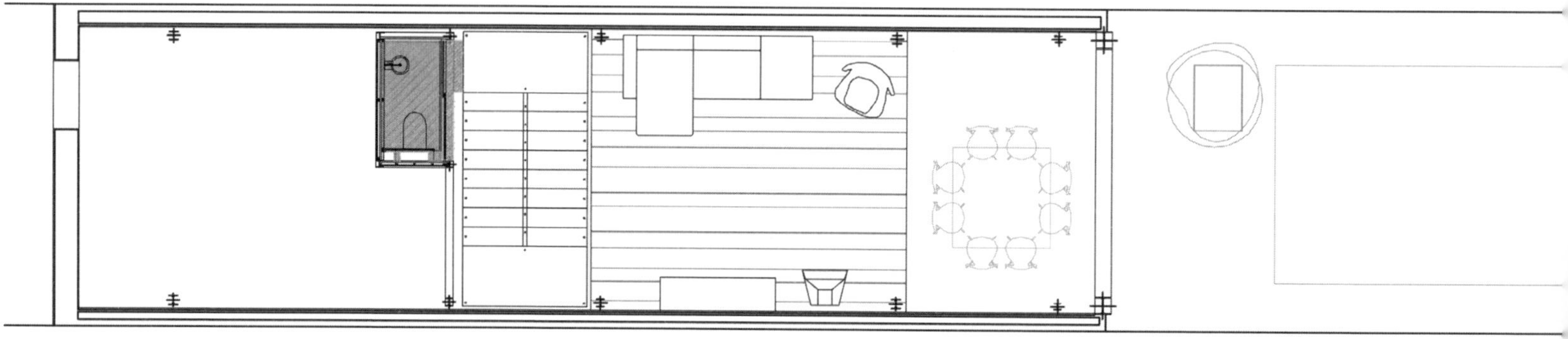

First floor plan
Primera planta

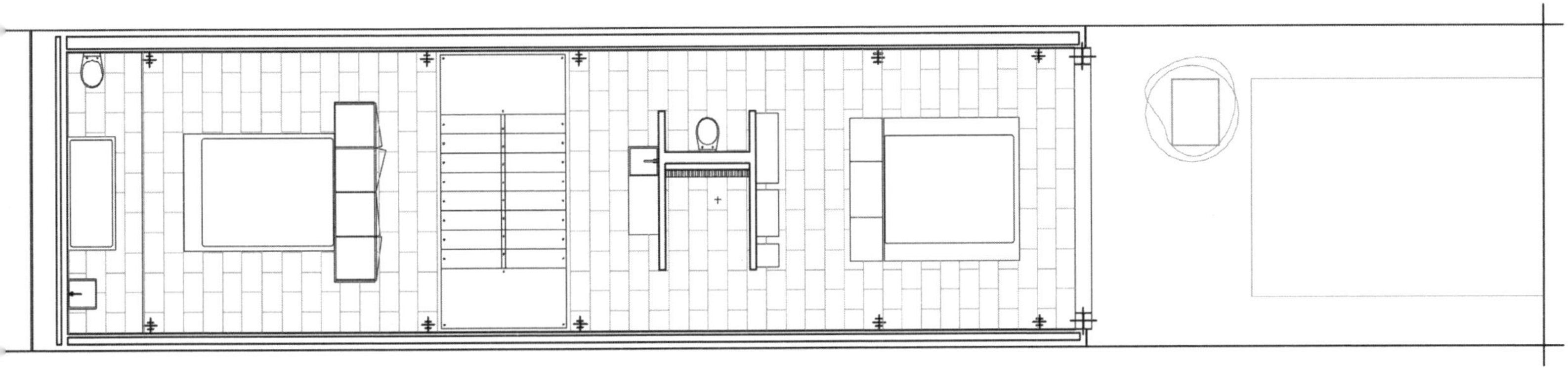

Second floor plan
Segunda planta

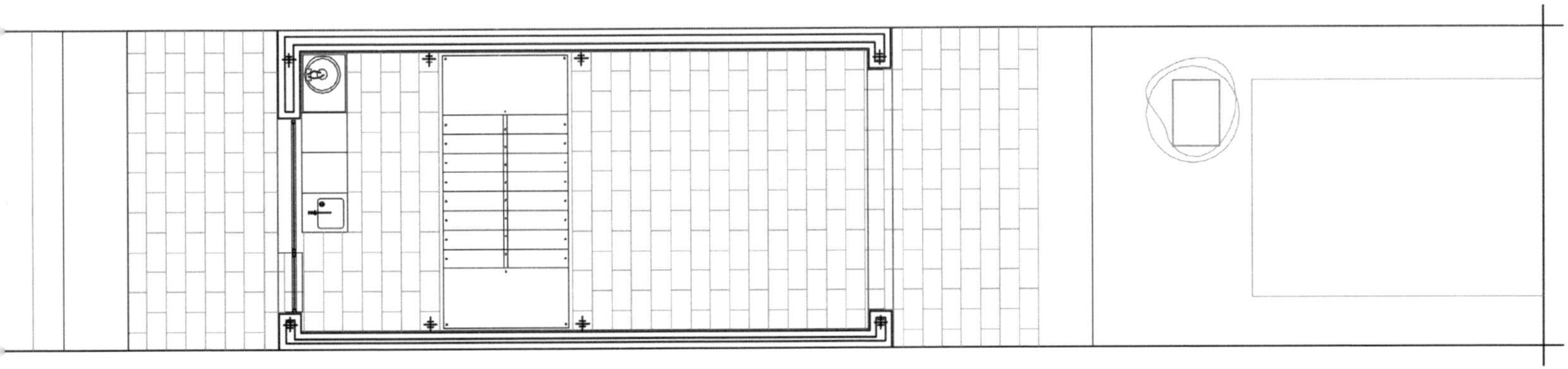

Third floor plan
Tercera planta

A house Between Party Walls in Lloret

Anne Bugugnani, Mònica Pascual
Lloret de Mar, Spain
Photos © Eugeni Pons

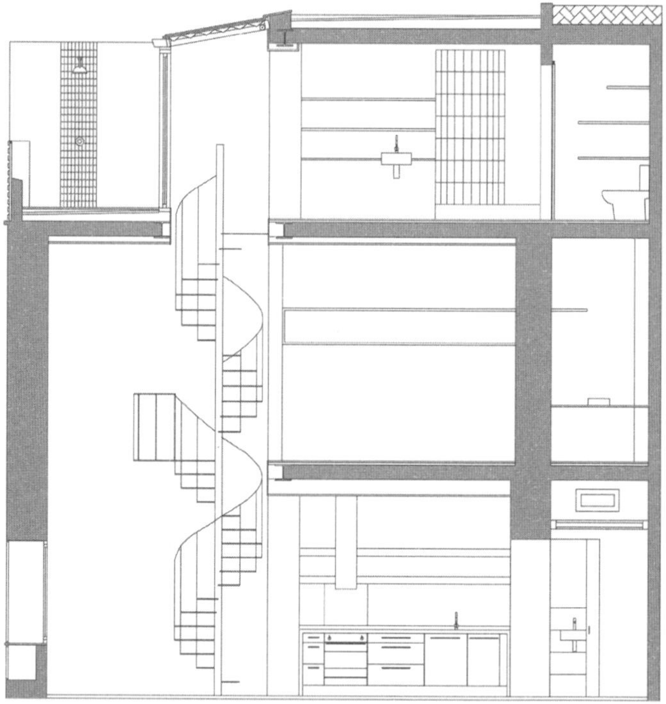

Longitudinal section A-A'
Sección longitudinal A-A'

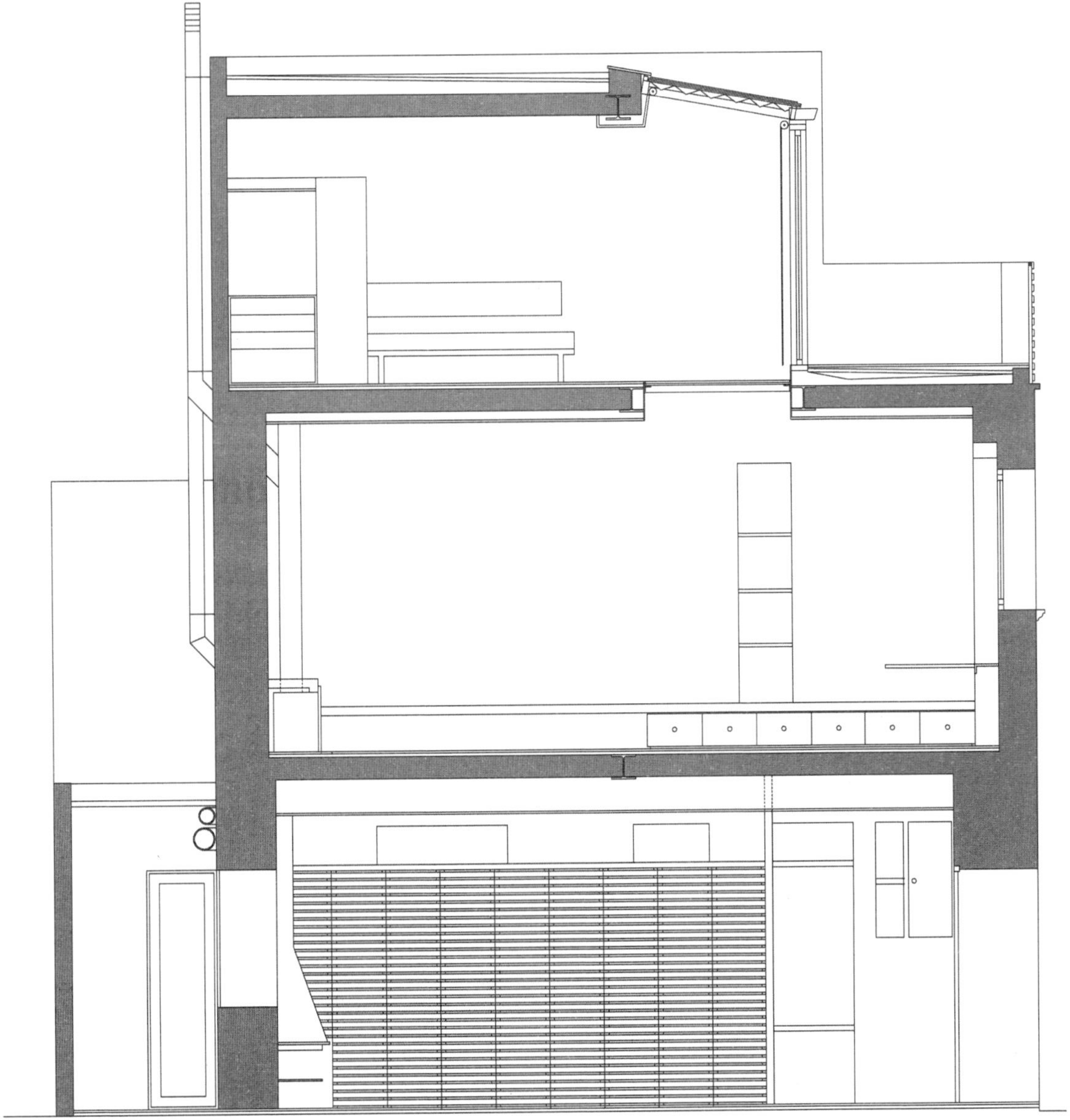

Longitudinal section B-B'
Sección longitudinal B-B'

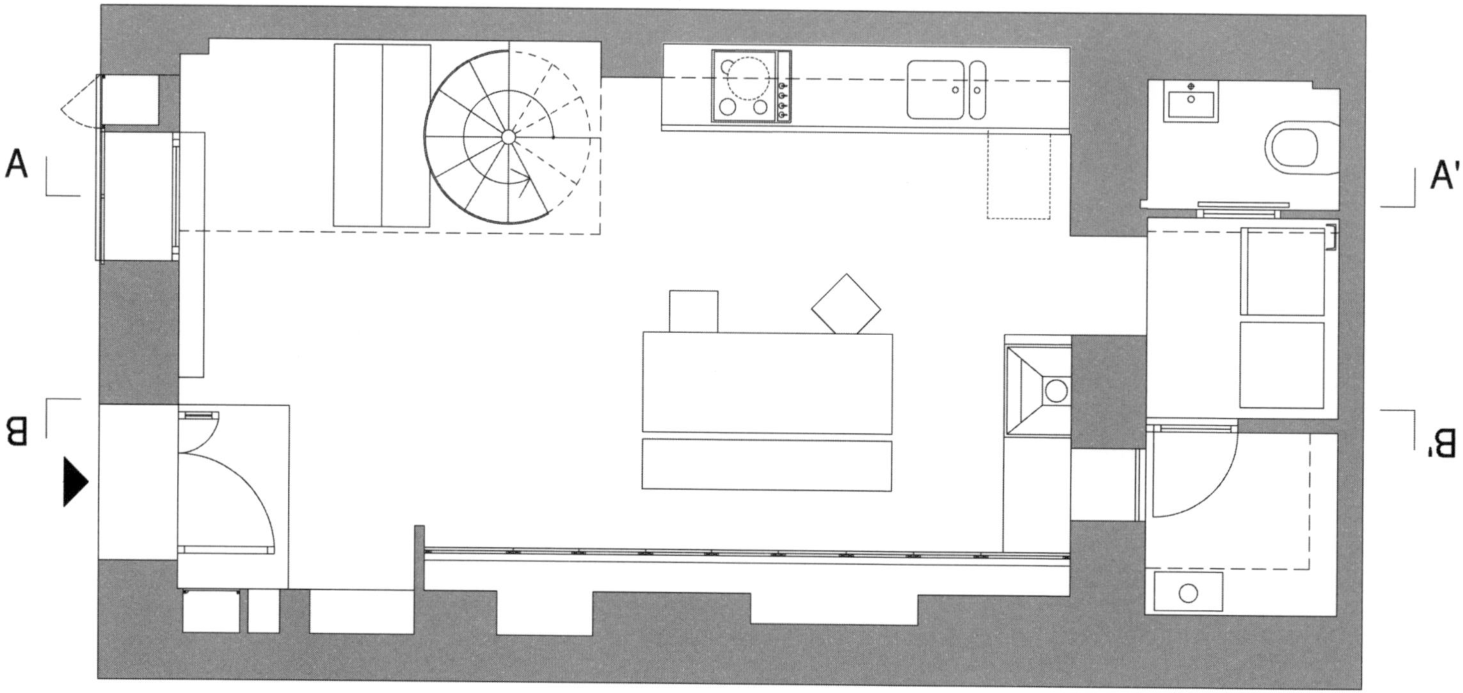

Ground floor plan
Planta baja

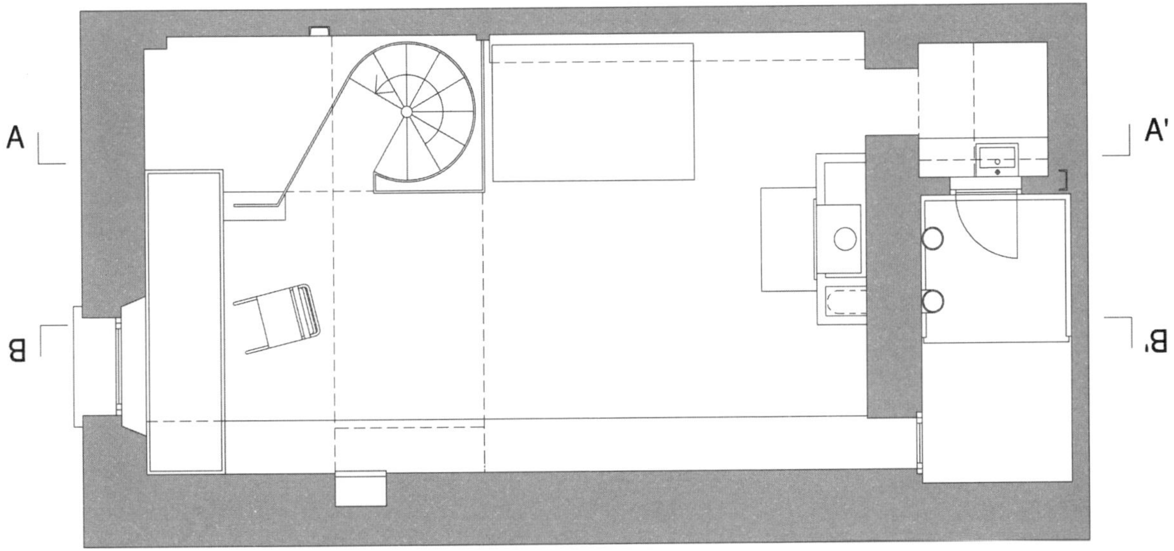

First floor plan
Primera planta

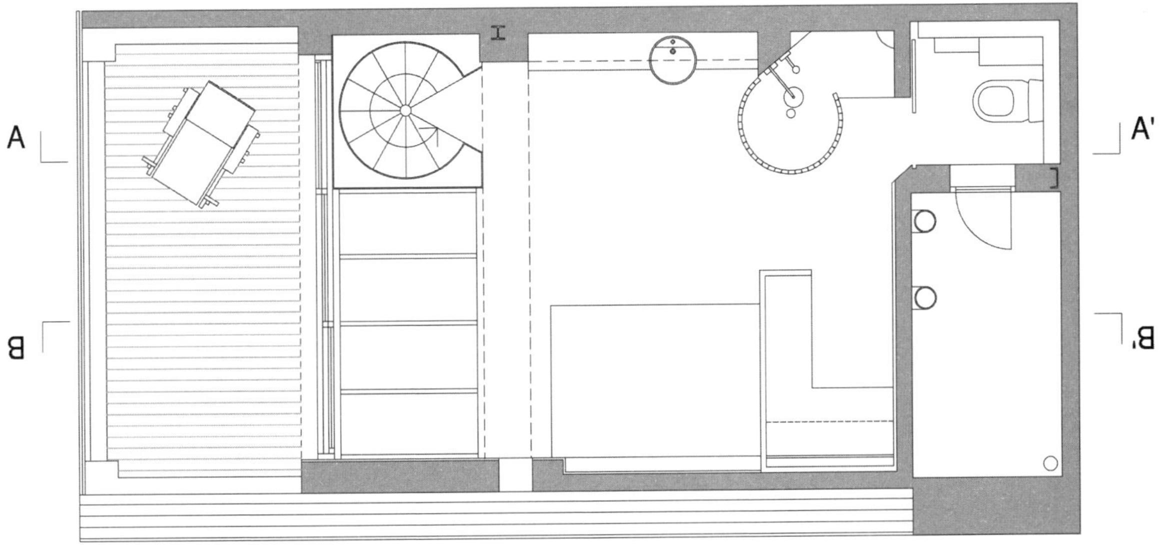

Second floor plan
Segunda planta

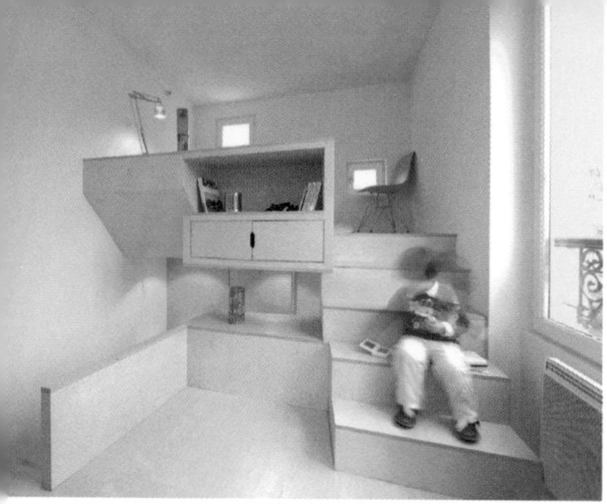

Chatou House

h2o Architectes
Chatou, France
Photos © Stéphane Chalmeau

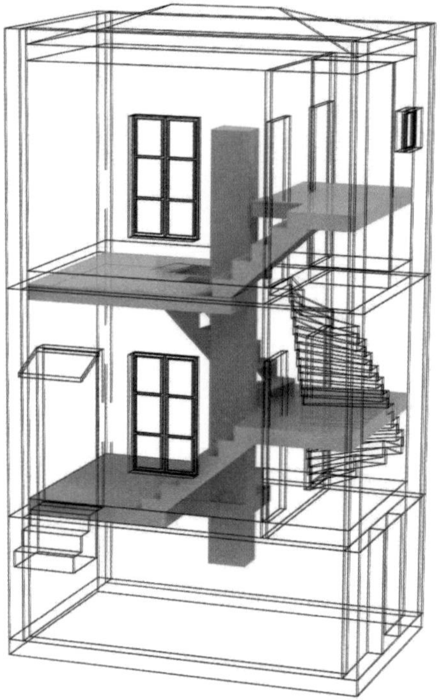

Staircase design development diagram
Diagrama de desarrollo del diseño de escaleras

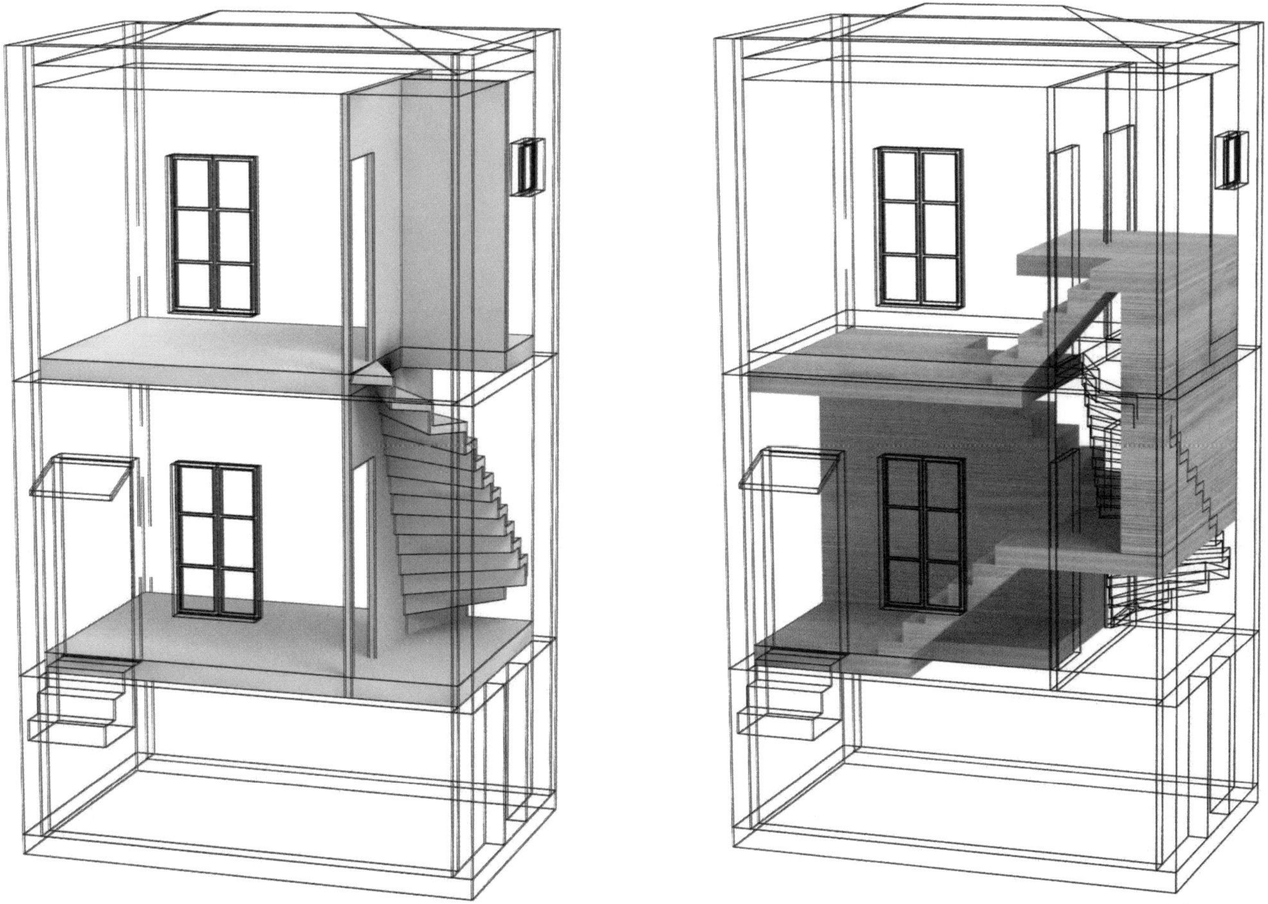

Staircase design development diagram
Diagrama de desarrollo del diseño de escaleras

House in Mosman

Emili Fox / Fox Johnston architects
Sydney, Australia
Photos © Eric Sierins

Location diagram
Diagrama de situación

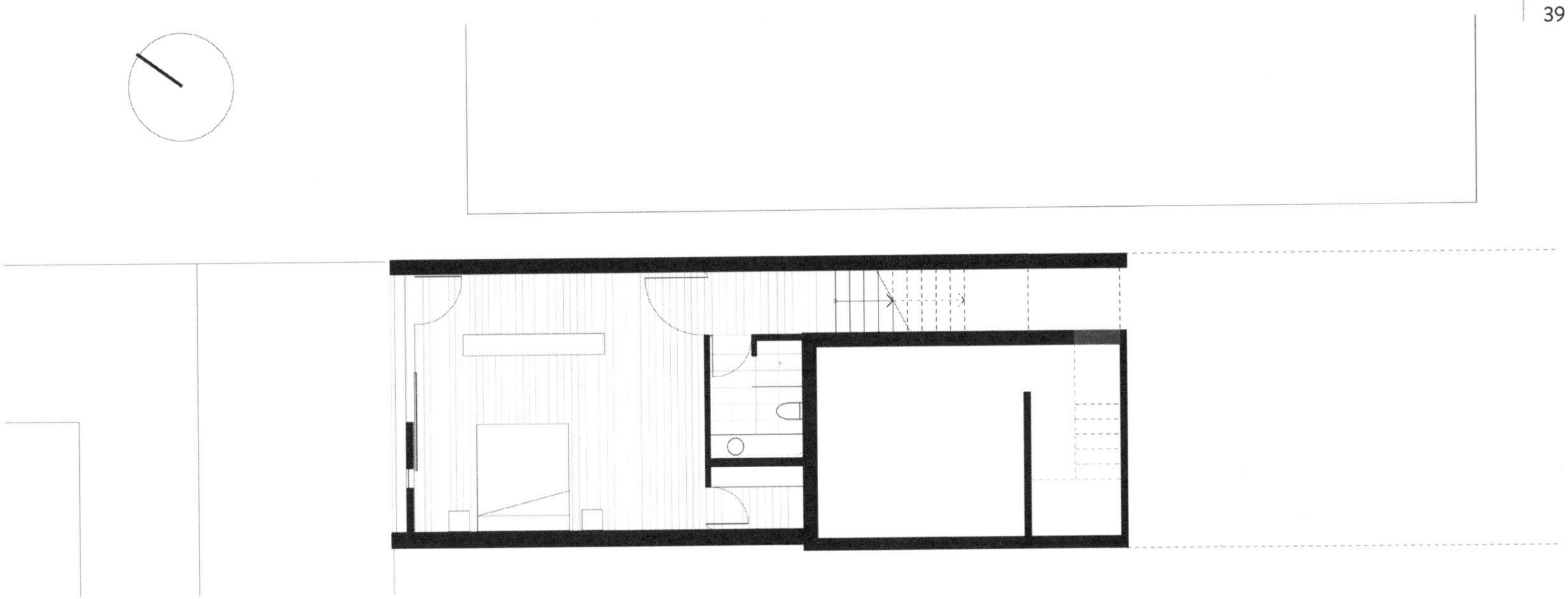

Ground floor plan
Planta baja

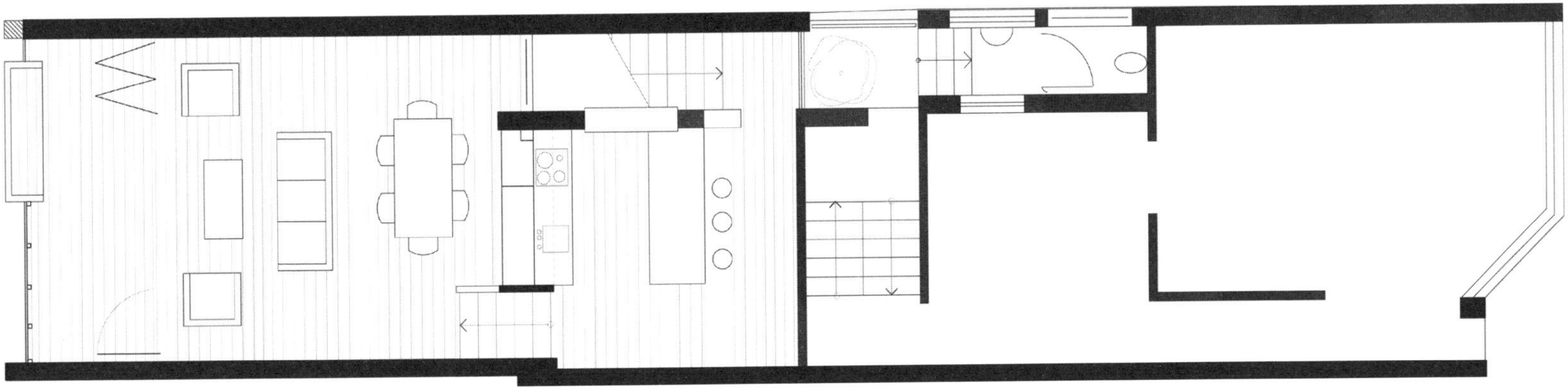

First floor plan
Primera planta

The Vertical House

Lorcan O'Herlihy Architects
Venice (Los Angeles), USA
Photos © Michael Weschler

Diagram of the wall facings
Diagrama del revestimiento de las fachadas

Longitudinal section
Sección longitudinal

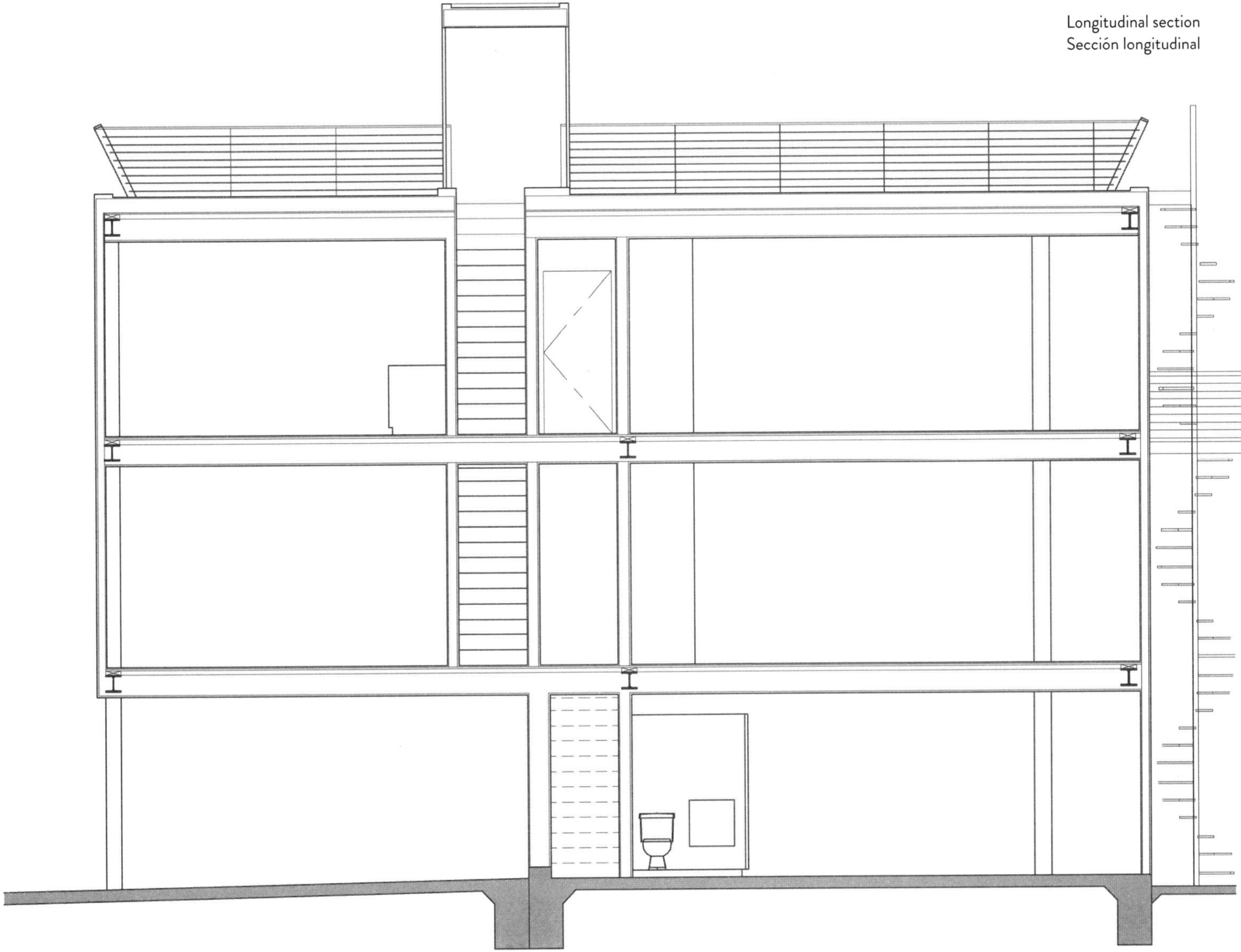

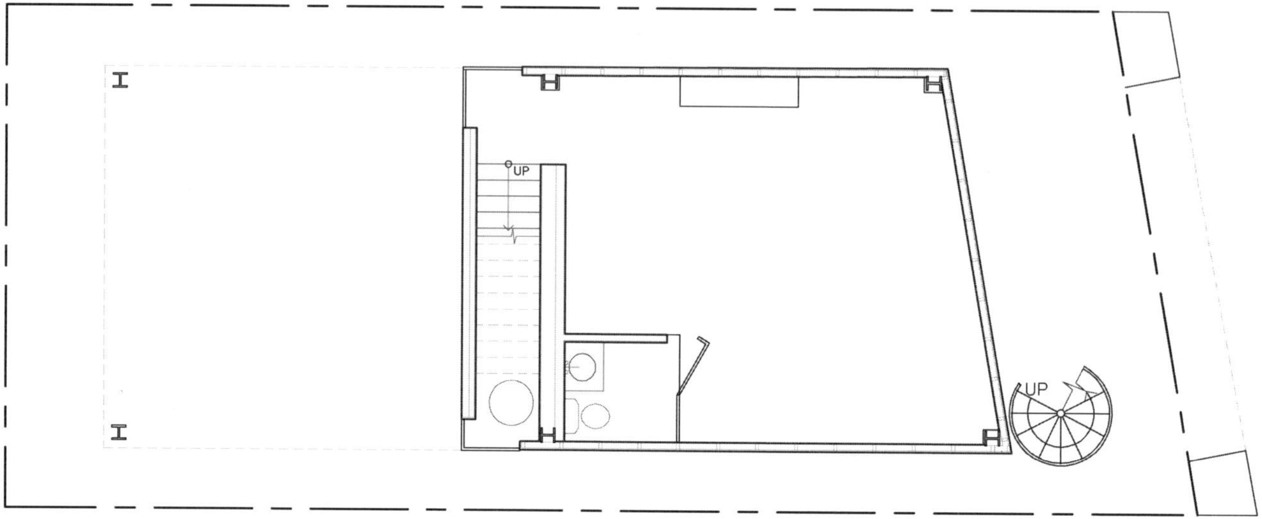

Ground floor plan
Planta baja

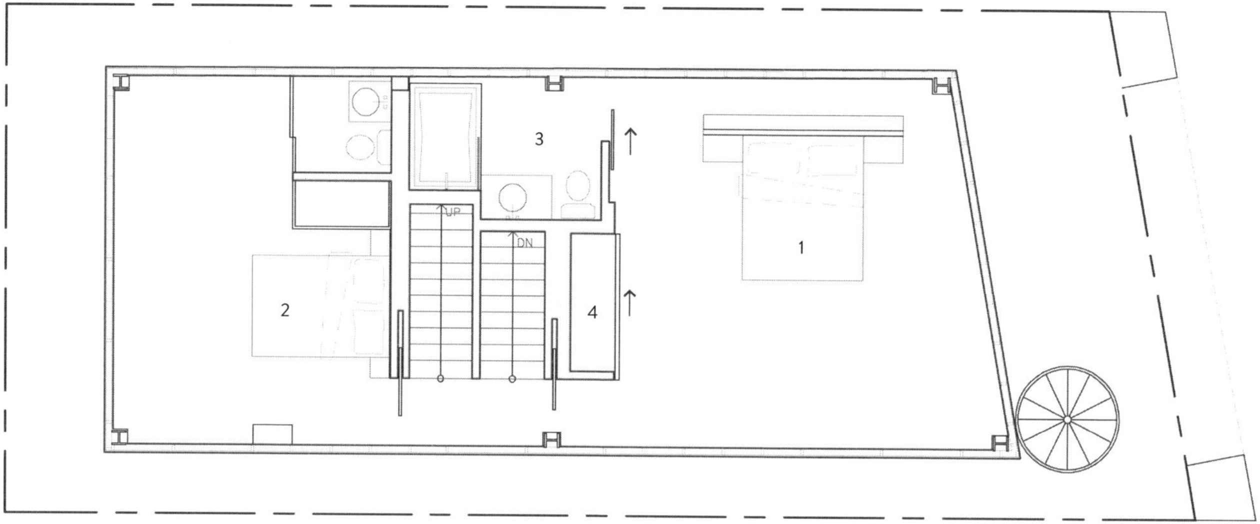

Second floor plan
Segunda planta

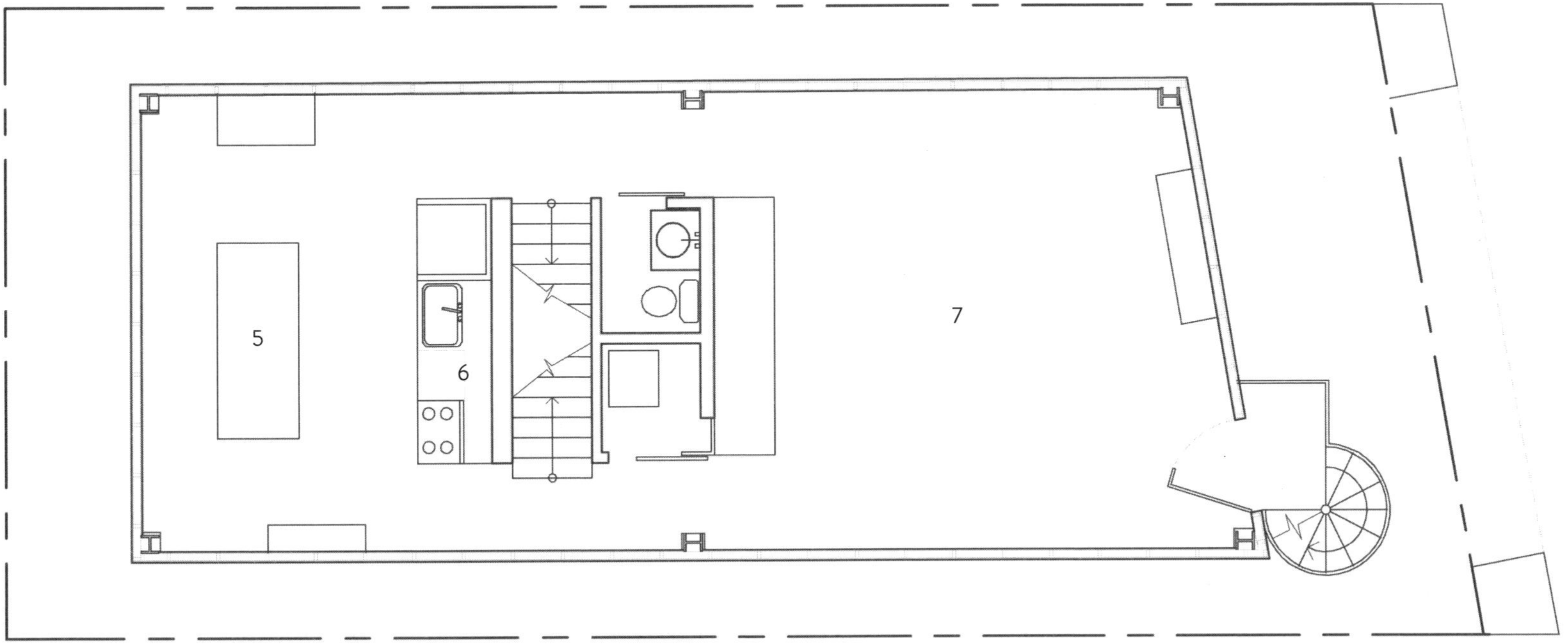

Third floor plan
Tercera planta

1. Master bedroom	1. Dormitorio principal
2. Guest bedroom	2. Dormitorio de invitados
3. Bathroom	3. Cuarto de baño
4. Closet	4. Armario
5. Dinning room	5. Comedor
6. Kitchen	6. Cocina
7. Living room	7. Sala de estar

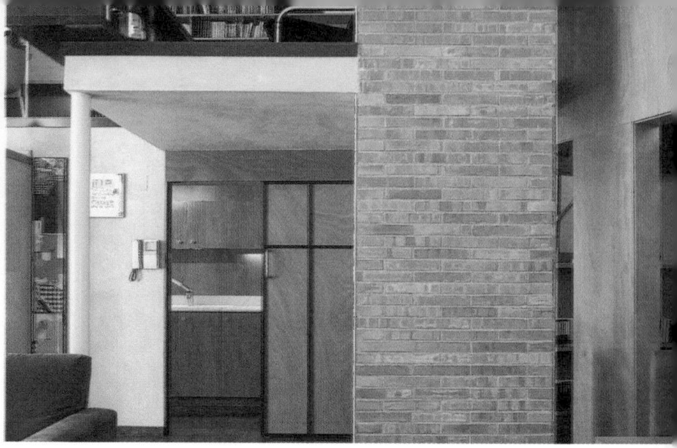

House in Sant Sadurní

Josep Juvé
Sant Sadurní d'Anoia, Spain
Photos © Eugeni Pons

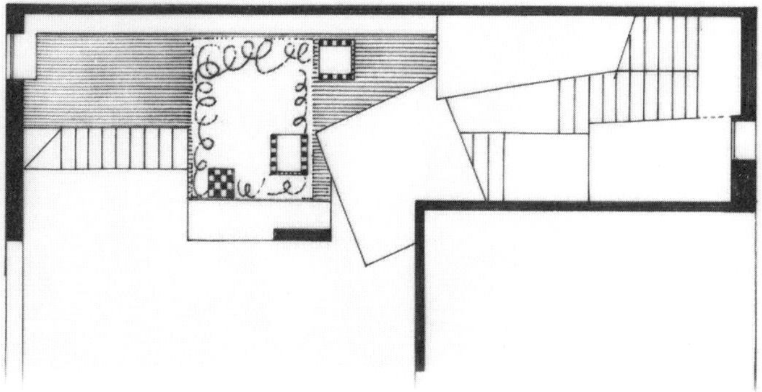

Entrance floor plan
Planta de acceso

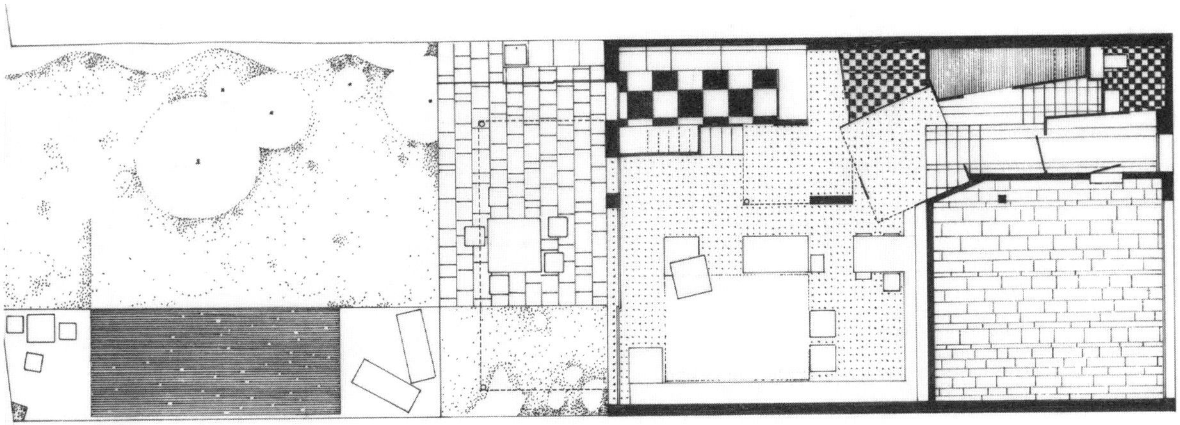

Ground floor plan
Planta baja

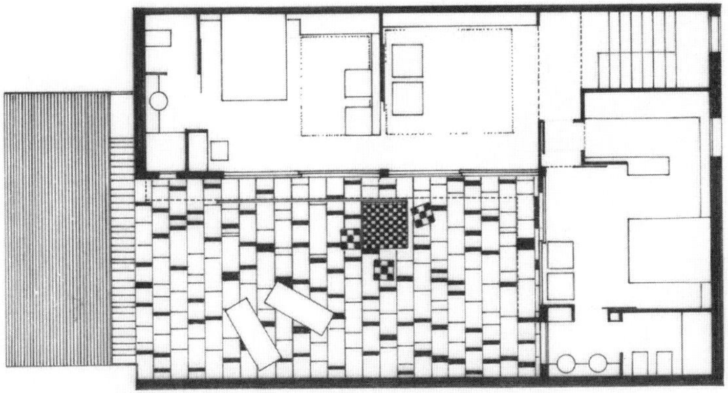

First floor plan
Primera planta

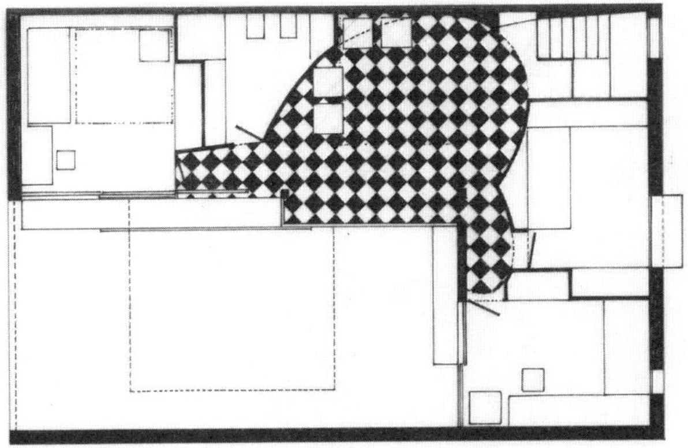

Second floor plan
Segunda planta

Minimum House

Yasuhiro Yamashita / Shinji Haraguchi / Atelier Tekuto
Saitama, Japan
Photos © Makoto Yoshida

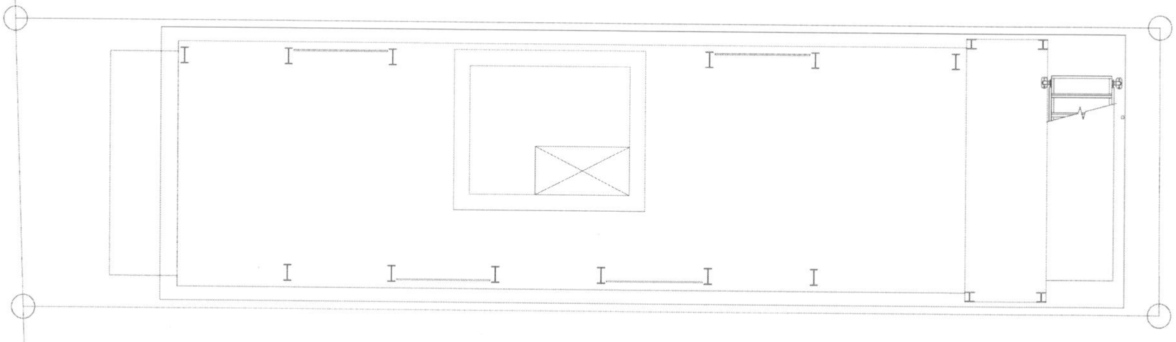

First floor plan
Primera planta

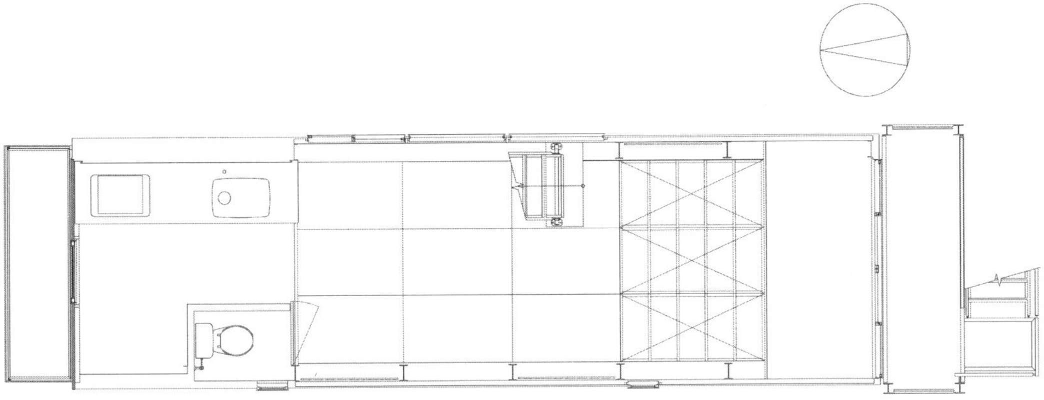

Second floor plan
Segunda planta

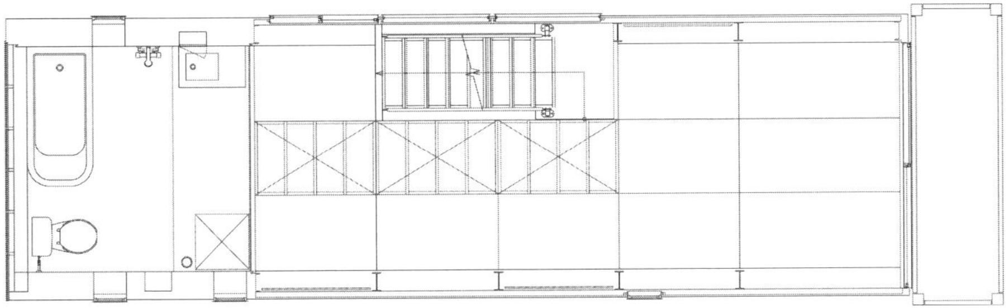

Third floor plan
Tercera planta

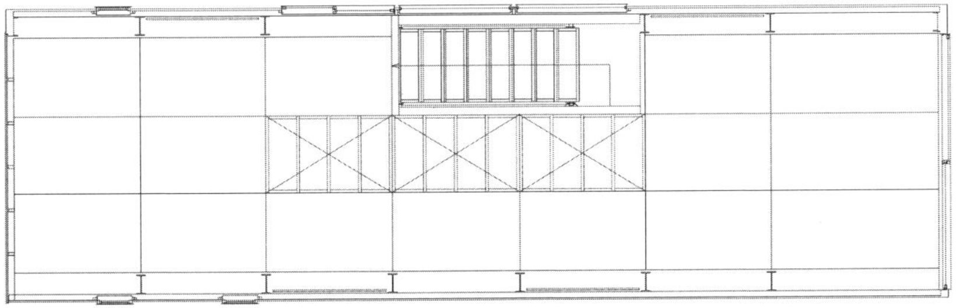

Fourth floor plan
Cuarta planta

MR House

Jordi Badia / BAAS arquitectes
Premià de Mar, Spain
Photos © Eugeni Pons

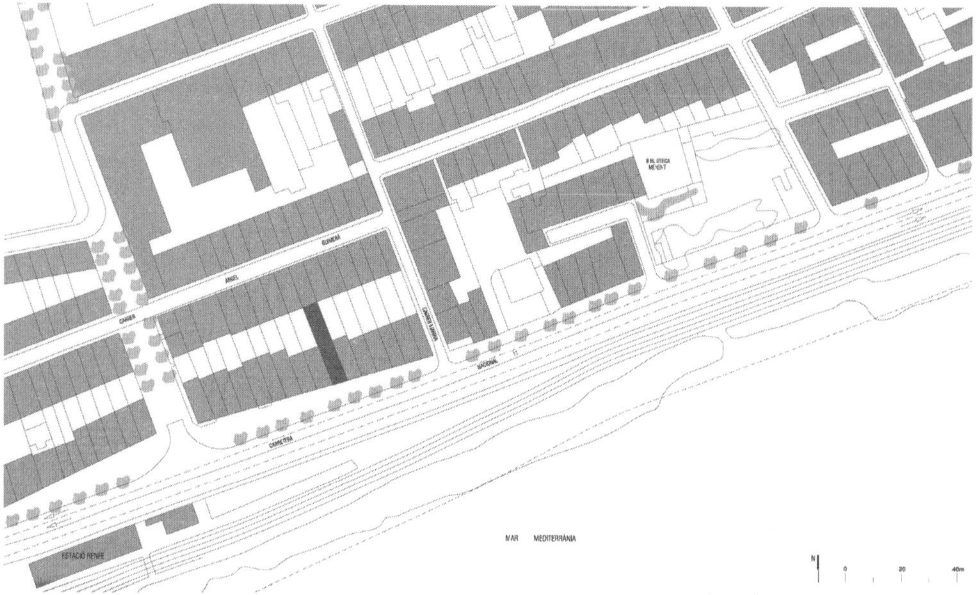

Site plan
Plano de situación

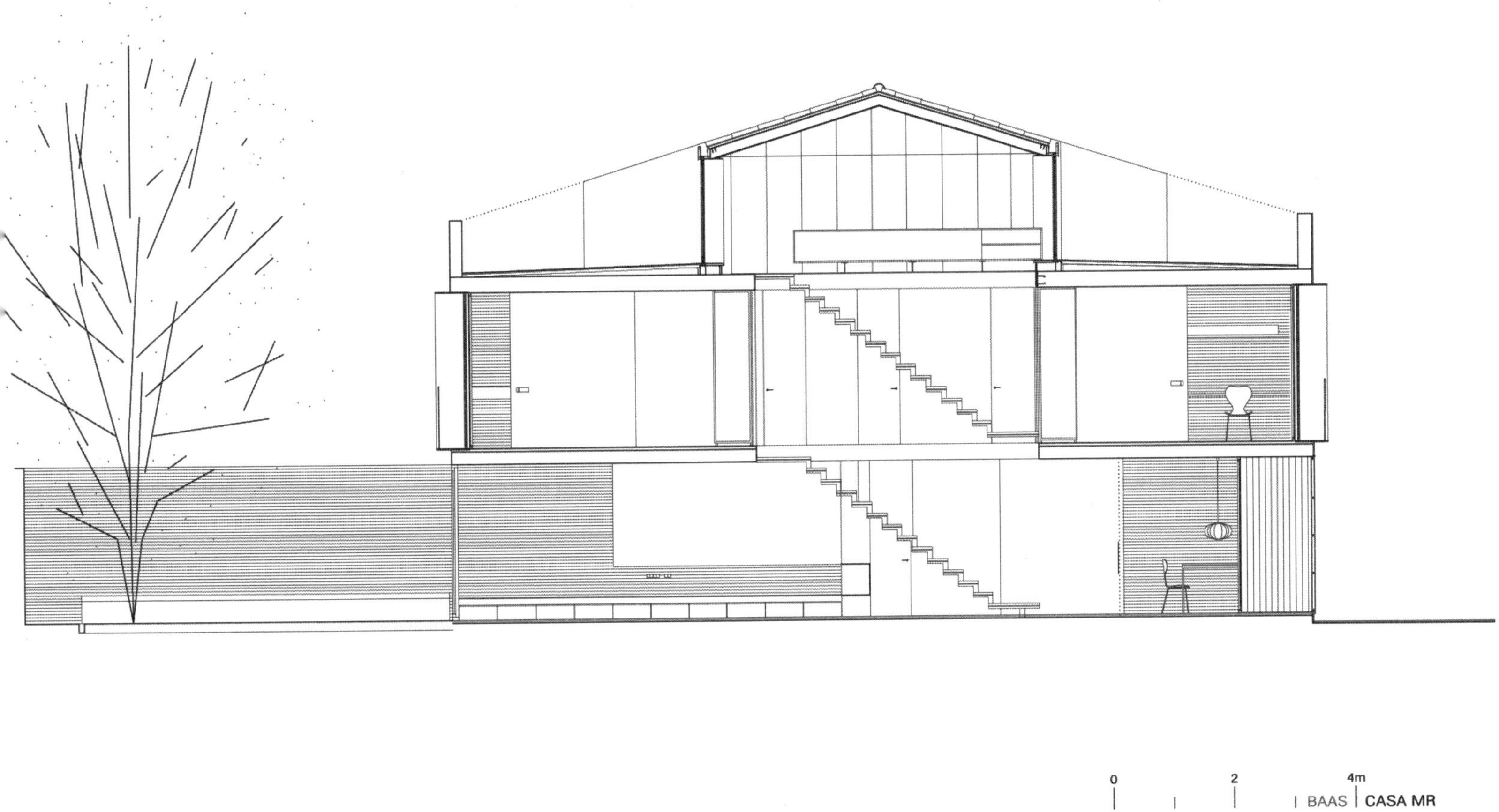

Longitudinal section
Sección longitudinal

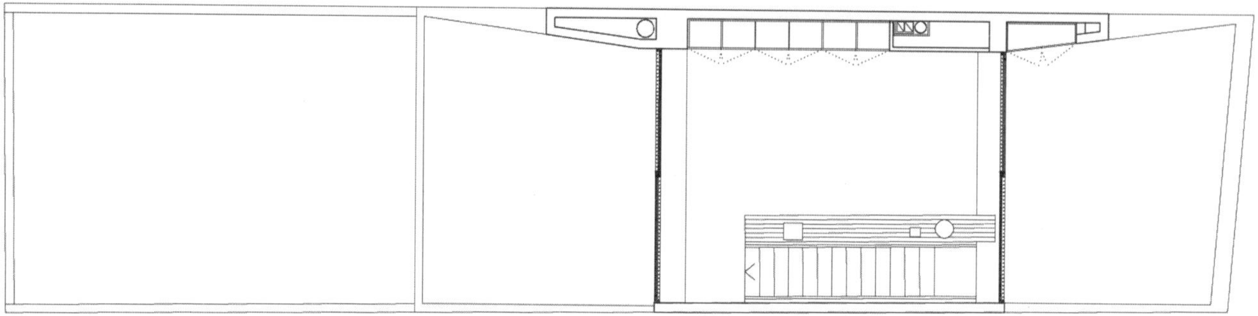

Second floor plan
Segunda planta

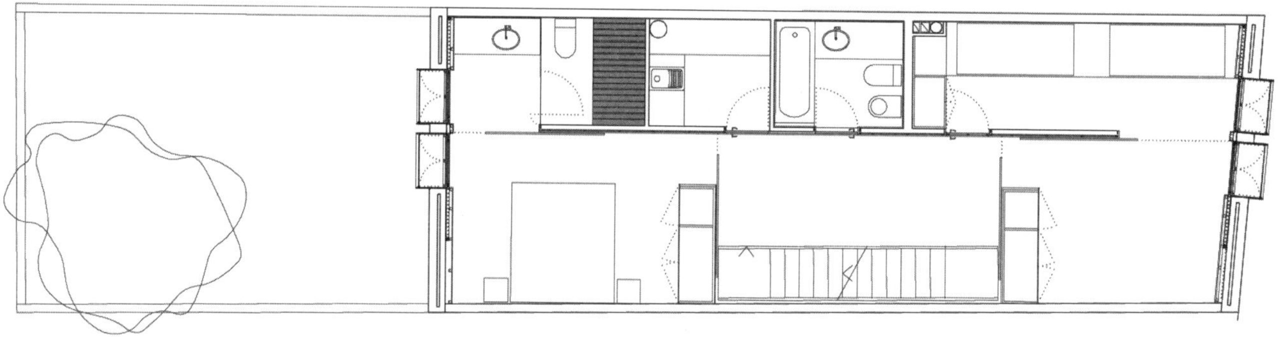

First floor plan
Primera planta

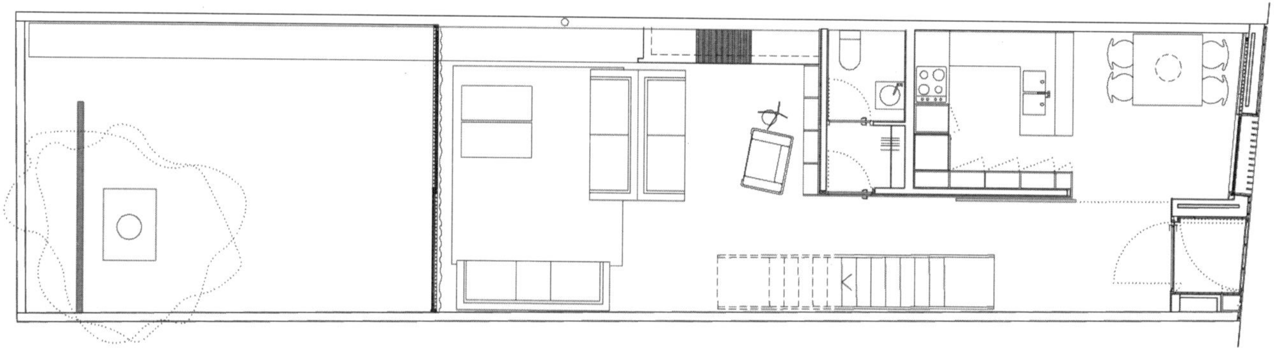

Ground floor plan
Planta baja

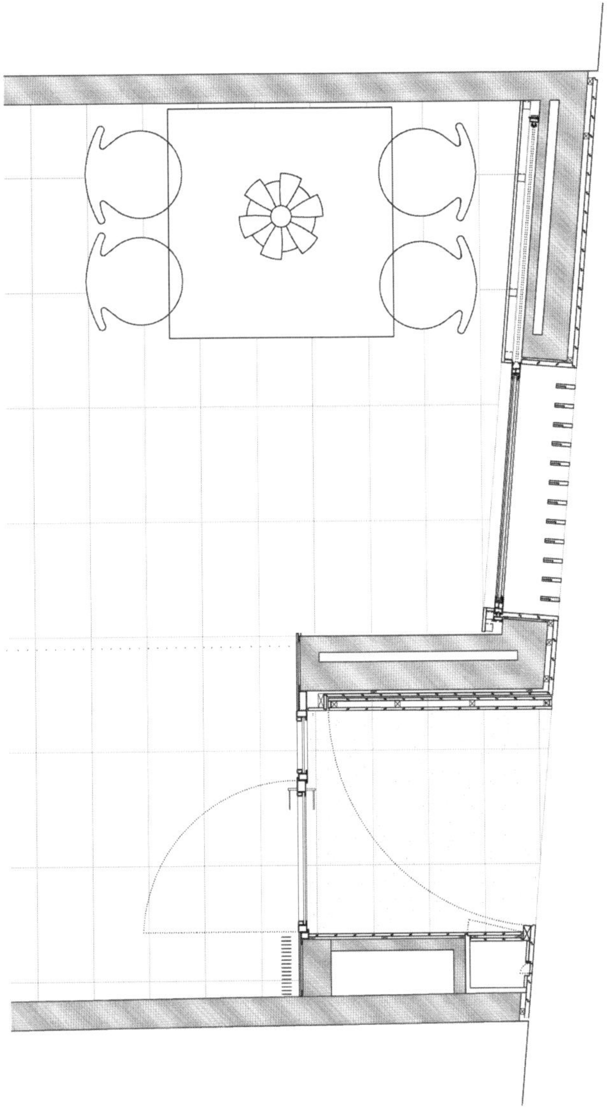

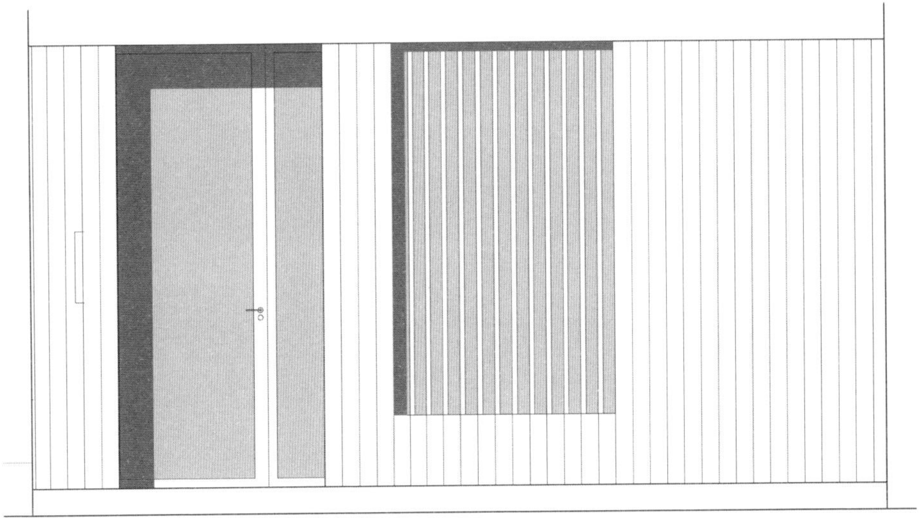

Details of the entrance
Detalles de la entrada

House T

Hiroyuki Shinozaki Architects
Tokyo, Japan
Photos © Hiroyasu Sakaguchi

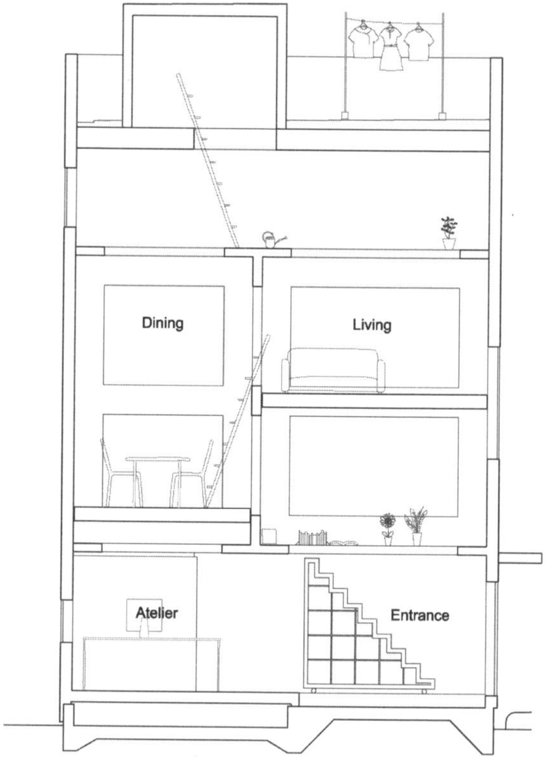

Longitudinal section
Sección longitudinal

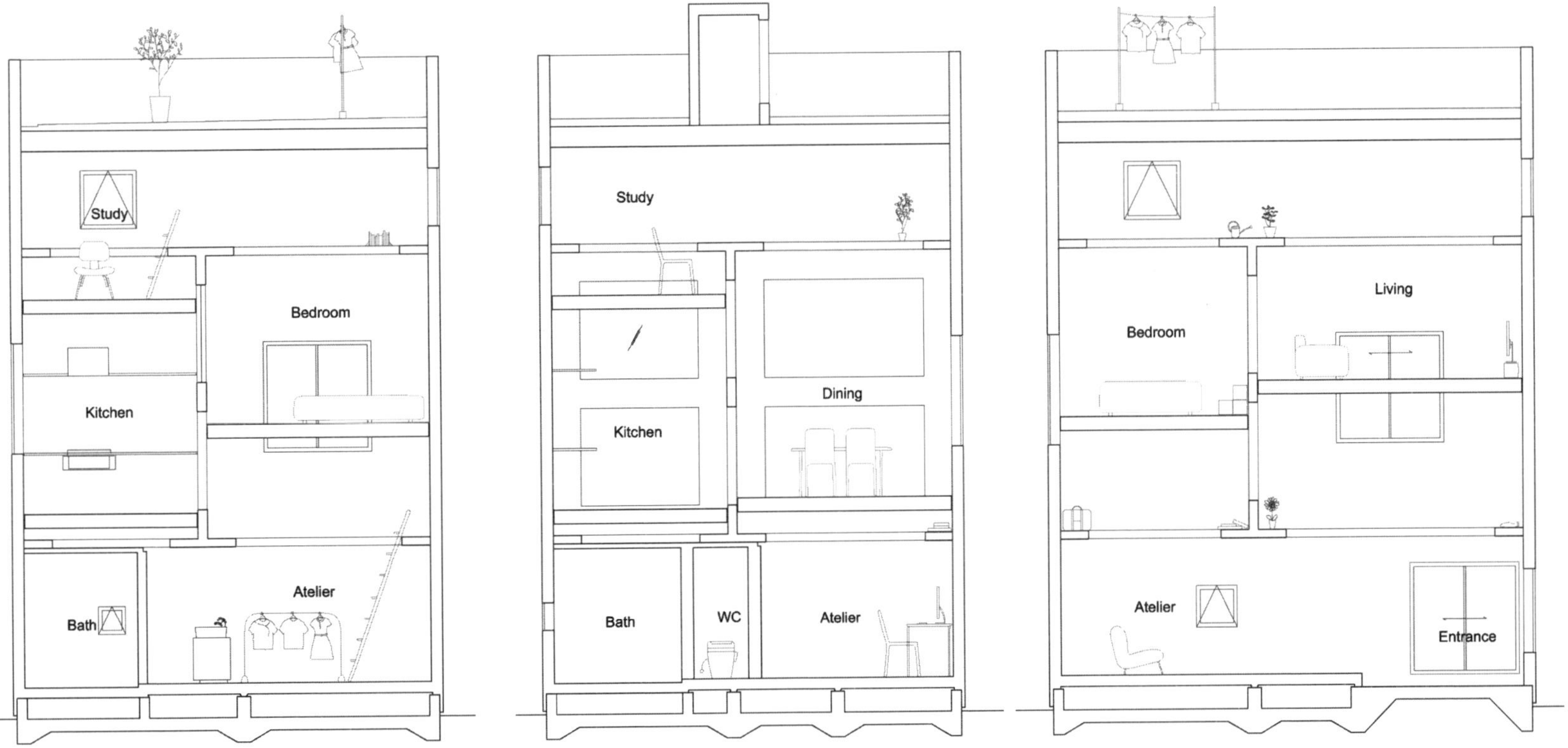

Longitudinal section
Sección longitudinal

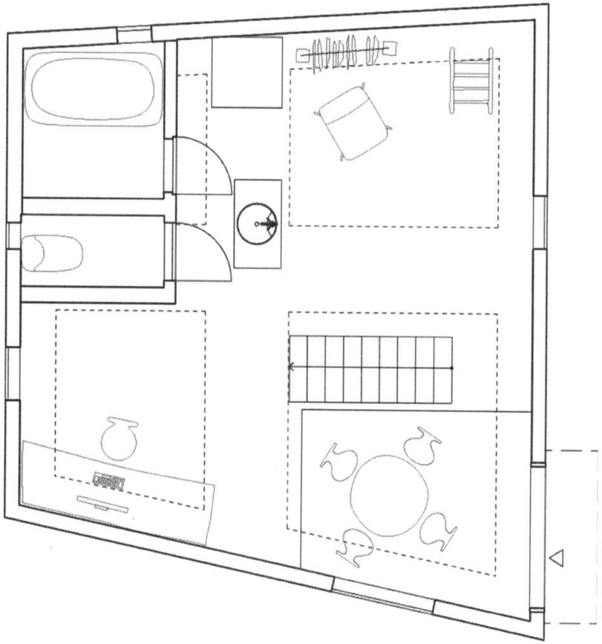

Main floor
Planta baja

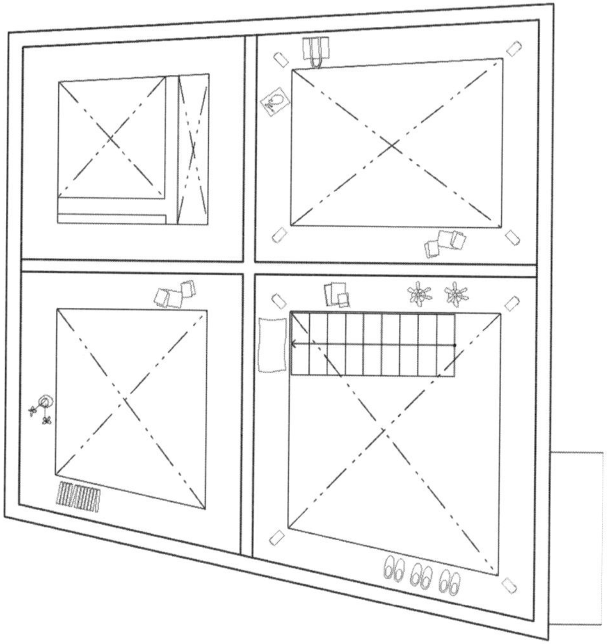

Second floor plan
Segunda planta

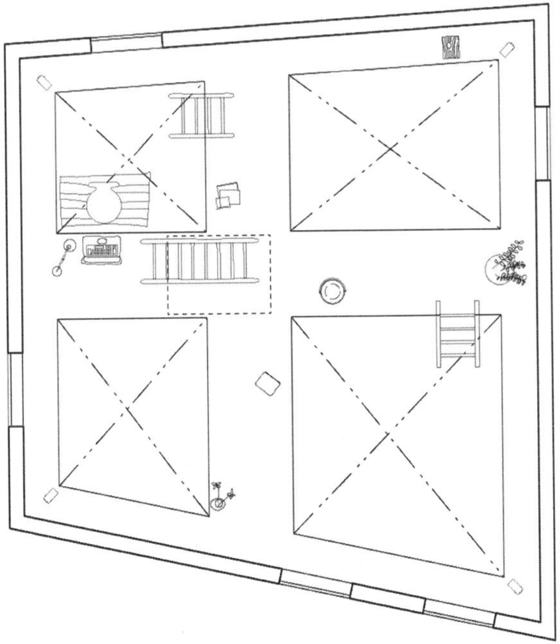

Third floor plan
Tercera planta

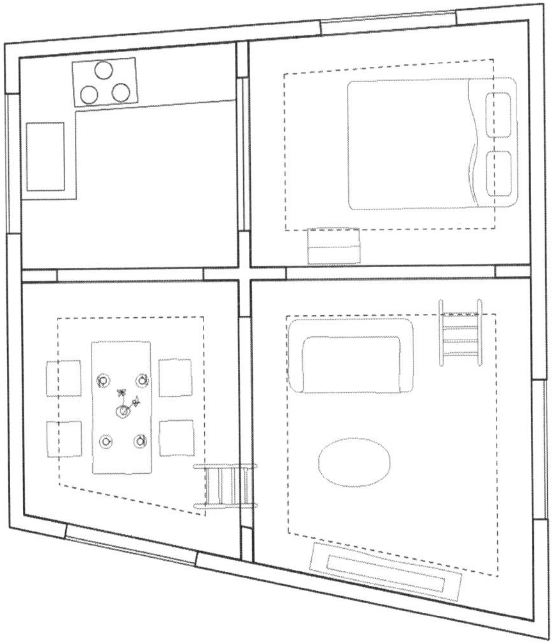

Loft

Tsuchida House

Intentionallies
Kobe, Japan
Photos © Mineo Sakata

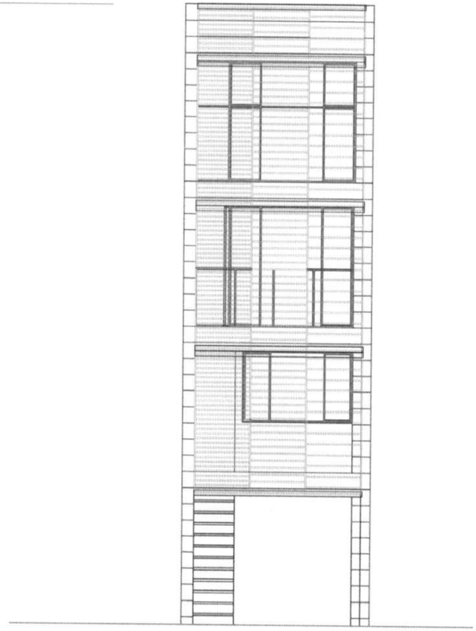

Elevations
Alzados

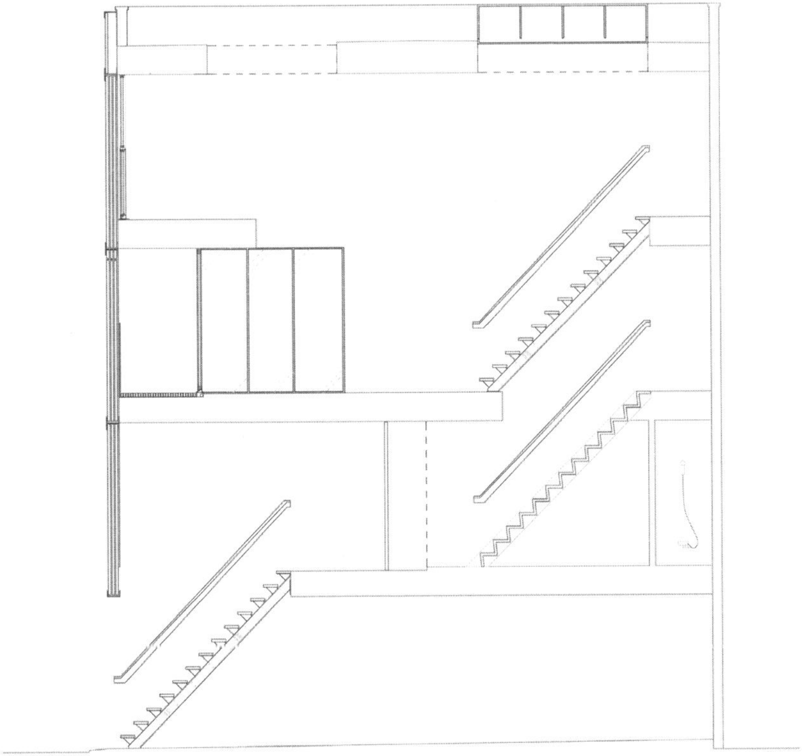

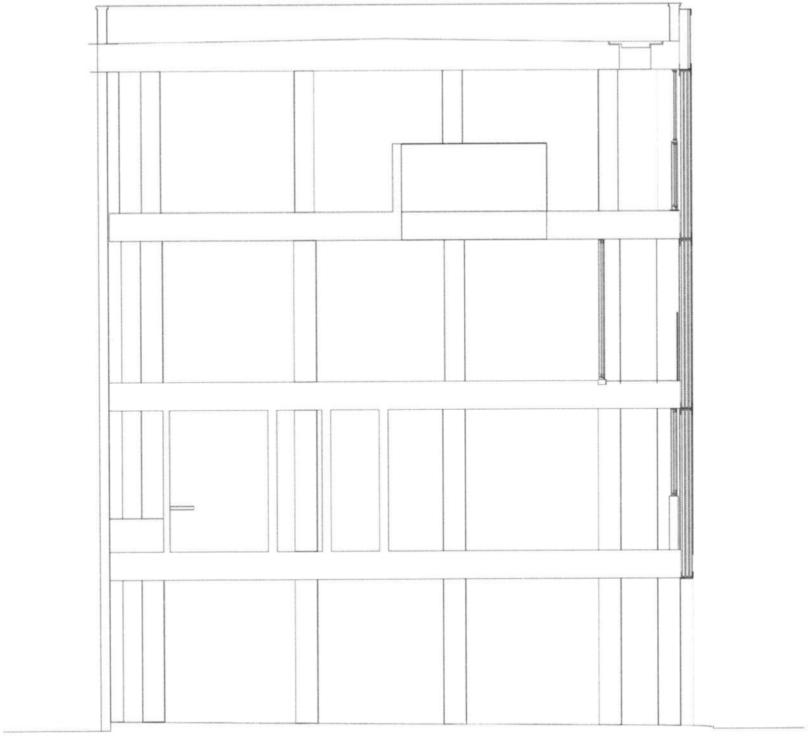

Longitudinal sections
Secciones longitudinales

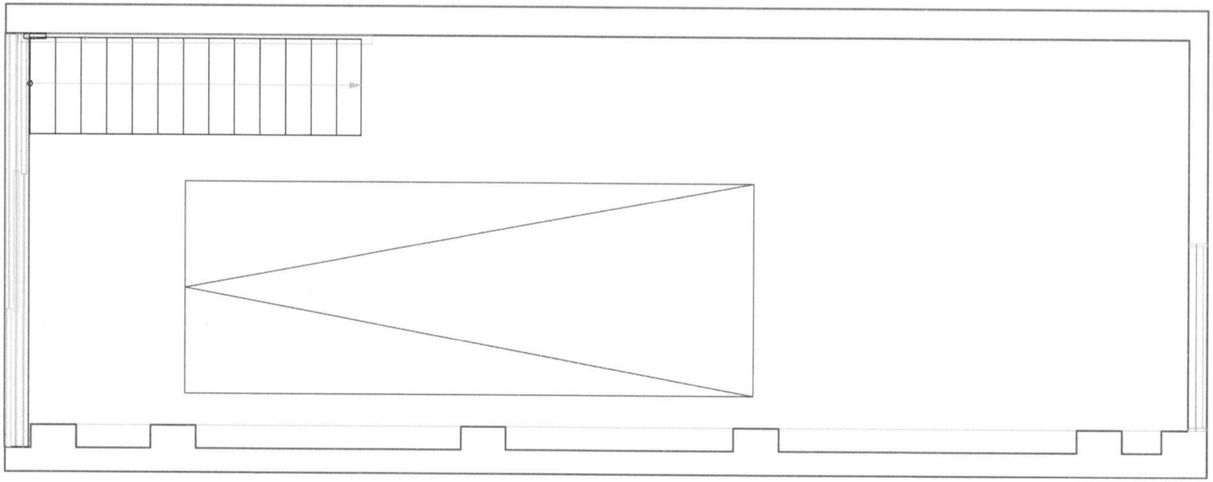

Ground floor plan
Planta baja

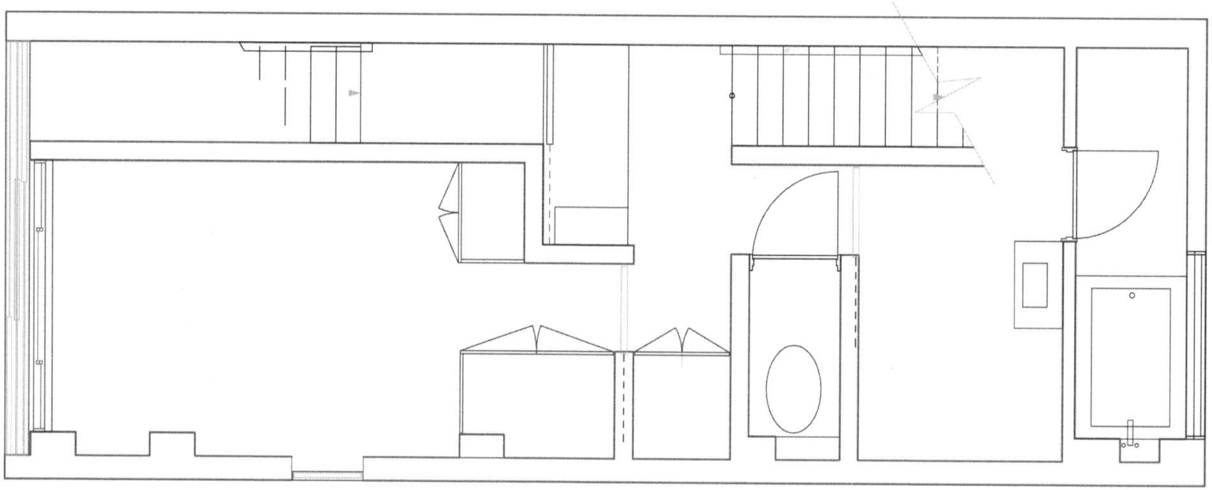

First floor plan
Primera planta

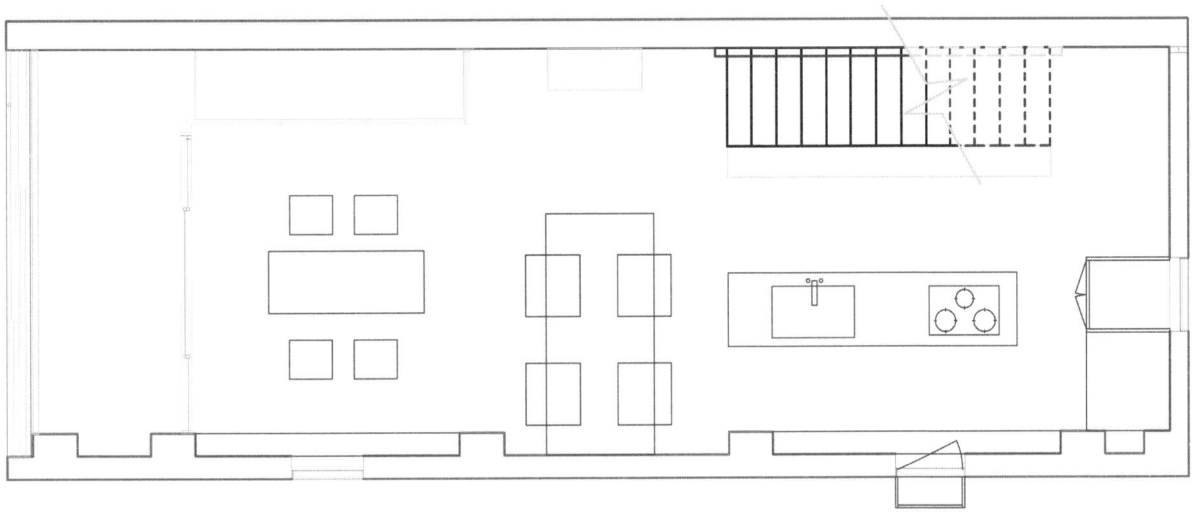

Second floor plan
Segunda planta

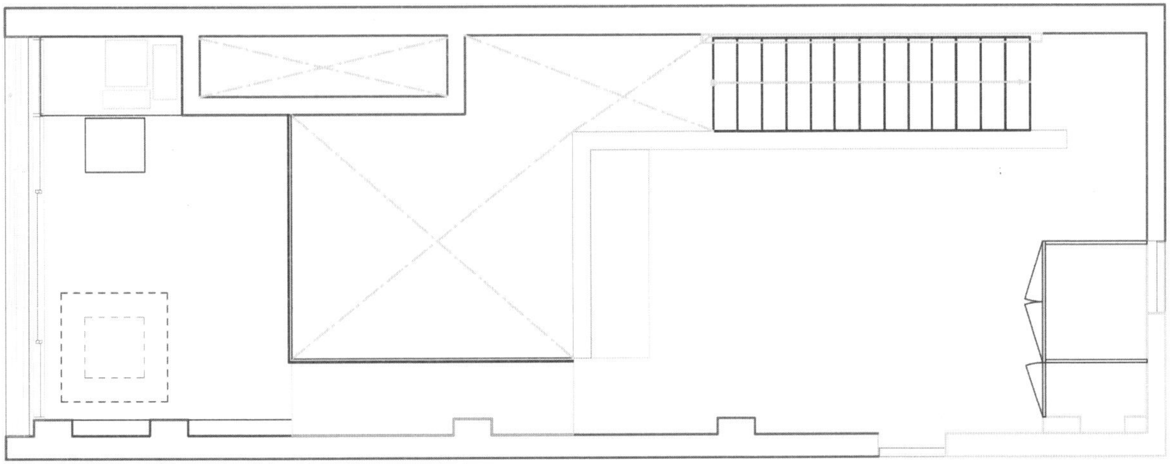

Third floor plan
Tercera planta

F House

Williams Burton Architects
Adelaide, Australia
Photos © James Knowler

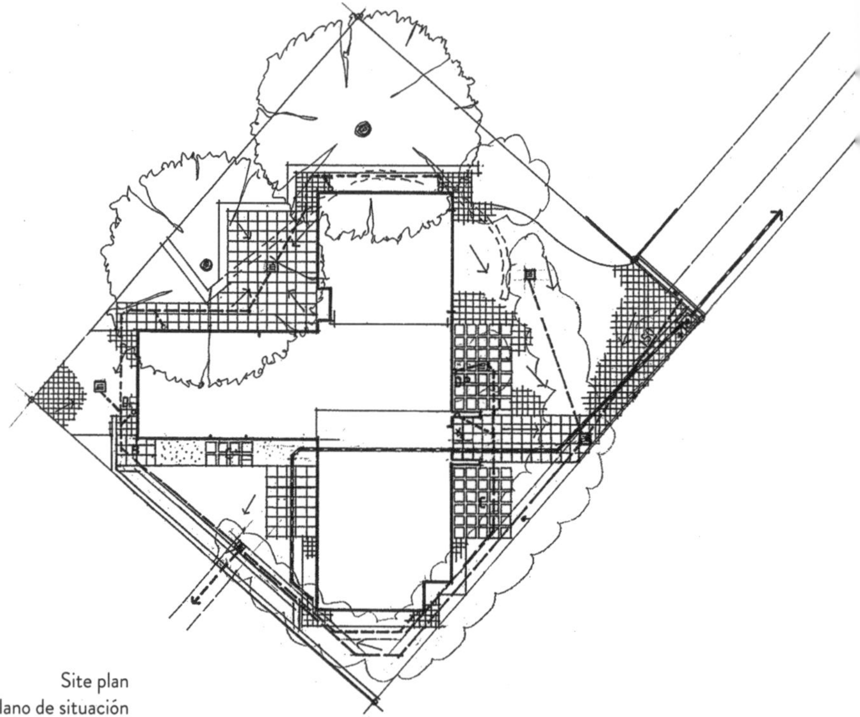

Site plan
Plano de situación

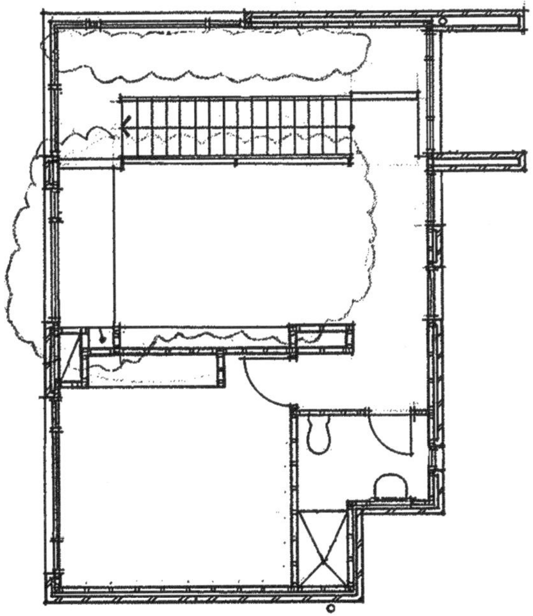

First floor plan
Primera planta

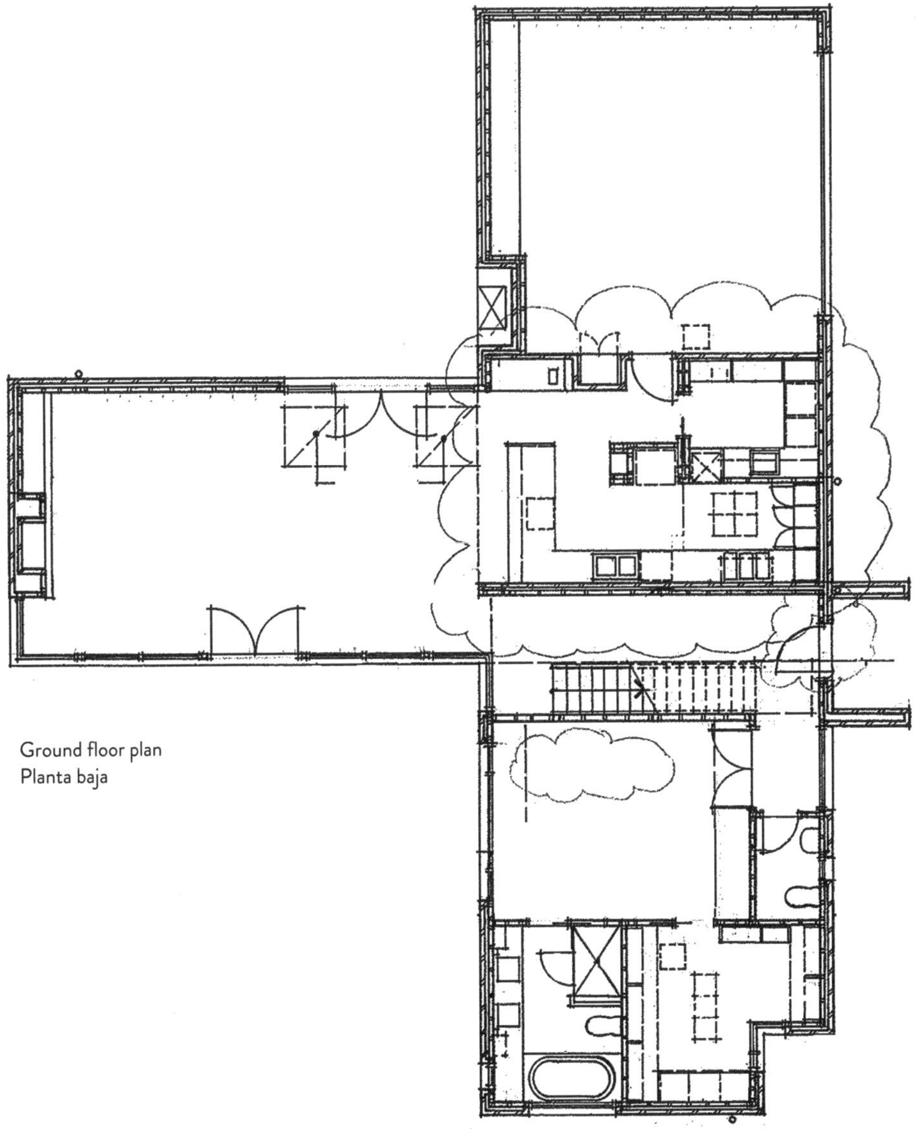

Ground floor plan
Planta baja

Living Space for Two Artists

Tony Fretton Architects
London, United Kingdom
Photos © Helène Binet

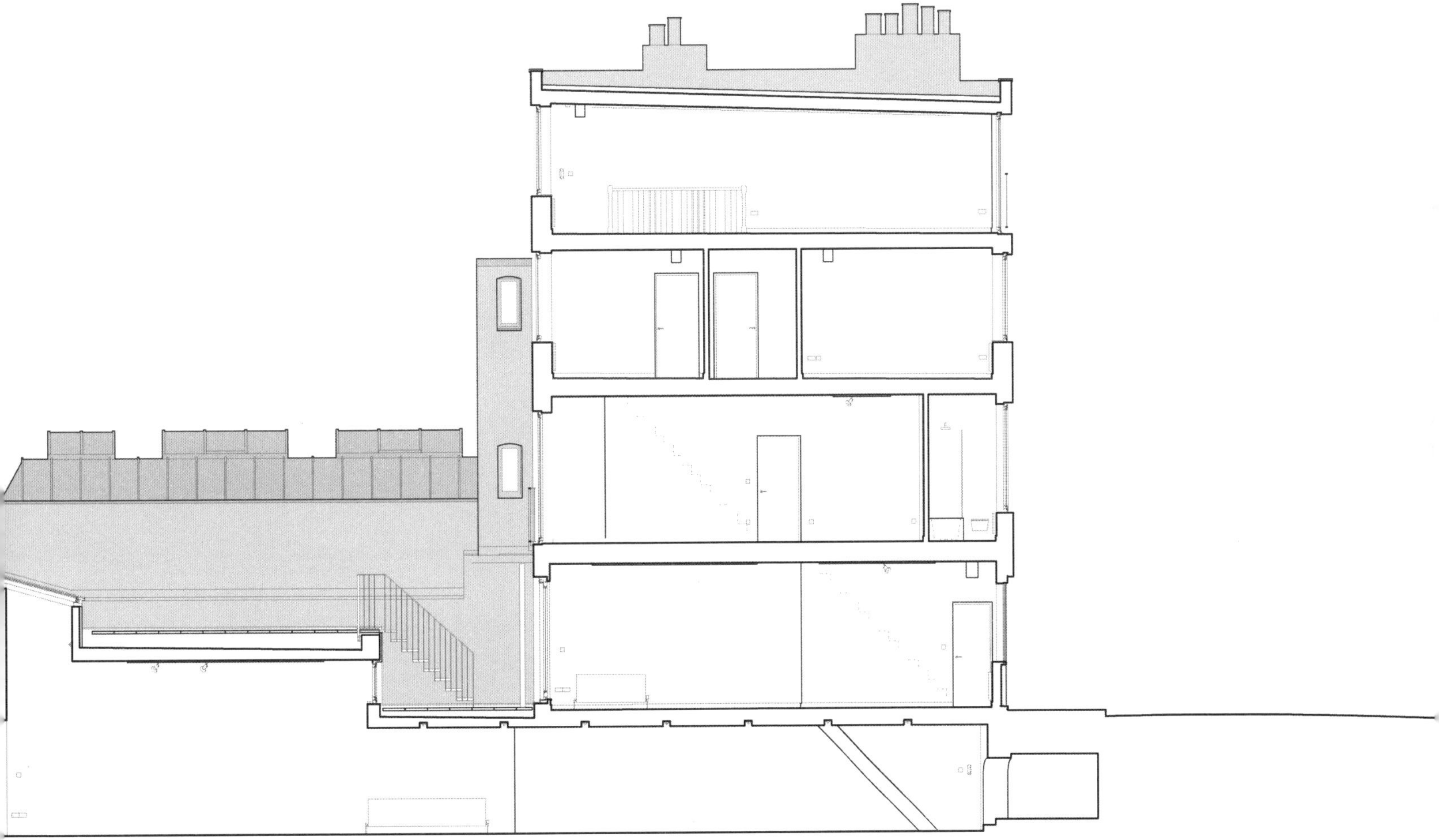

Longitudinal section
Sección longitudinal

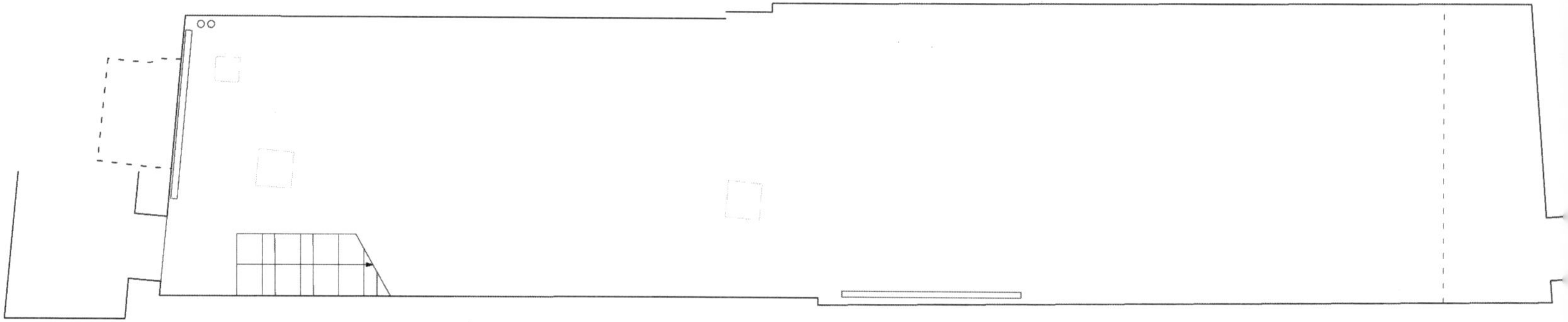

Basement floor plan
Sótano

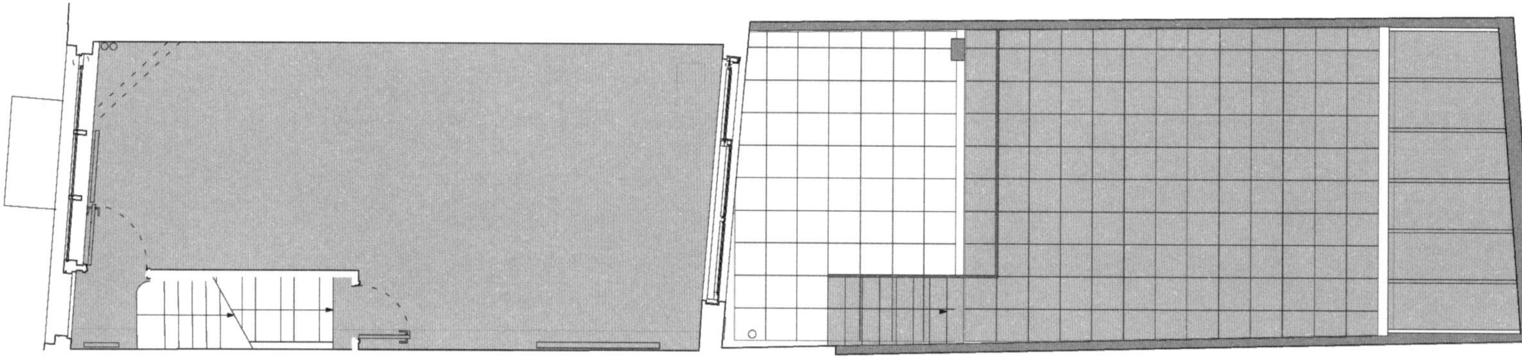

Ground floor plan
Planta baja

First floor plan
Primera planta

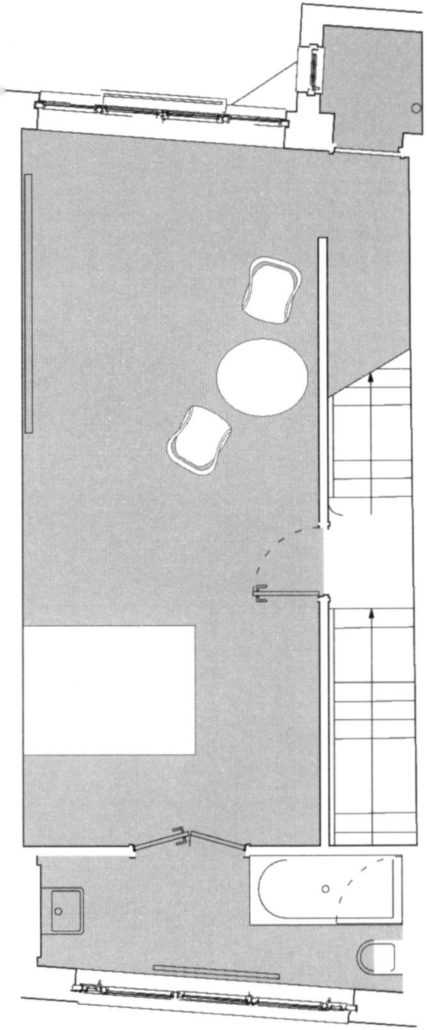

Second floor plan
Segunda planta

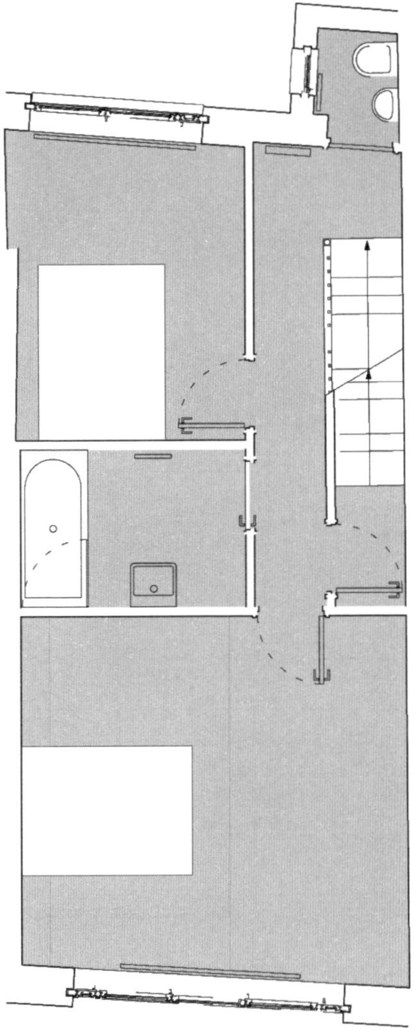

Third floor plan
Tercera planta

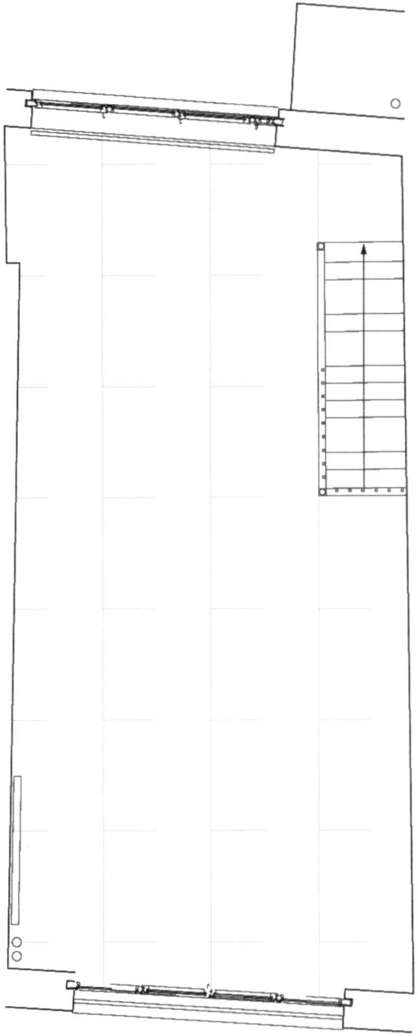

Duplex on Chattanooga Street

Zack | De Vito Architecture
San Francisco (California), USA
Photos © Massimiliano Bozonella

Elevation
Alzado

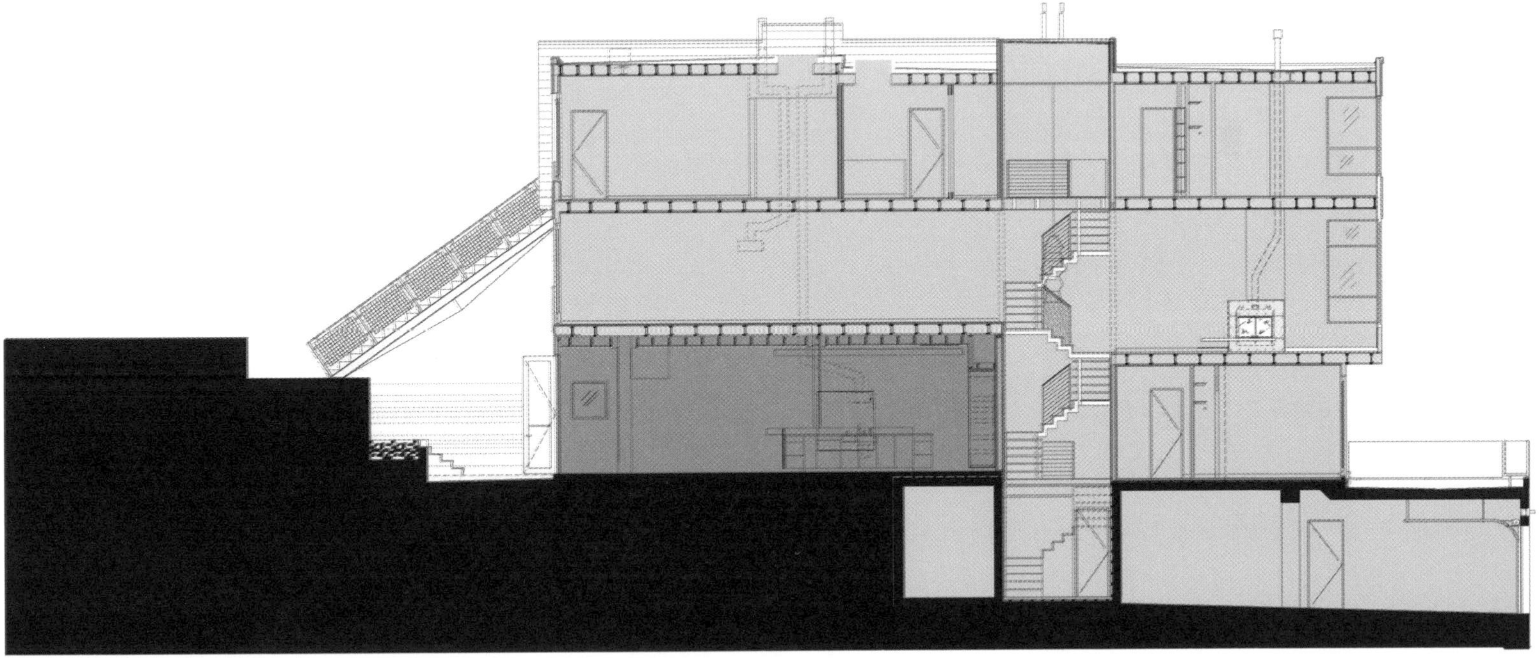

Longitudinal section
Sección longitudinal

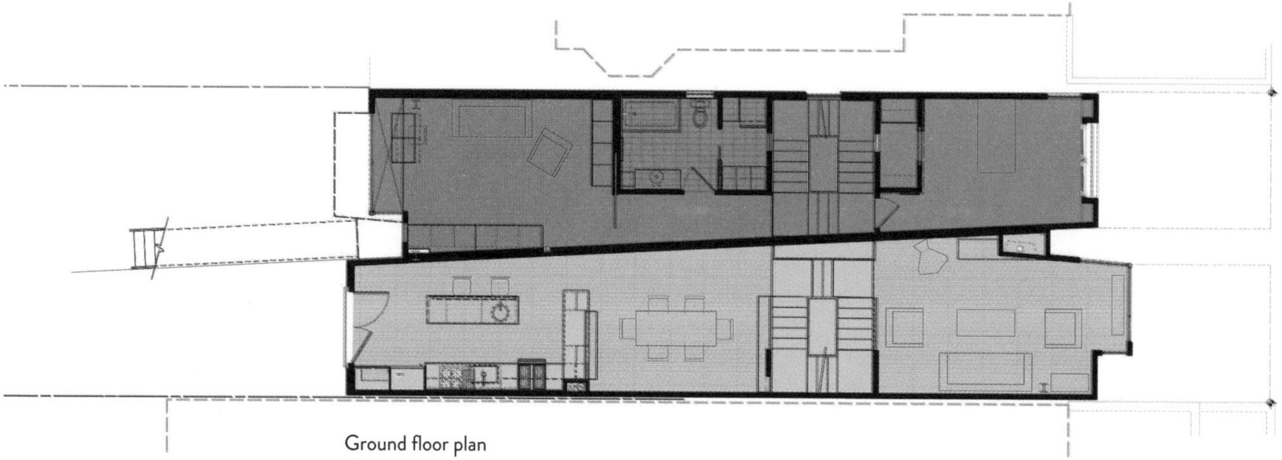

Ground floor plan
Planta baja

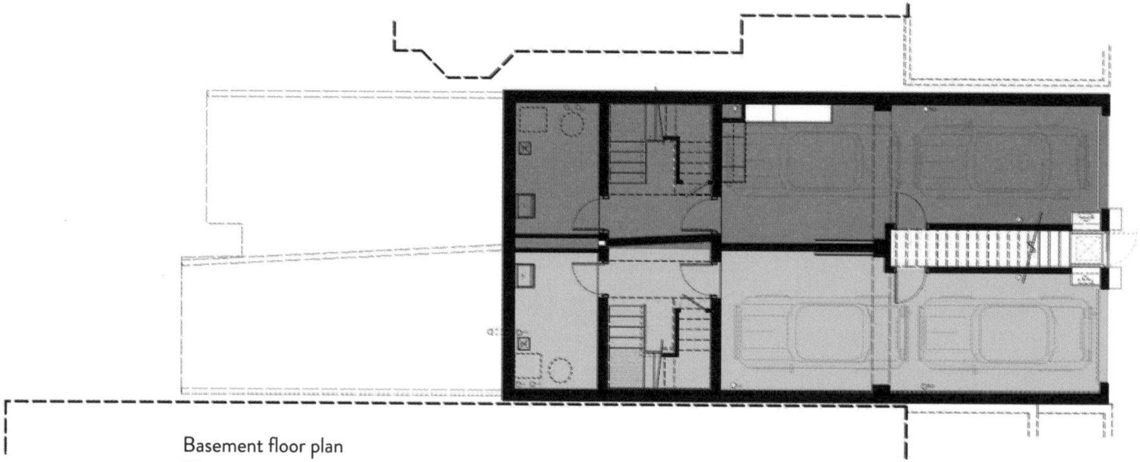

Basement floor plan
Sótano

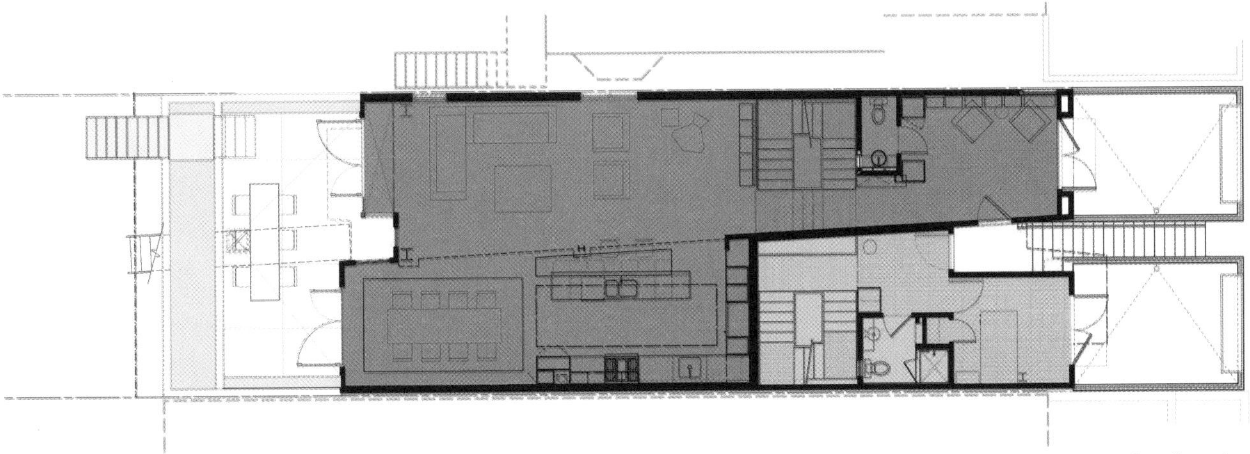

First floor plan
Primera planta

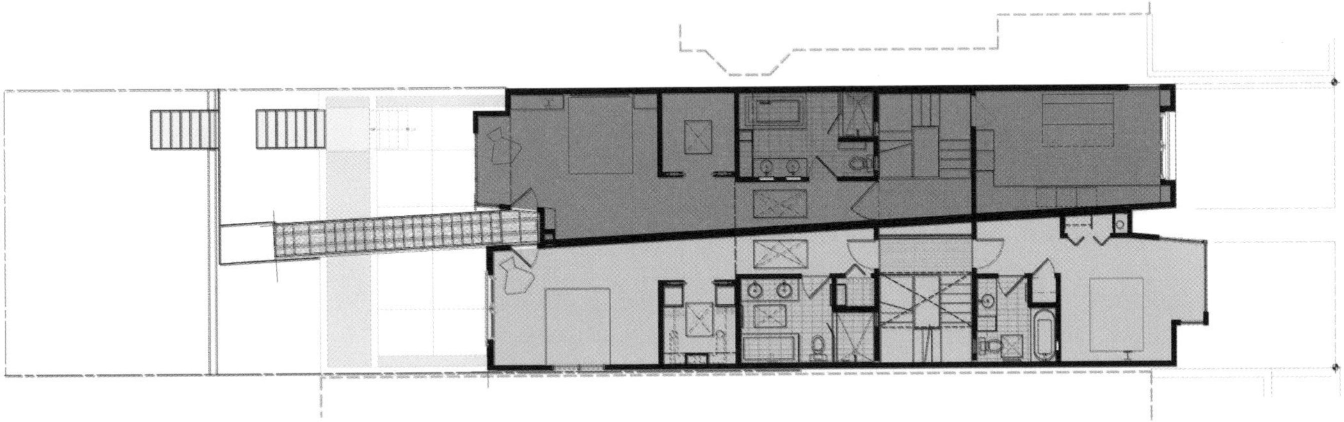

Second floor plan
Segunda planta

Gillipsi Airaghi

A+D Architecture
San Francisco (California), USA
Photos © Roger Casas

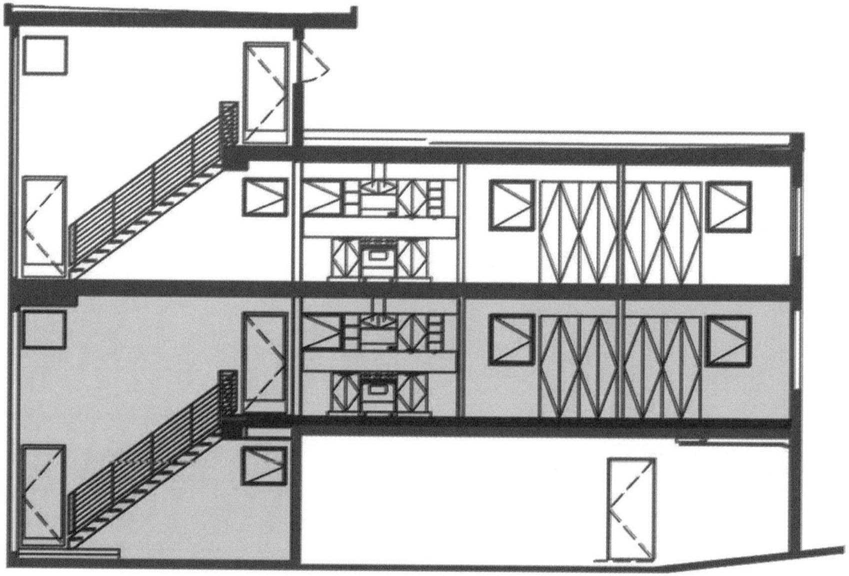

Cross section
Sección transversal

Elevations
Alzados

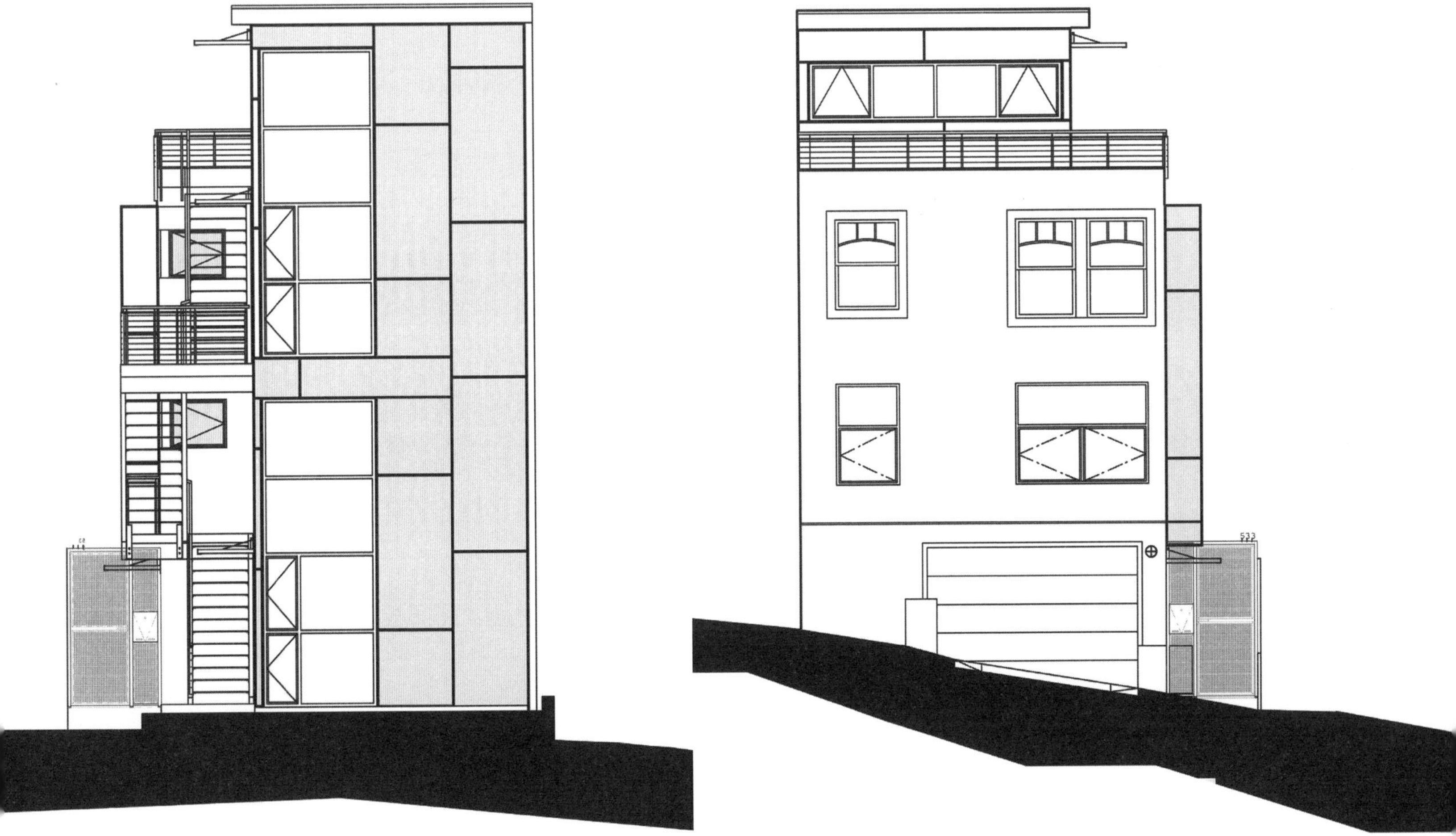

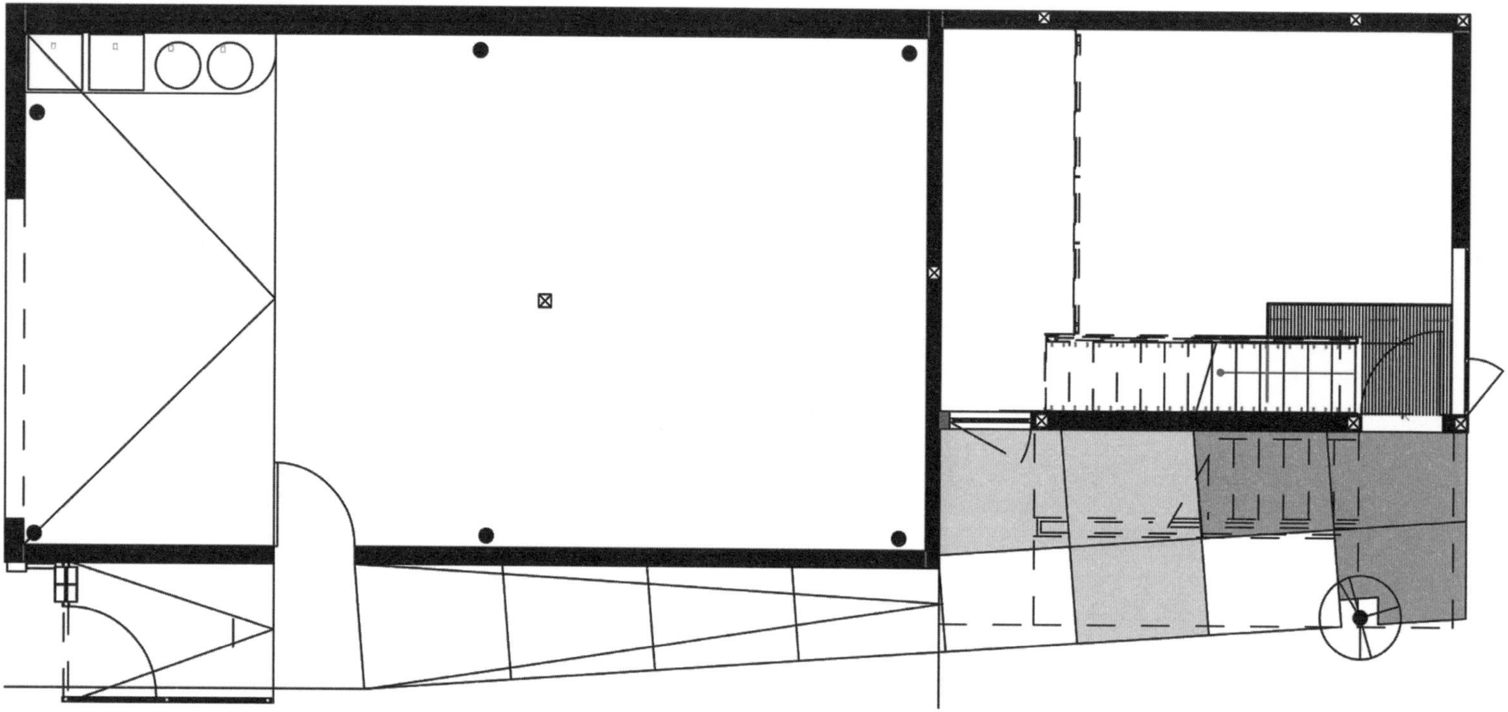

Ground floor plan
Planta baja

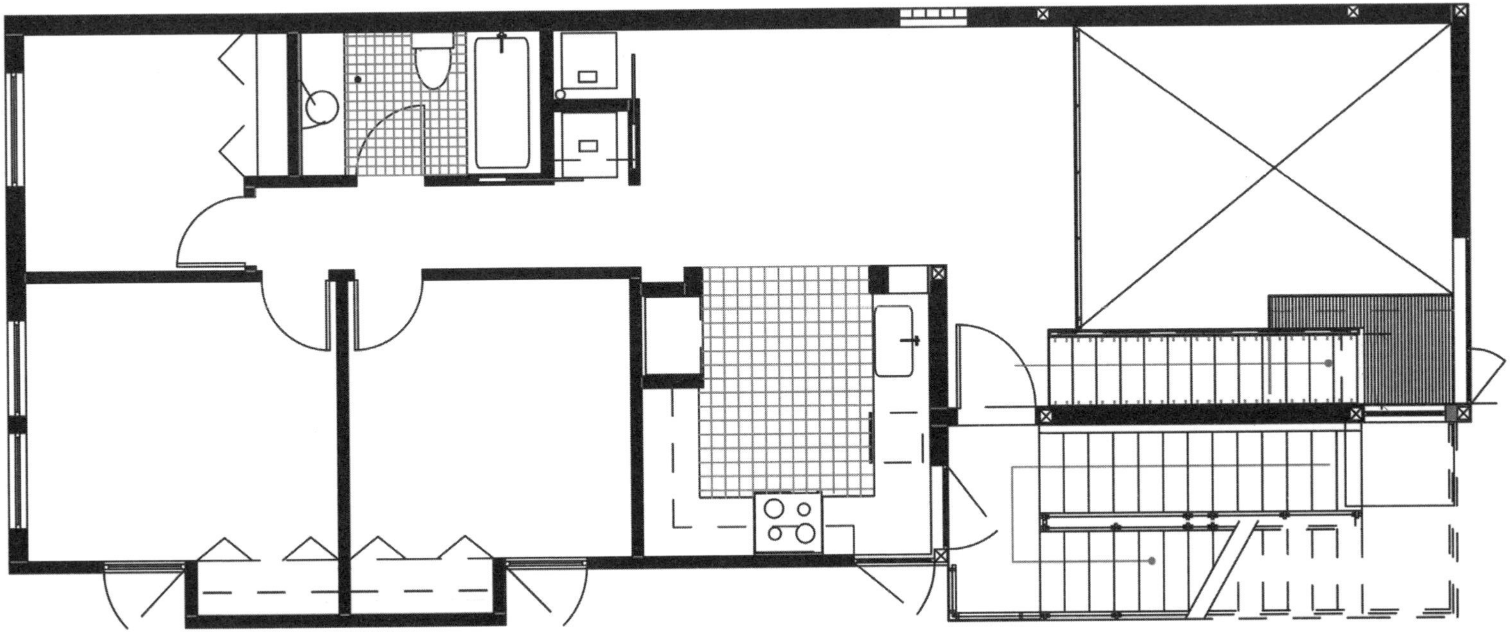

First floor plan
Primera planta

House in Russian Hill

Leddy Maytum Stacy Architects
San Francisco (California), USA
Photos © Richard Barnes

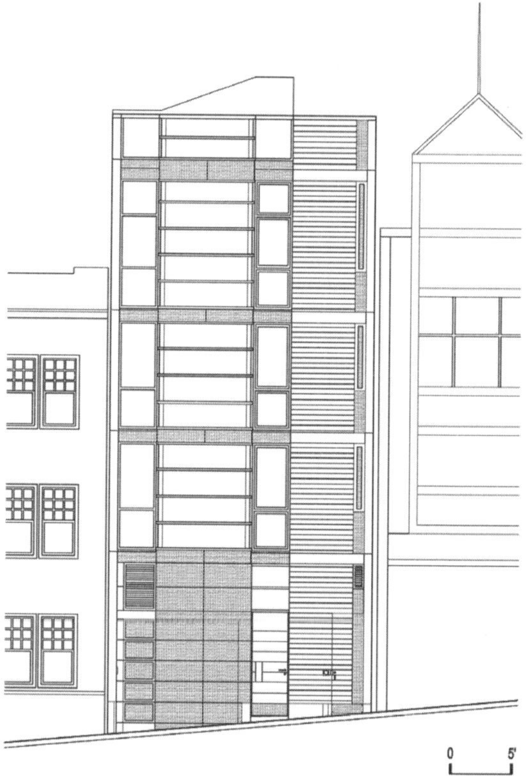

Street elevation
Alzado calle

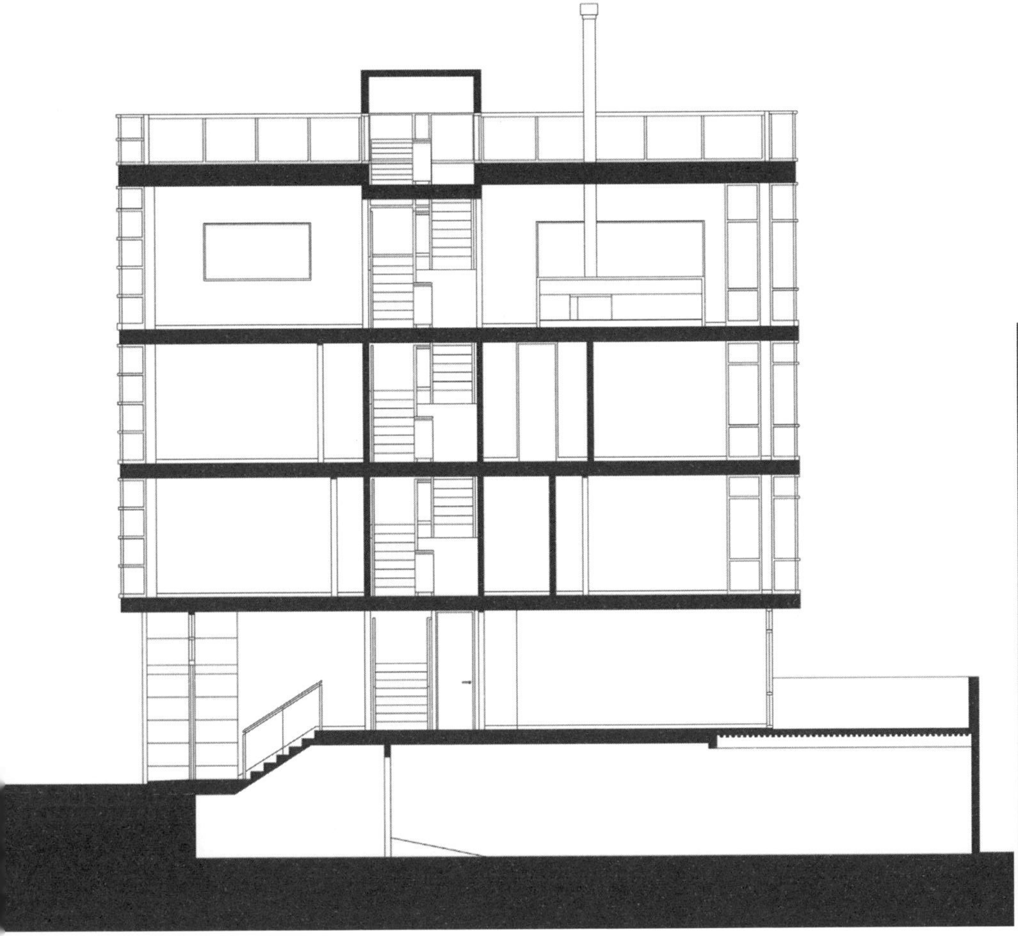

Longitudinal section
Sección longitudinal

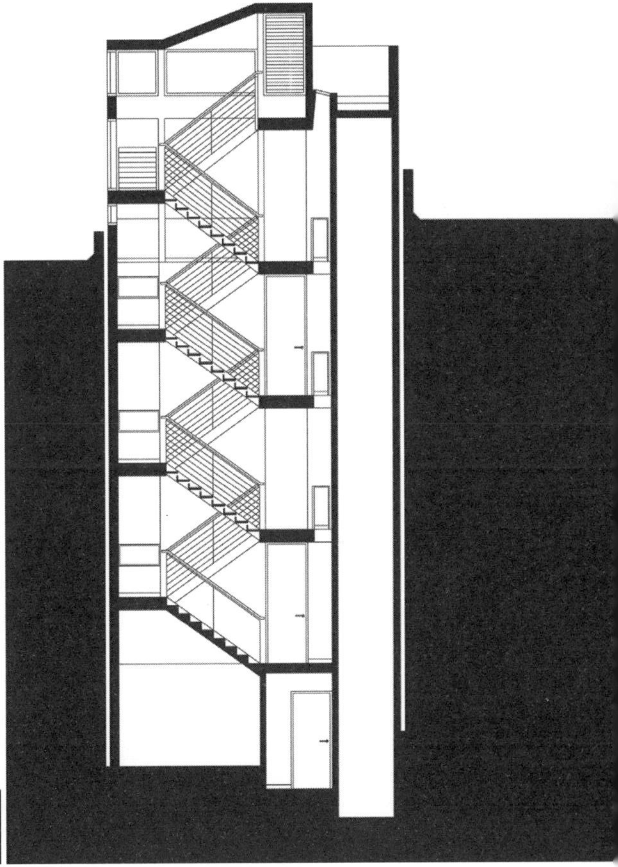

Cross section
Sección transversal

1.Bedroom 01
2.Office
3.Bedroom 02
4.Bathroom
5.Laundry

1.Dormitorio 01
2.Despacho
3.Dormitorio 02
4.Baño
5.Lavandería

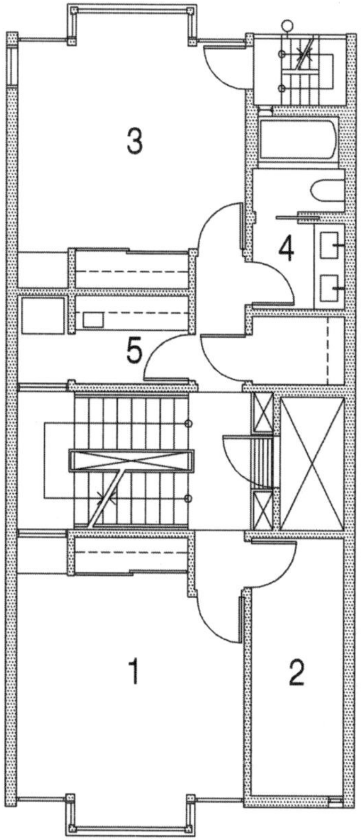

Second floor plan
Segunda planta

1.Entry
2.Trash
3.Storage
4.Family room
5.Kitchenette
6.Bath
7.Patio

1. Entrada
2. Basura
3. Almacenamiento
4. Habitación familiar
5. Cocina
6. Baño
7. Patio

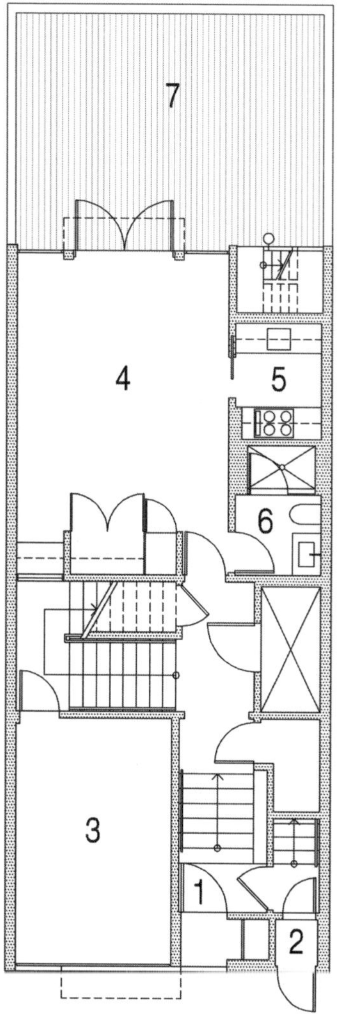

First floor plan
Primera planta

1.Garage
2.Fitness room
3.Storage

1. Garaje
2. Sala de fitness
3. Almacenamiento

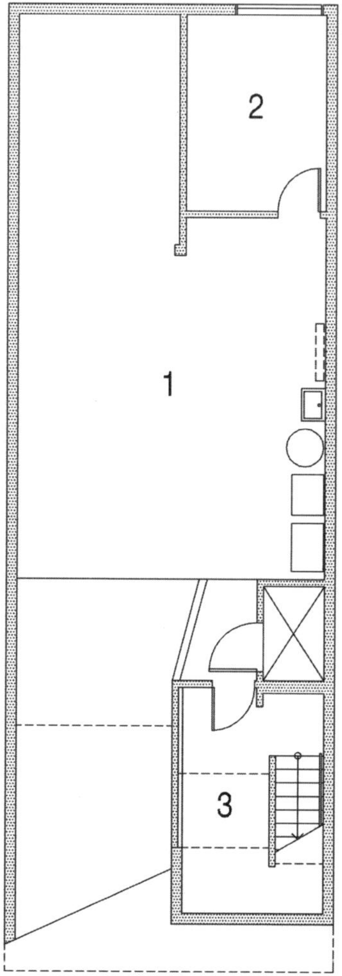

Basement floor plan
Sótano

Attic floor plan
Planta del ático

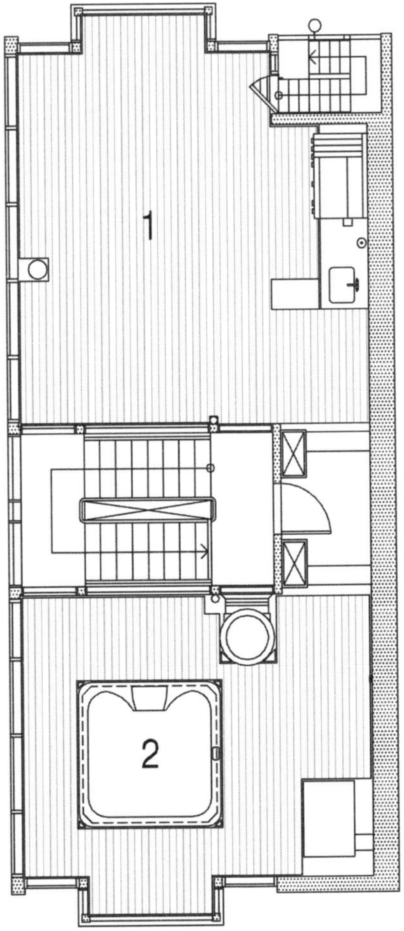

1.Wood deck
2.Spa

1. Cubierta de madera
2. Spa

Fourth floor plan
Cuarta planta

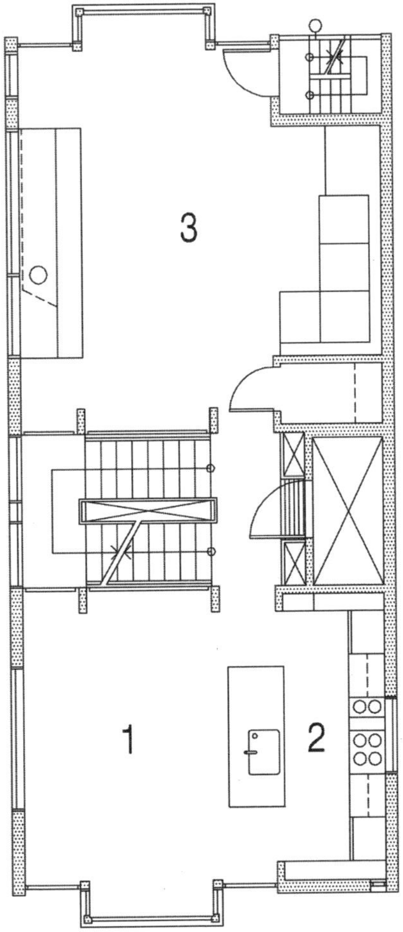

1.Dining room
2.Kitchen
3.Living room

1. Comedor
2. Cocina
3. Sala de estar

Third floor plan
Tercera planta

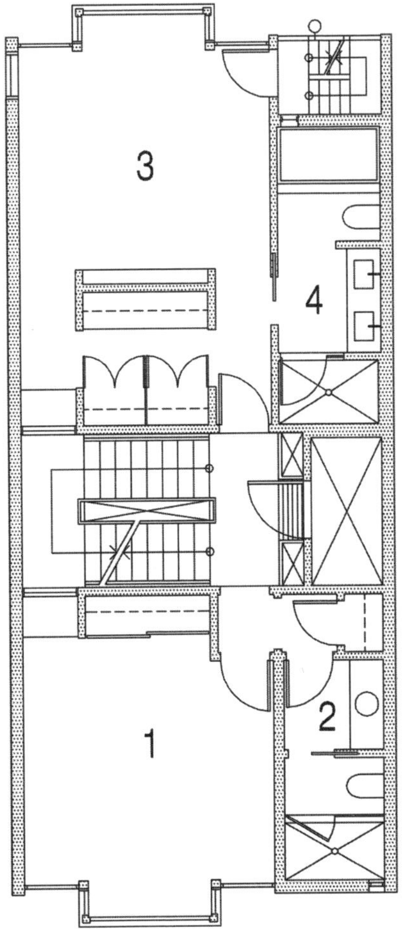

1.Bedroom 03
2.Bathroom
3.Master bedroom
4.Master bathroom

1. Dormitorio 03
2. Baño
3. Dormitorio principal
4. Baño principal.

Martin House

CCS Architecture
San Francisco (California), USA
Photos © Tim Griffith

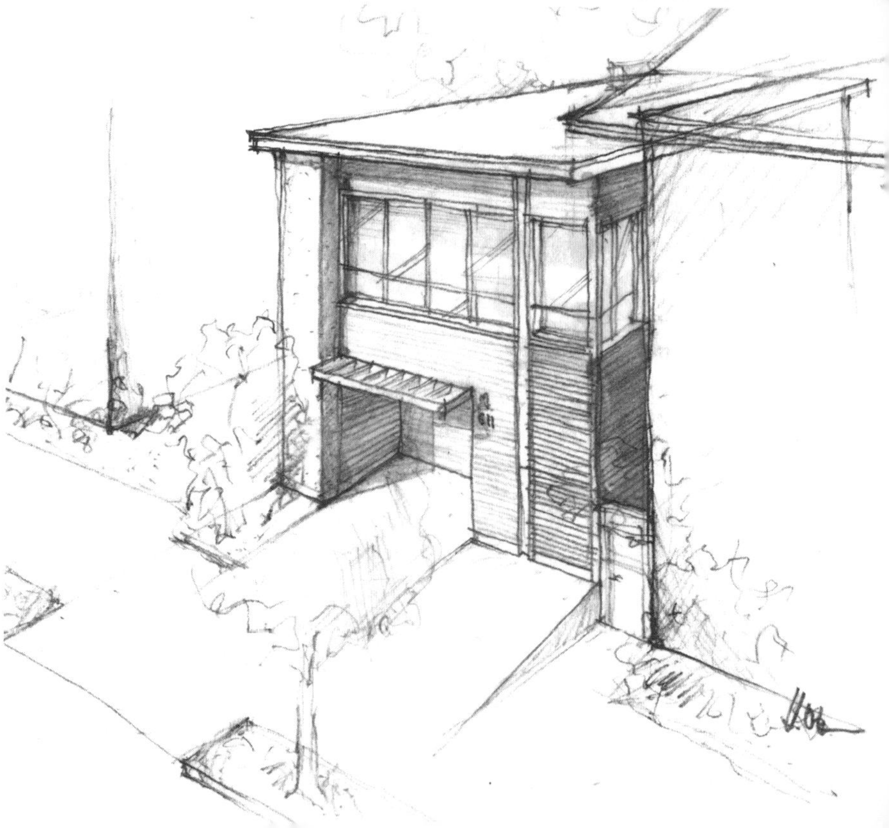

Sketch
Boceto

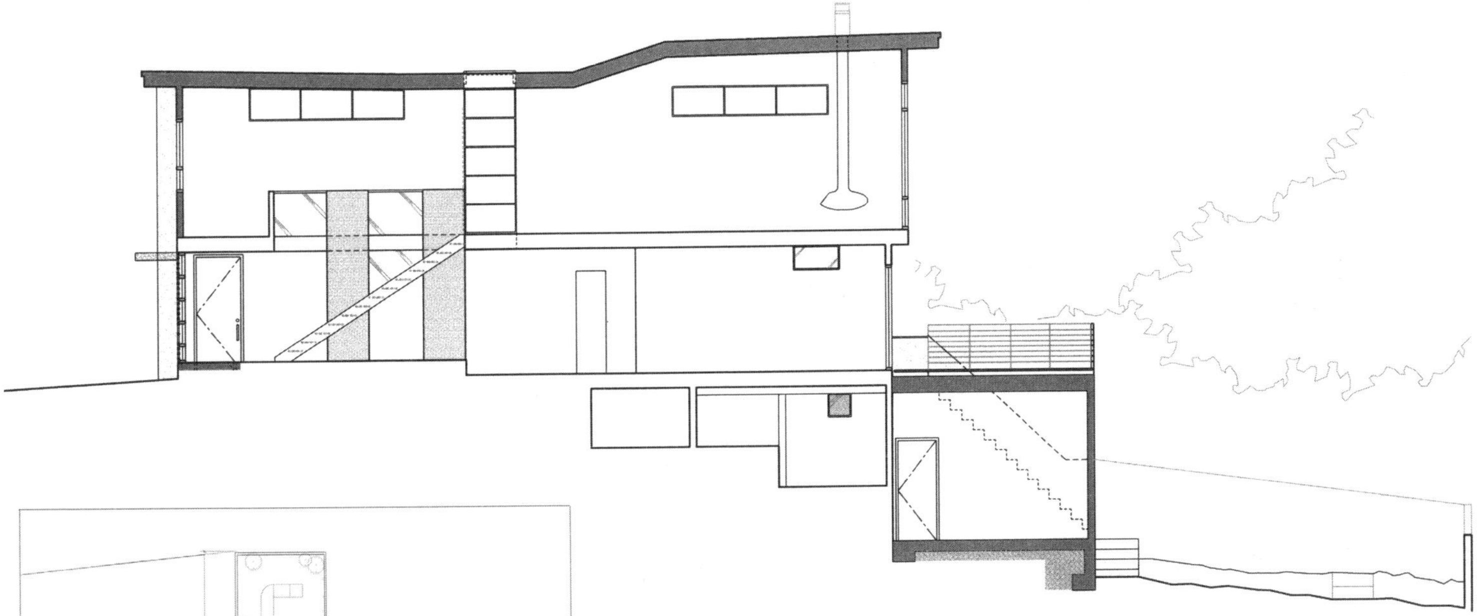

Longitudinal section
Sección longitudinal

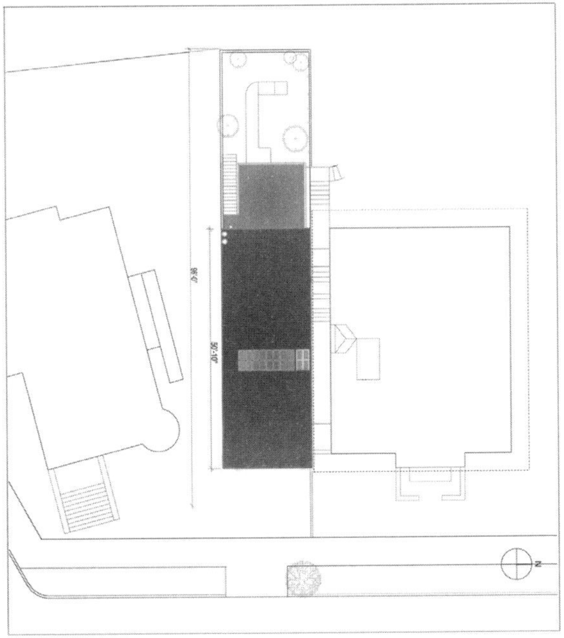

Site plan
Plano de situación

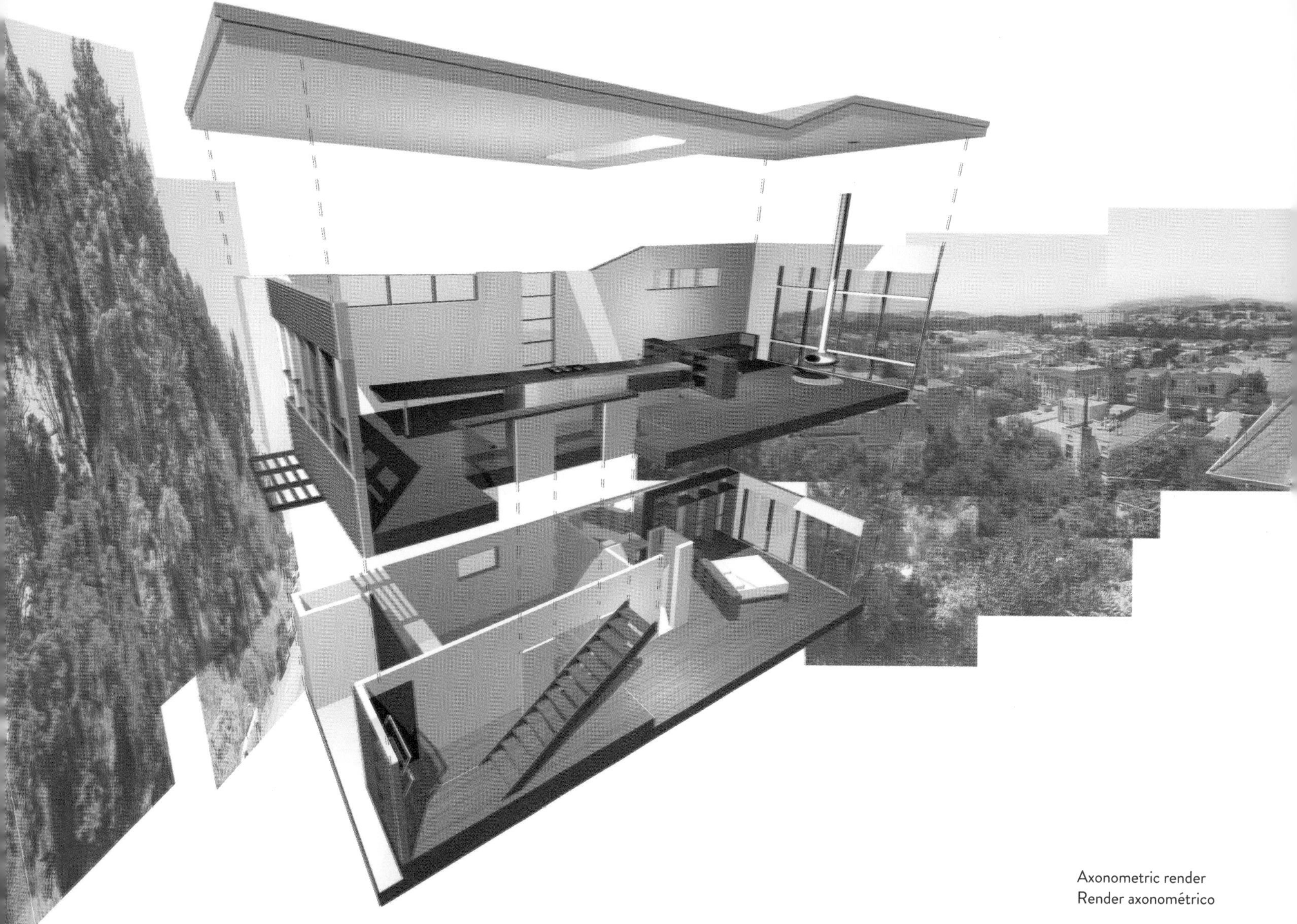

Axonometric render
Render axonométrico

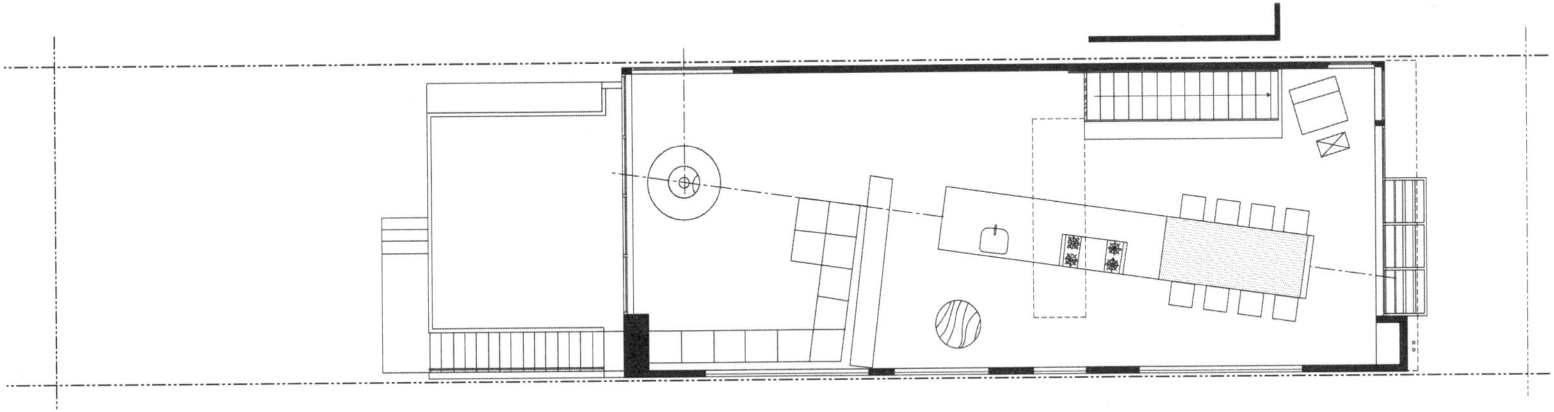

Second floor plan
Segunda planta

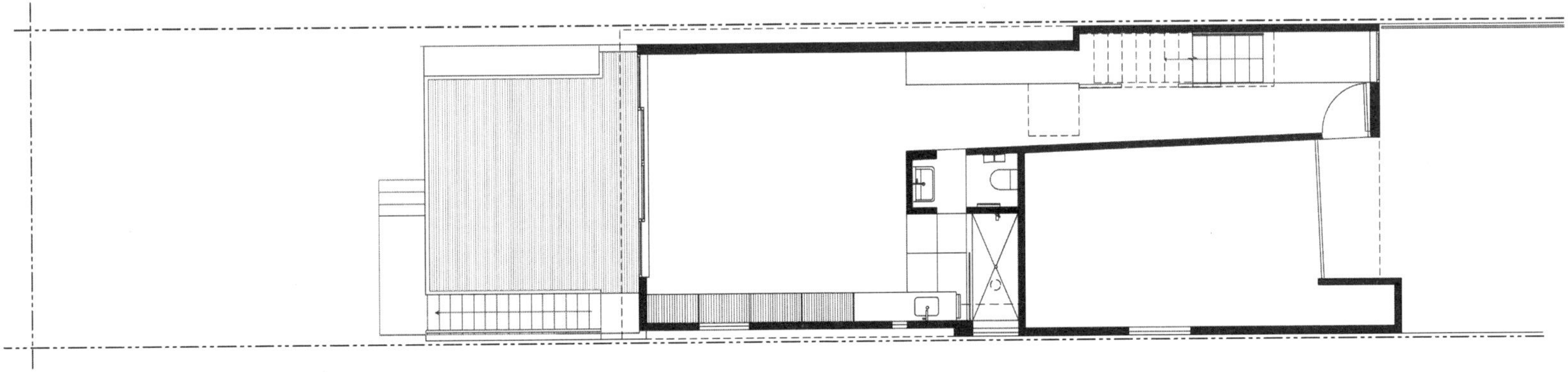

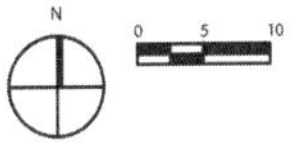

First floor plan
Primera planta

Alexandra Residence

Naturehumaine Architecture Design
Montreal, Canada
Photos © Adrien Williams

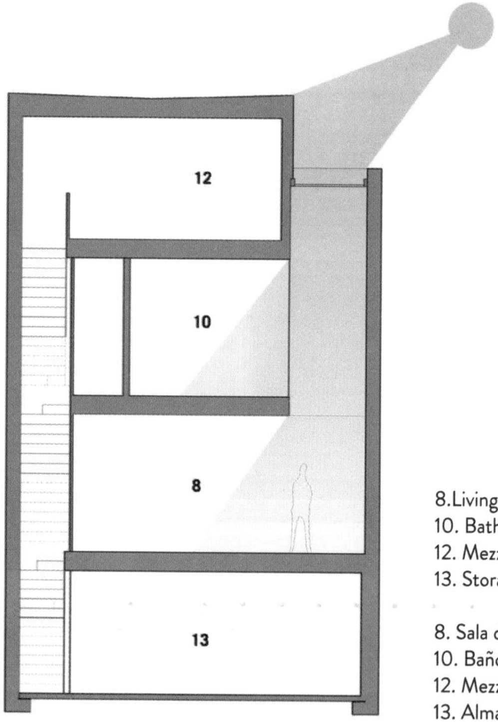

Cross section
Sección transversal

8. Living room
10. Bathroom
12. Mezzanine / Office
13. Storage

8. Sala de estar
10. Baño
12. Mezzanine / Oficina
13. Almacenamiento

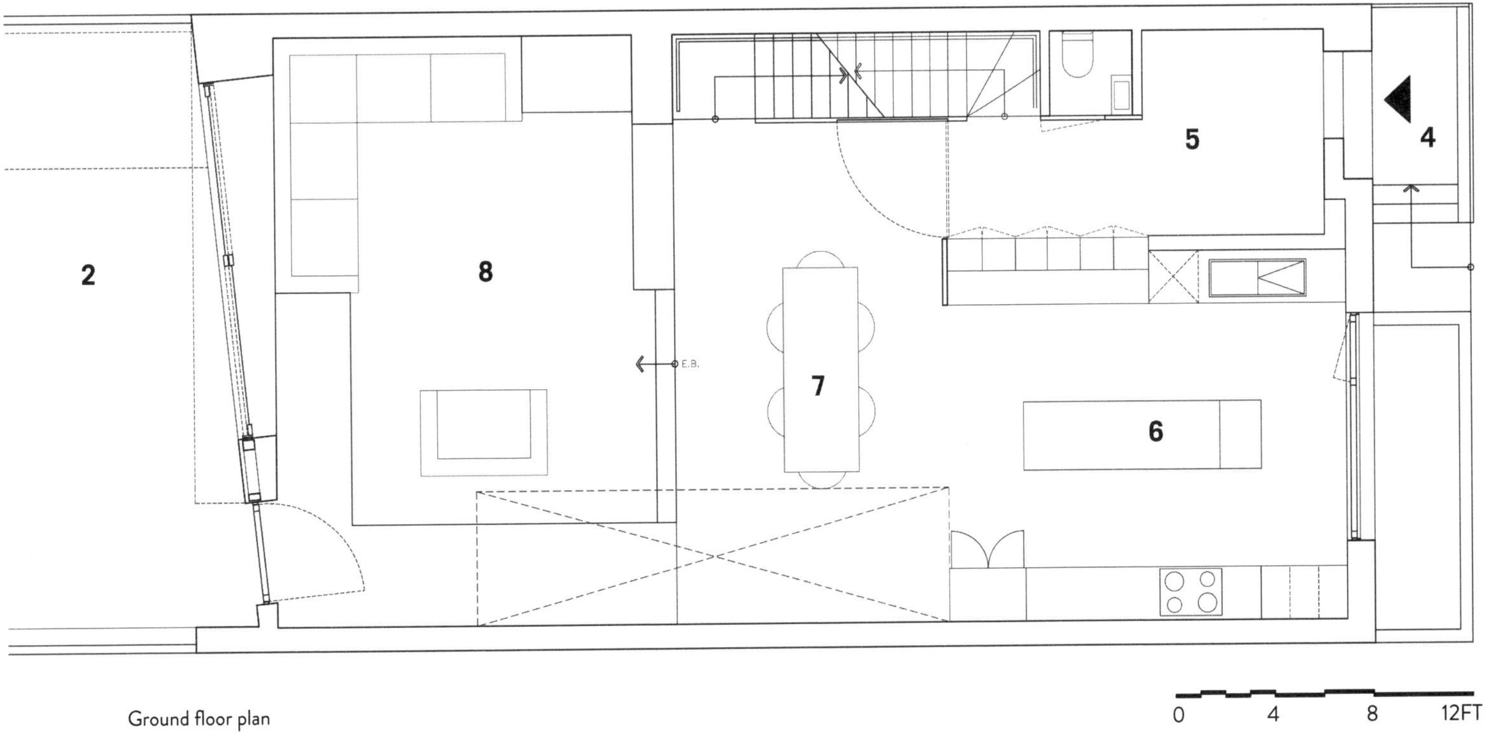

Ground floor plan
Planta baja

2.Patio	2. Patio
4.Entrance	4. Entrada
5.Vestibule	5. Portal
6.Kitchen	6. Cocina
7.Dining room	7. Comedor
8.Living room	8. Sala de estar

Longitudinal section
Sección longitudinal

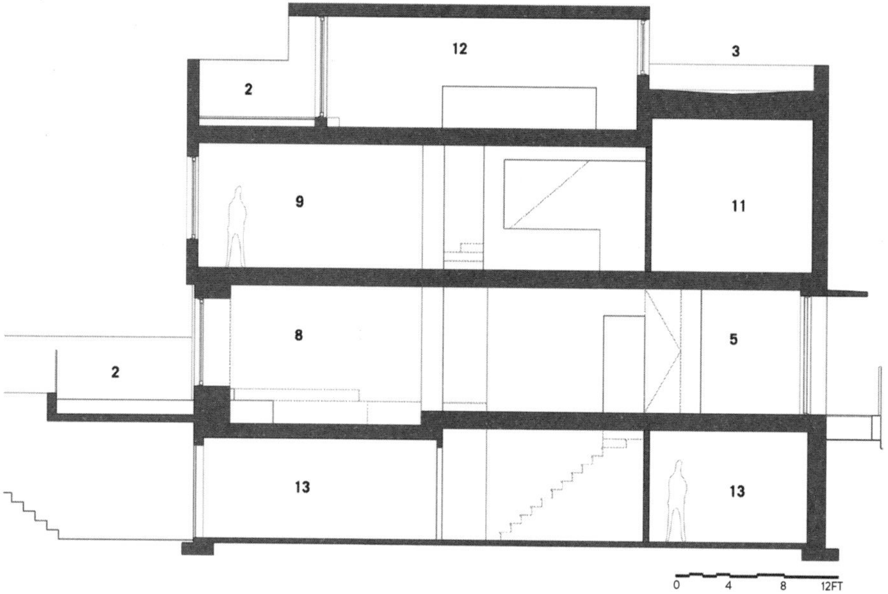

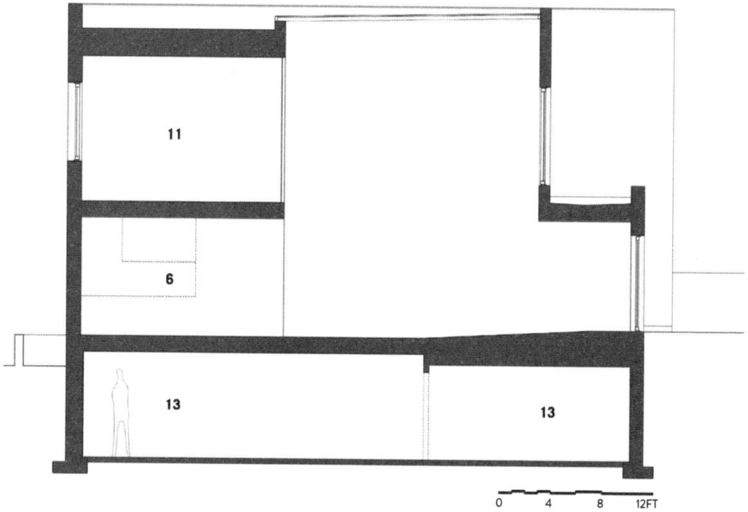

1. Garden
2. Patio
3. Green roof
4. Entrance
5. Vestibule
6. Kitchen
7. Dining room
8. Living room
9. Master bedroom
10. Bathroom
11. Bedroom
12. Mezzanine
13. Storage

1. Jardín
2. Patio
3. Techo verde
4. Entrada
5. Portal
6. Cocina
7. Comedor
8. Sala de estar
9. Dormitorio principal
10. Baño
11. Dormitorio
12. Entresuelo
13. Almacenamiento

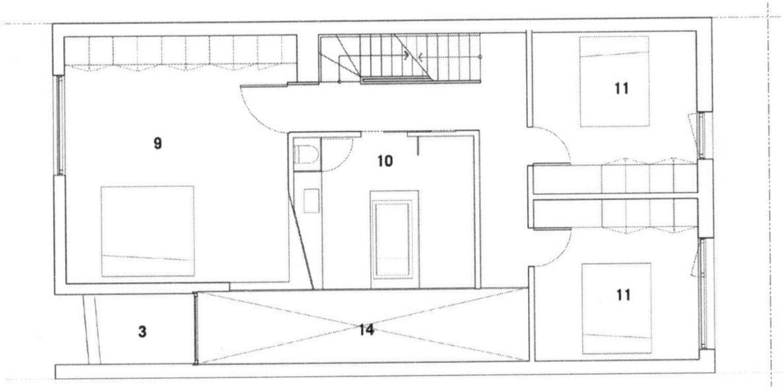

Second floor plan
Segunda planta

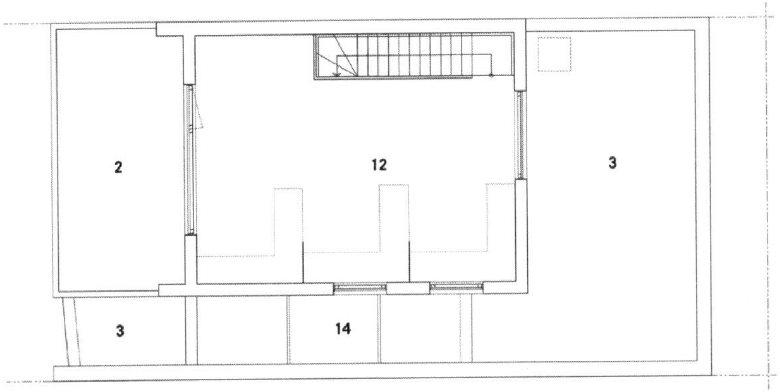

Mezzanine floor plan
Planta entresuelo

2. Patio
3. Green roof
9. Bedroom
10. Bathroom
11. Bedroom
12. Mezzanine
14. Skylight

2. Patio
3. Techo verde
9. Habitación
10. Baño
11. Dormitorio
12. Mezzanine
14. tragaluz

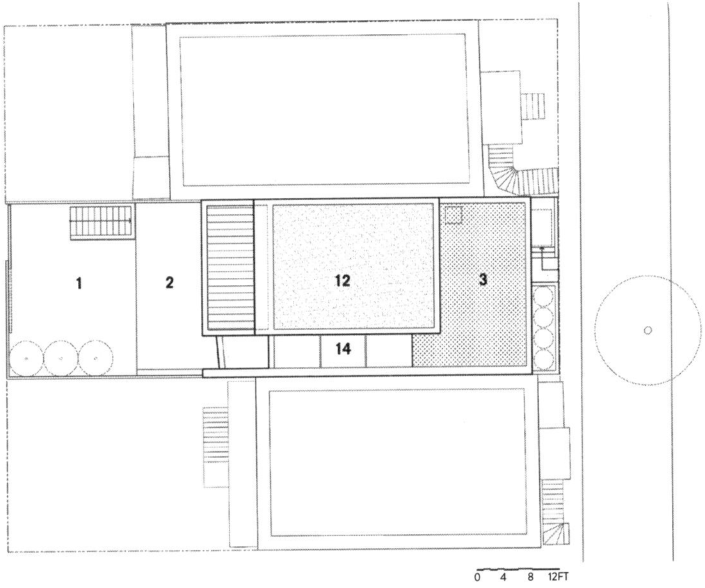

Site plan
Plano de situación

1. Garden
2. Patio
3. Green roof
12. Mezzanine
14. Skylight

1. Jardín
2. Patio
3. Techo verde
12. Entresuelo
14. Tragaluz

Kohler House

Zack | de Vito Architecture
San Francisco (California), USA
Photos © Massimiliano Bozonella + Roger Casas

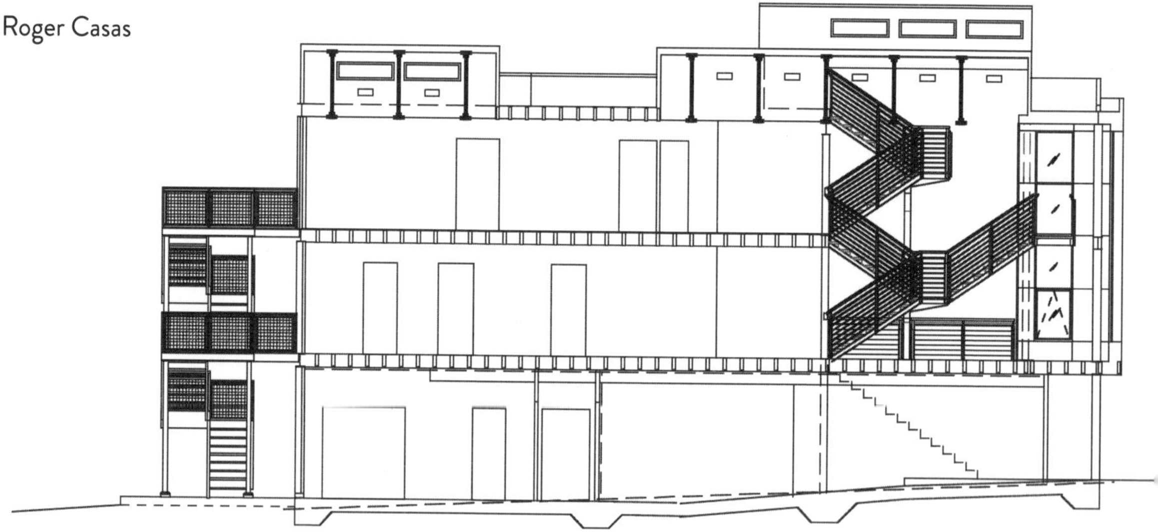

Longitudinal section
Sección longitudinal

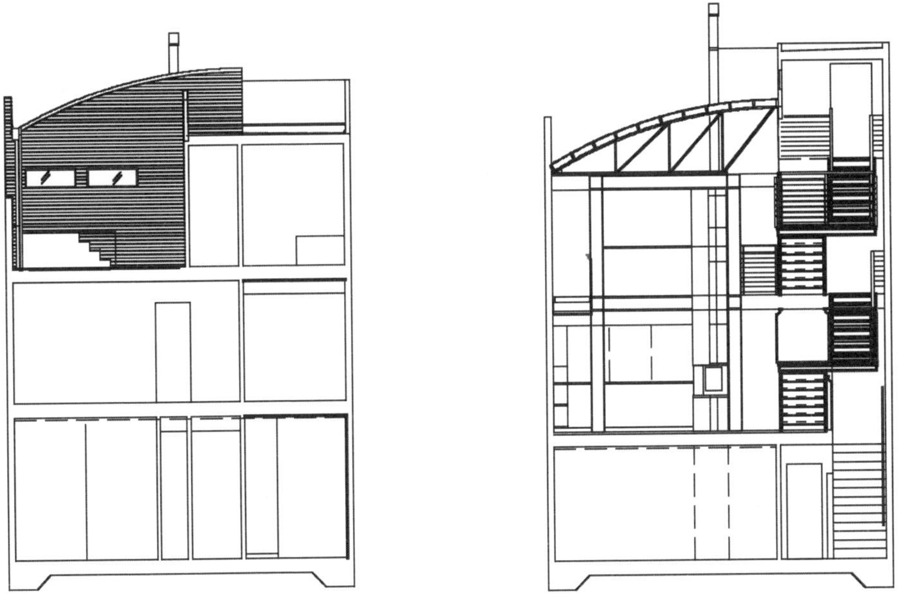

Cross sections
Secciones transversales

Street elevation
Alzado calle

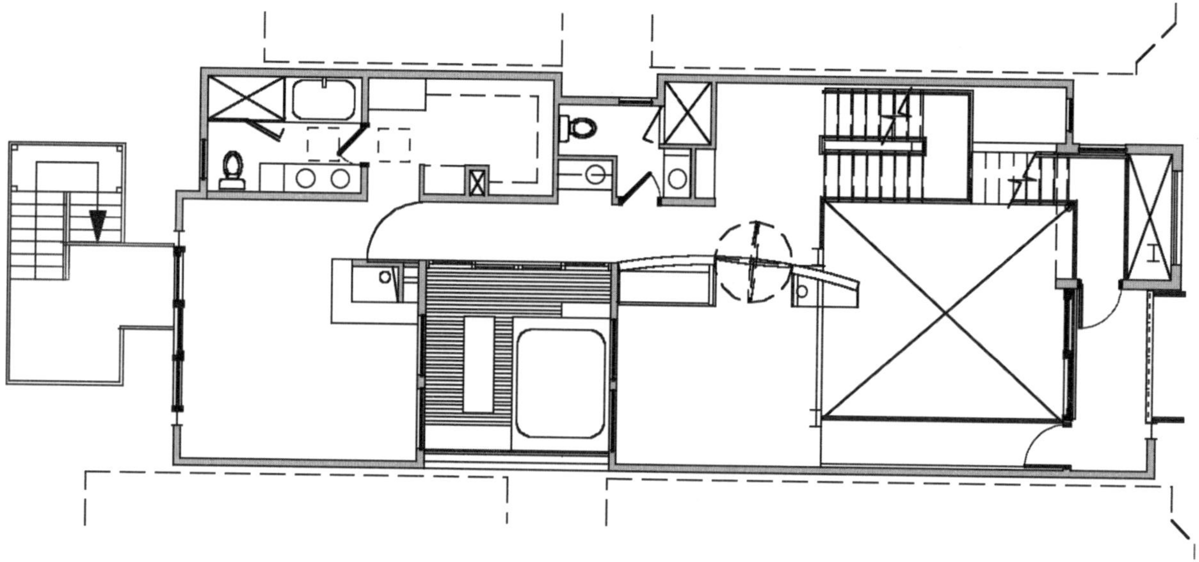

Second floor plan
Segunda planta

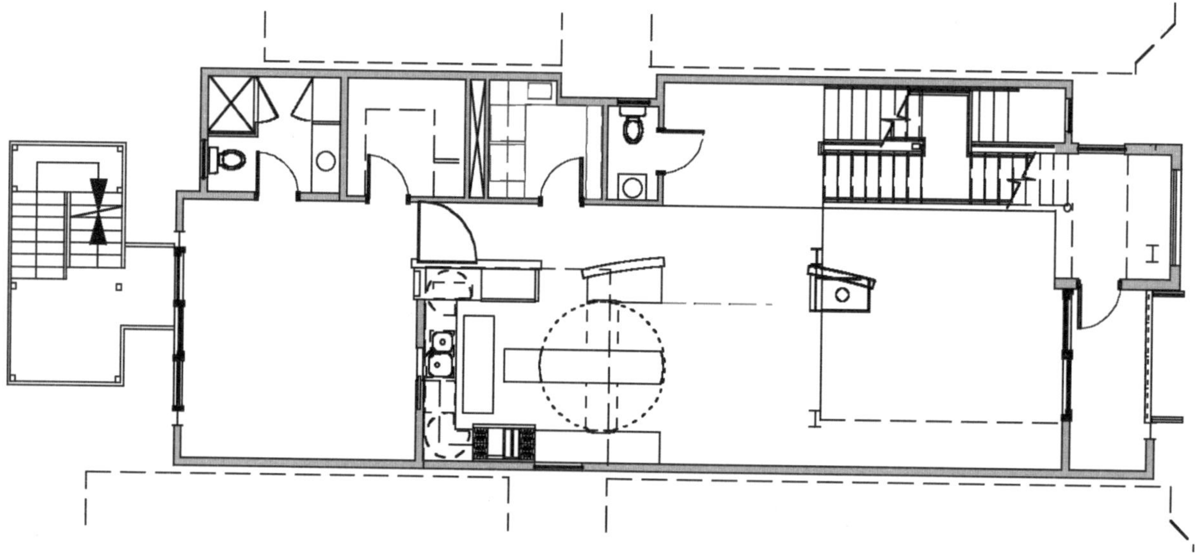

First floor plan
Primera planta

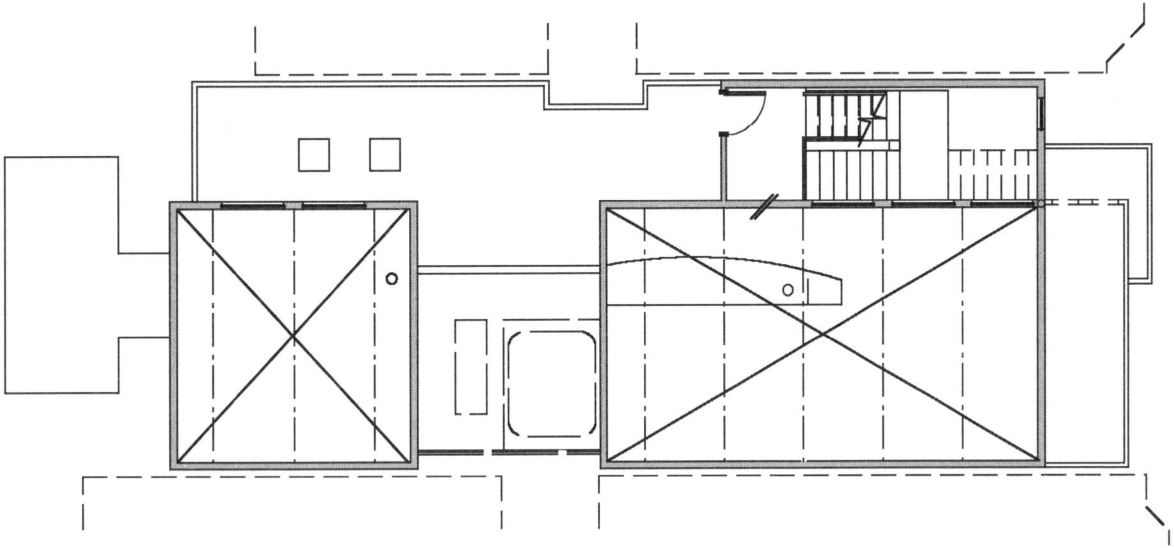

Attic floor plan
Planta del ático

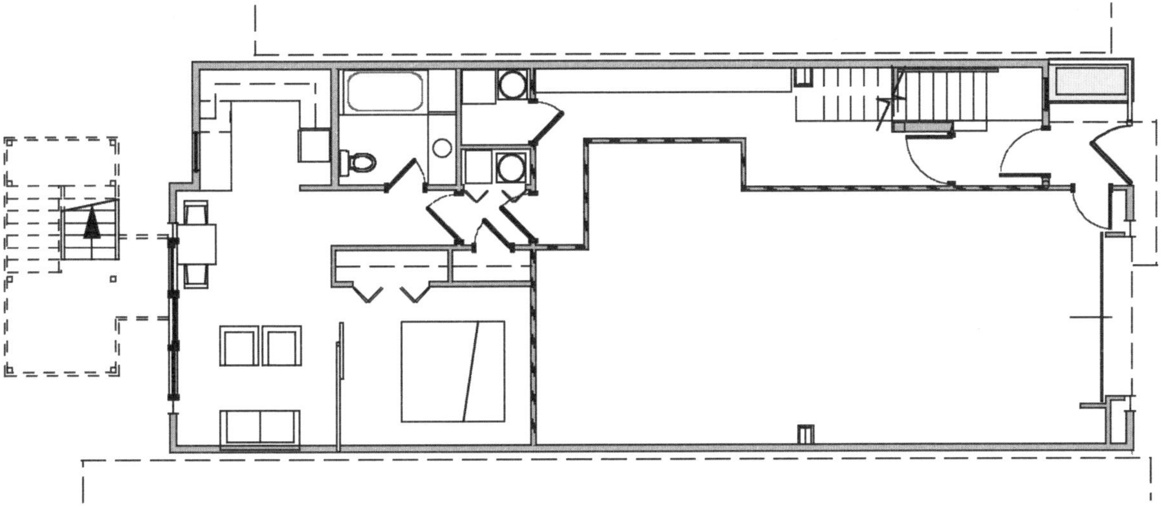

Ground floor plan
Planta baja

Two Duplexes in Campo del Principe

Ramón Fernández - Alonso Borrajo
Granada, Spain
Photos © Fernando Alda

Front elevation
Alzado frontal

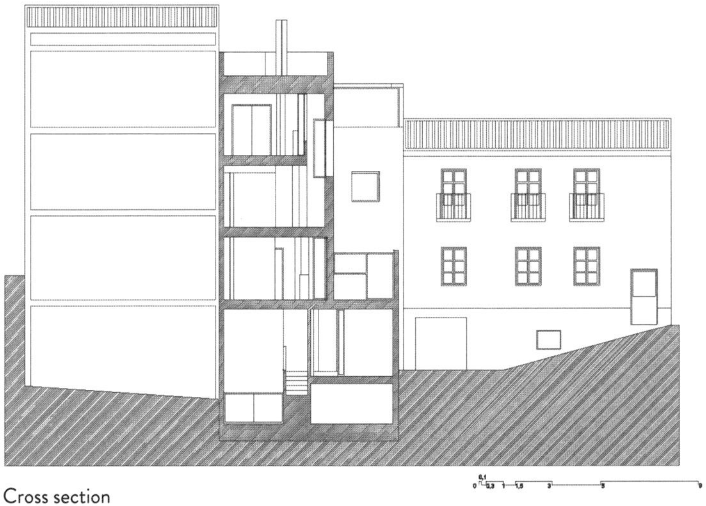

Cross section
Sección transversal

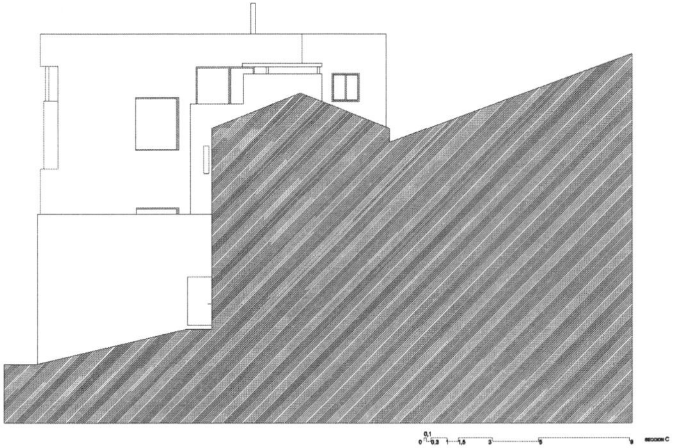

Lateral elevation
Alzado lateral

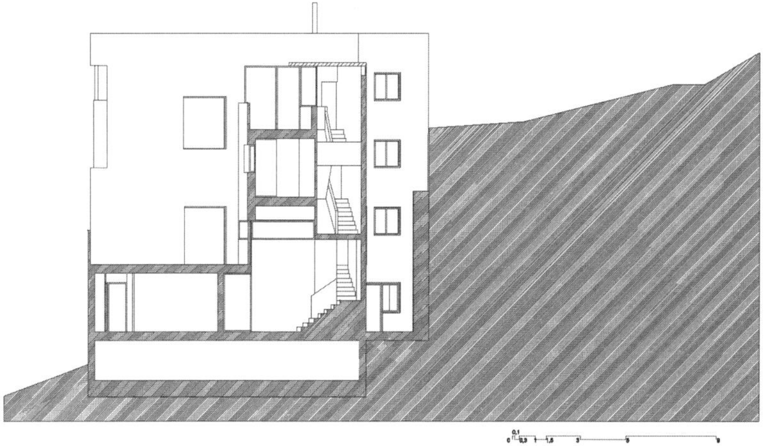

Longitudinal section
Sección longitudinal

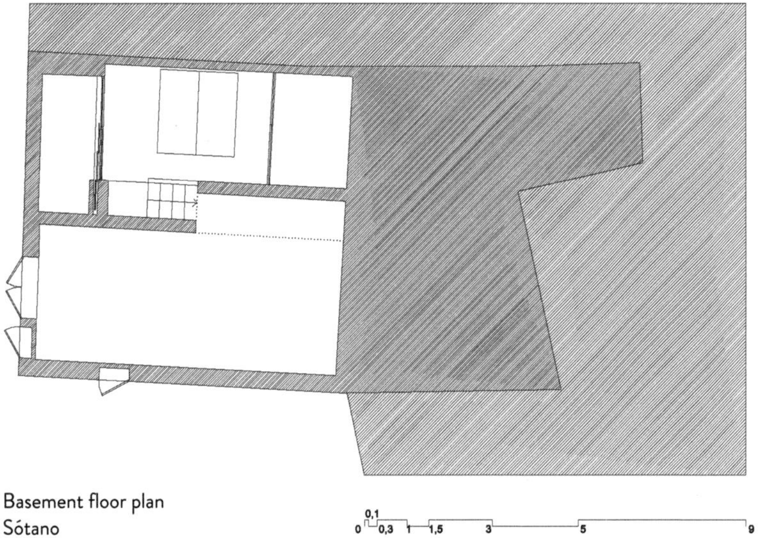

Basement floor plan
Sótano

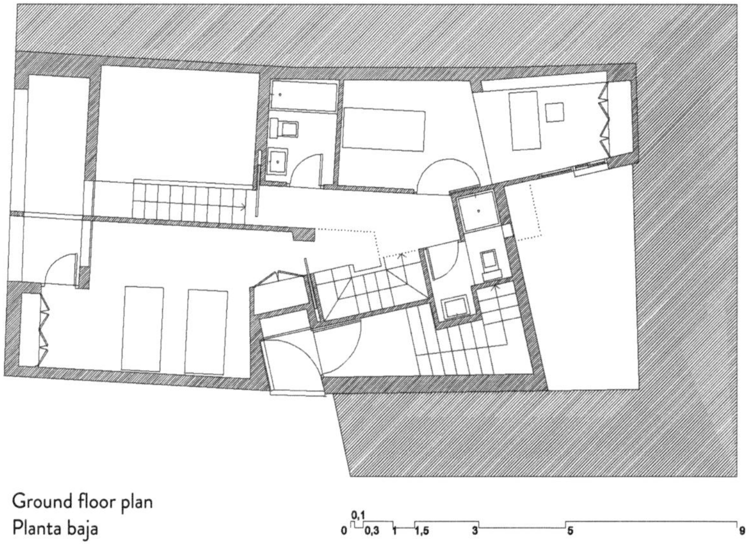

Ground floor plan
Planta baja

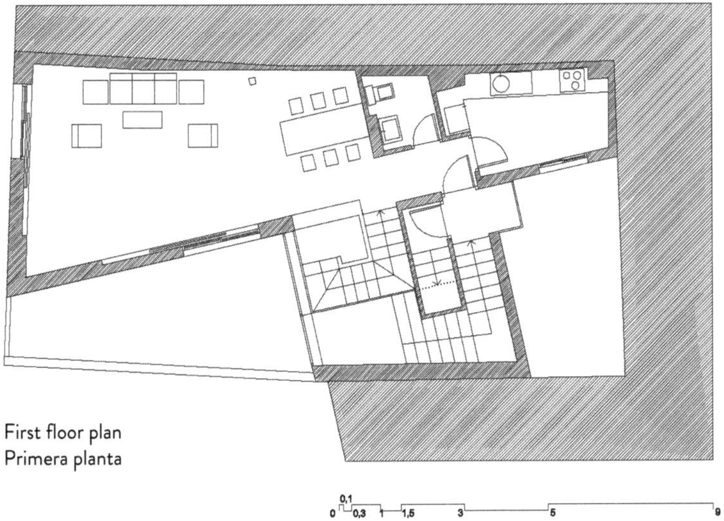

First floor plan
Primera planta

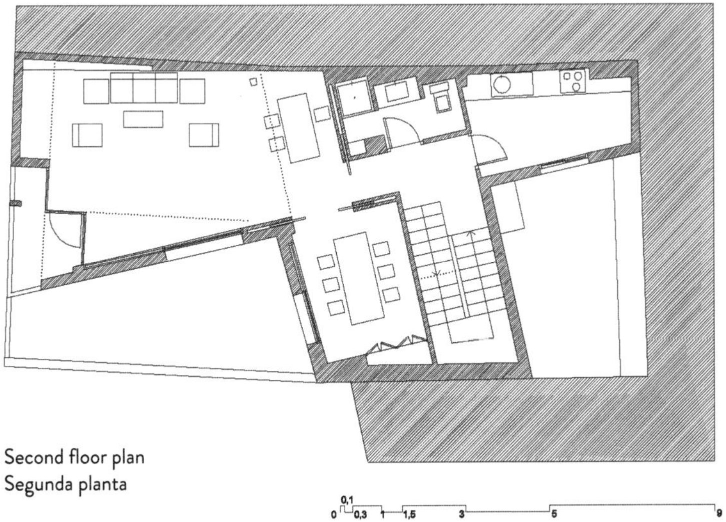

Second floor plan
Segunda planta

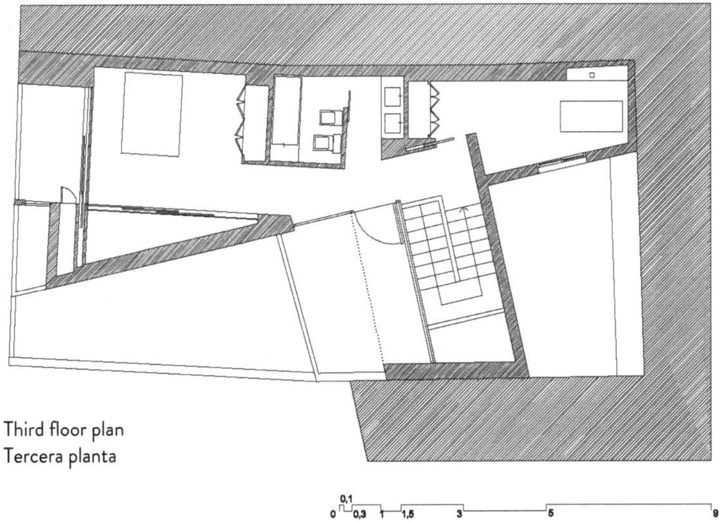

Third floor plan
Tercera planta

Stacked House

Naturehumaine Architecture Design
Montreal, Canada
Photos © Adrien Williams

Site plan
Plano de situación

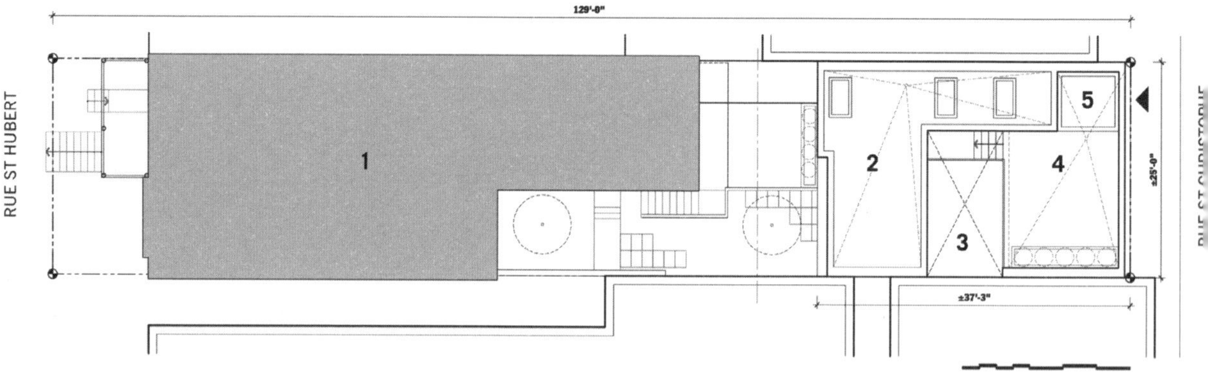

1. Existing two-floor building
2. Stacked house
3. Outdoor patio
4. Solarium
5. Spa

1. Edificio existente de dos pisos.
2. Casa apilada
3. Patio al aire libre
4. Solarium
5. Spa

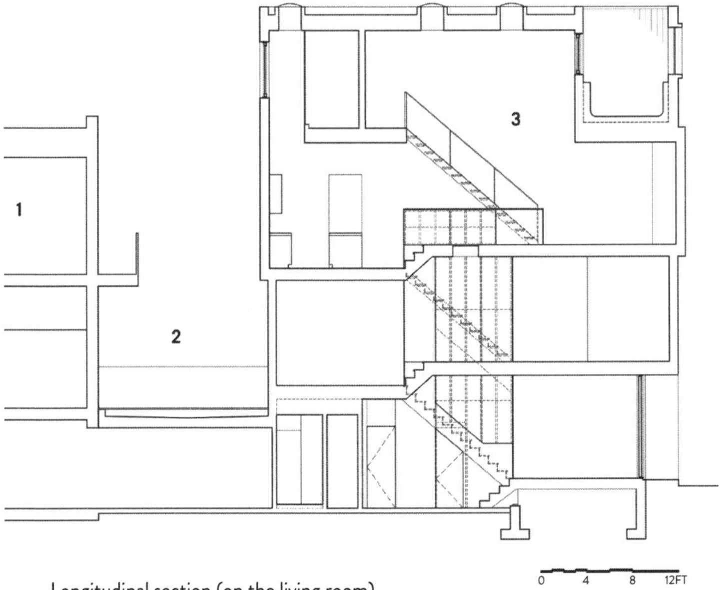

Longitudinal section (on the living room)
Sección longitudinal (en la sala de estar)

1. Neighboring building
2. Neighboring terrace
3. Stacked house

1. Edificio vecino
2. Terraza vecina
3. Casa apilada

Longitudinal section (on the inner courtyard)
Sección longitudinal (en el patio interior)

1. Inner courtyard
2. Terrace

1. Patio interior
2. Terraza

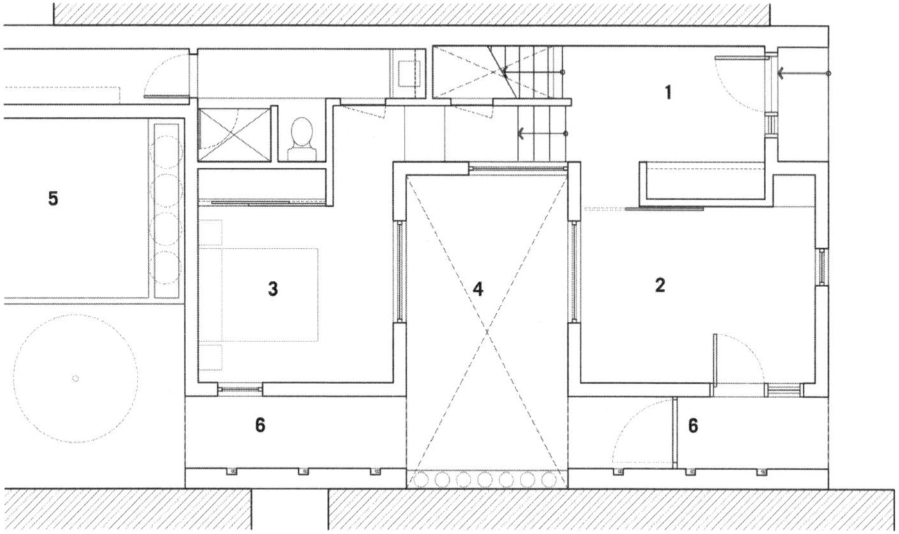

Ground floor plan
Planta baja

1. Entry
2. Atelier
3. Bedroom
4. Interior patio
5. Neighboring terrace
6. Direct access to the patio and garden
7. Bathroom
8. Kitchen
9. Dining room
10. Living room
11. Outdoor terrace
12. Master bedroom
13. Outdoor patio
14. Solarium
15. Spa

1. Entrada
2. Taller
3. Dormitorio
4. Patio interior
5. Terraza vecina
6. Acceso directo al patio y jardín
7. Baño
8. Cocina
9. Comedor
10. Sala de estar
11. Terraza al aire libre
12. Dormitorio principal
13. Patio al aire libre
14. Solarium
15. Spa

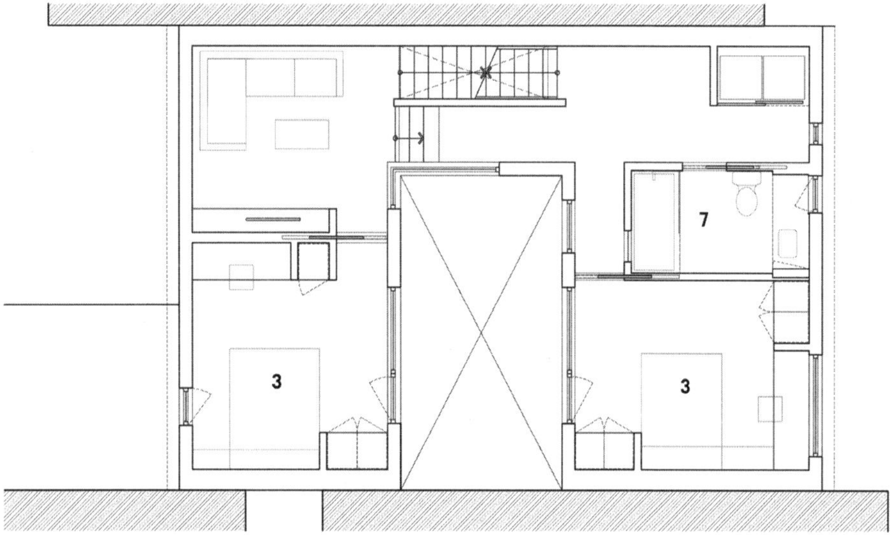

First floor plan
Primera planta

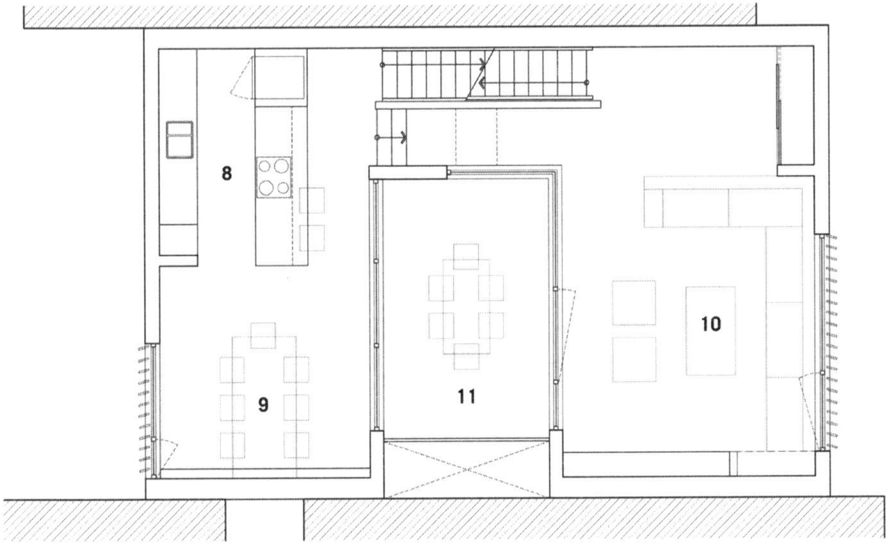

Second floor plan
Segunda planta

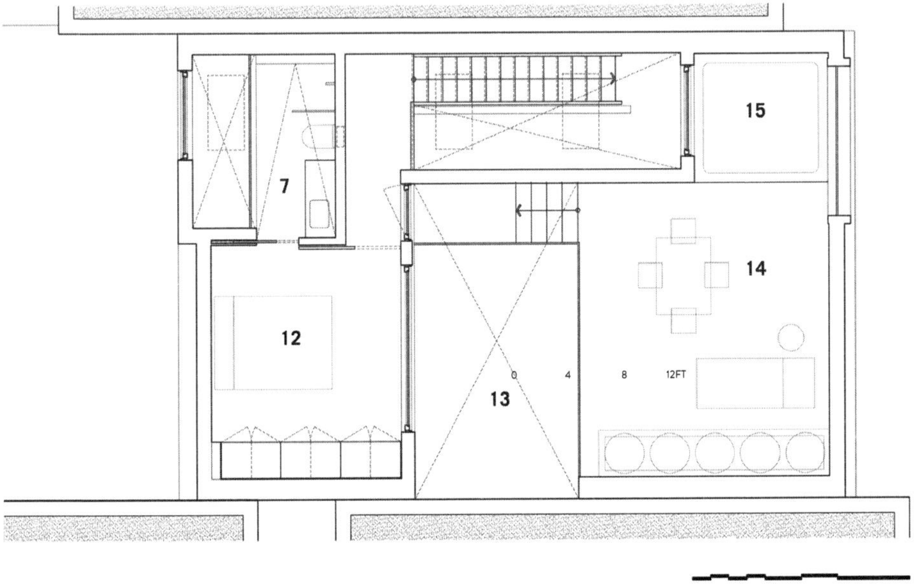

Third floor plan
Tercera planta

Bioclimatic Living Space in San Isidro

Elisa Valero
Granada, Spain
Photos © Fernando Alda

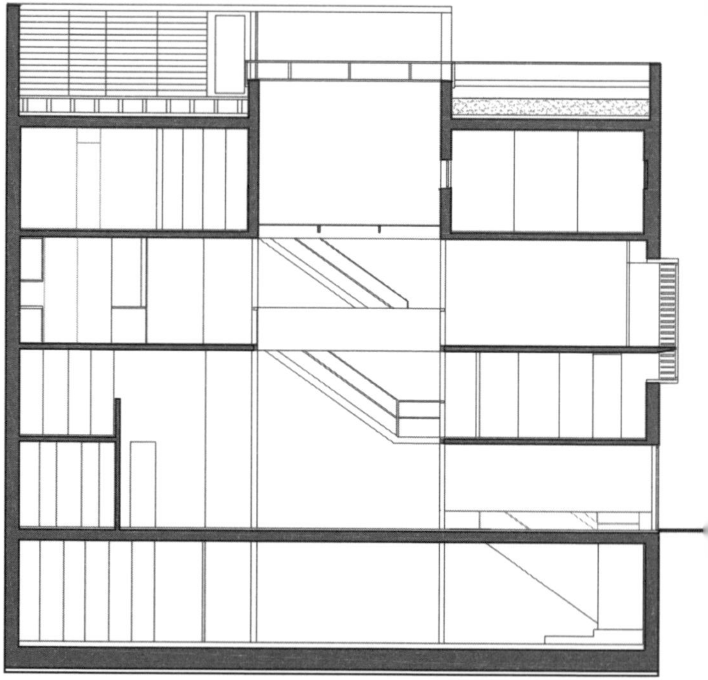

Longitudinal section
Sección longitudinal

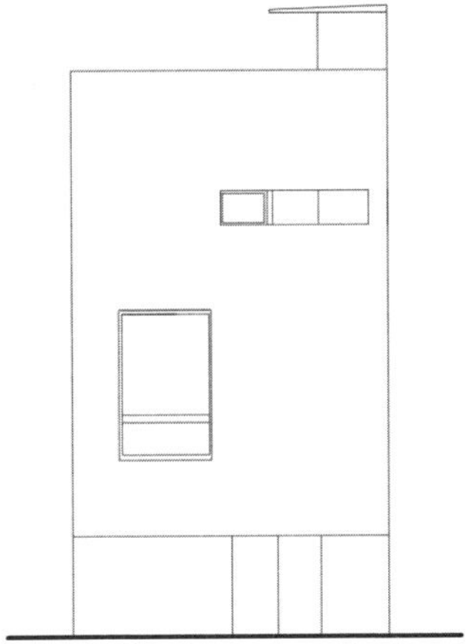

Front elevation
Alzado frontal

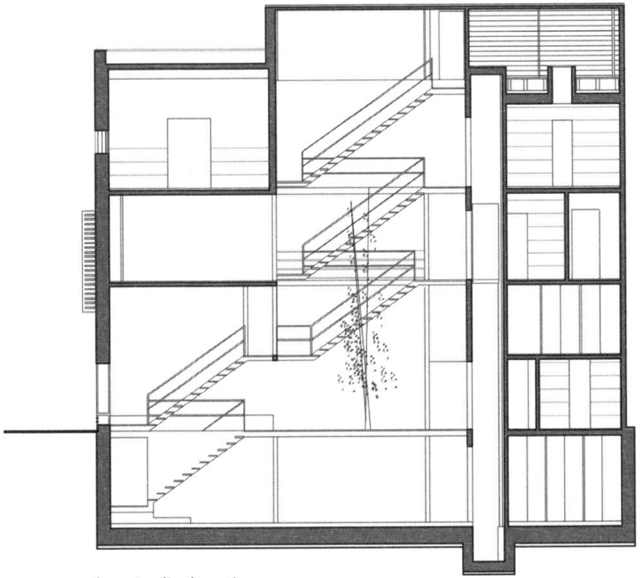

Longitudinal section
Sección longitudinal

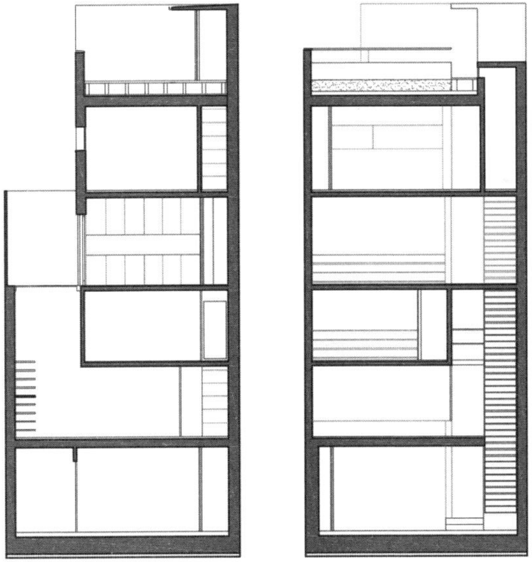

Cross sections
Secciones transversales

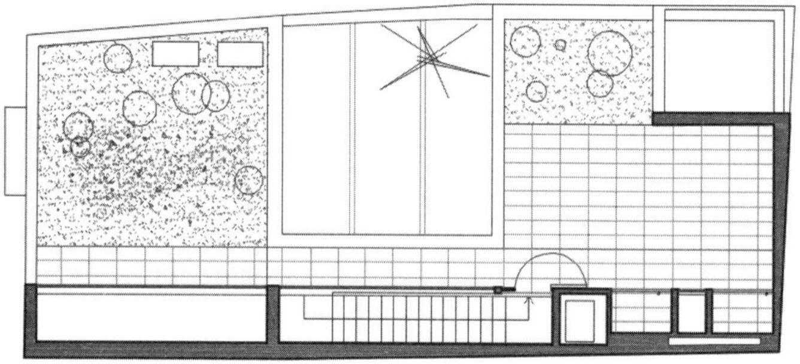

Fourth floor plan
Cuarta planta

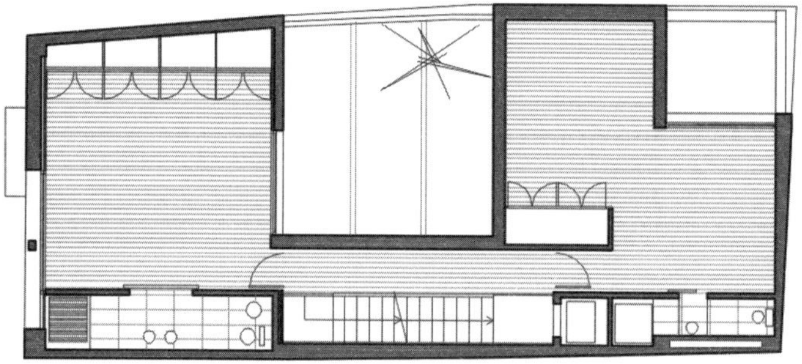

Third floor plan
Tercera planta

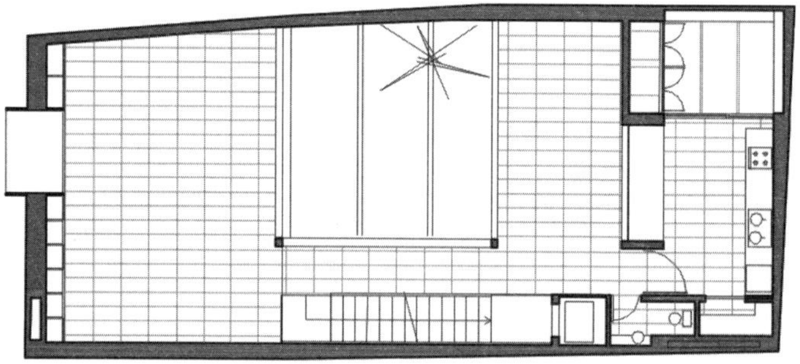

Second floor plan
Segunda planta

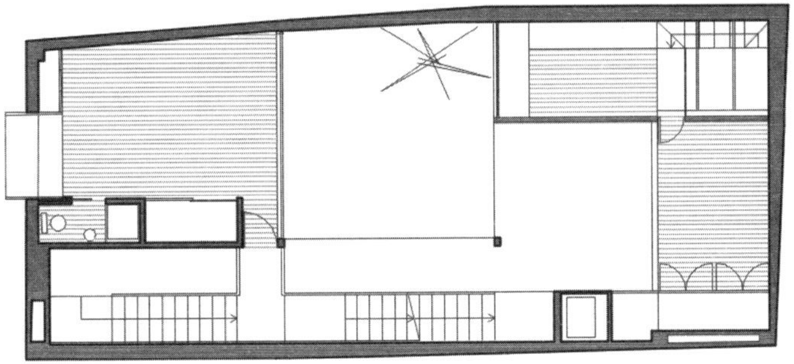

First floor plan
Primera planta

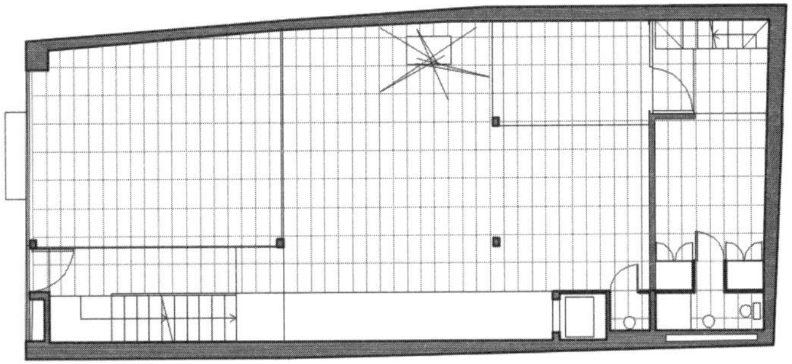

Ground floor plan
Planta baja

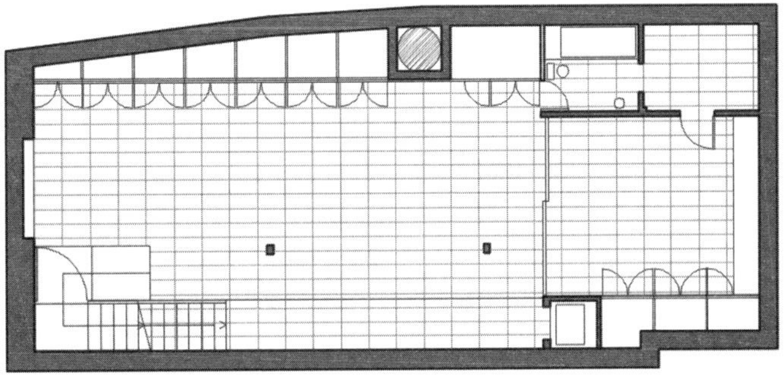

Basement floor plan
Sótano

Plastic House

Kengo Kuma & Associates
Tokyo, Japan
Photos © Mitsumasa Fujitsuka / Helico Co. Ltd.

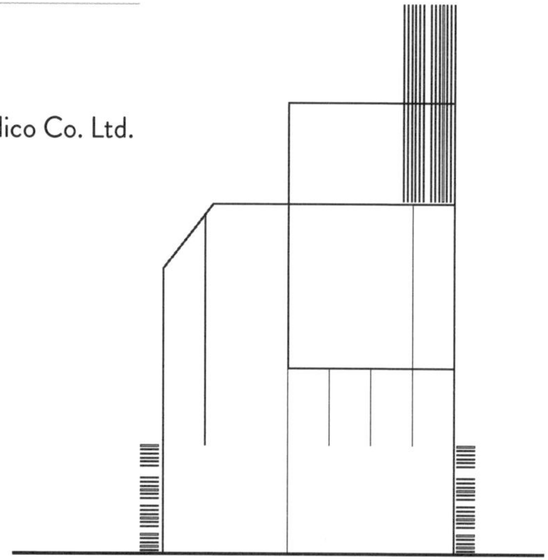

West elevation
Alzado oeste

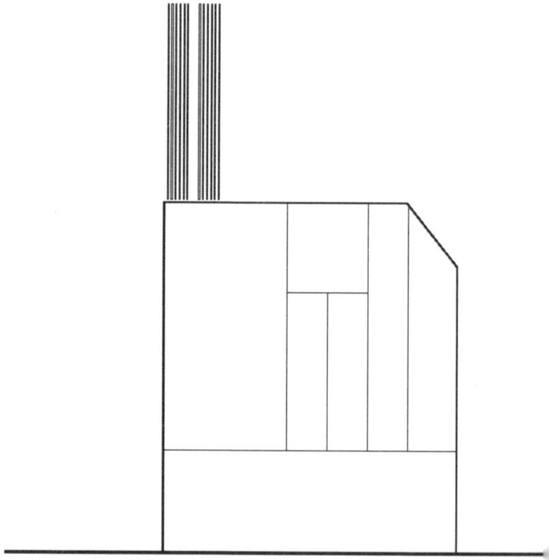

East elevation
Alzado este

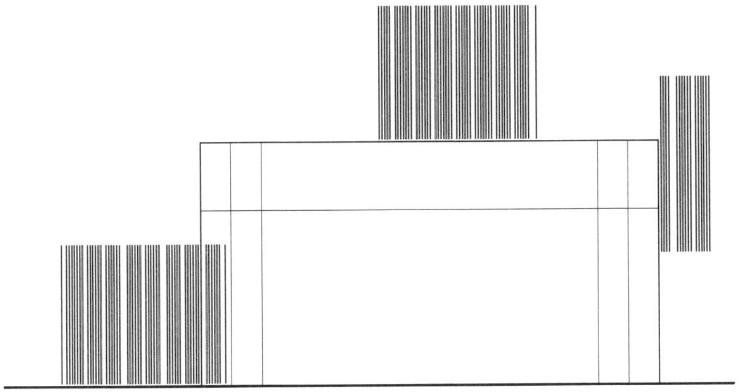

North elevation
Alzado norte

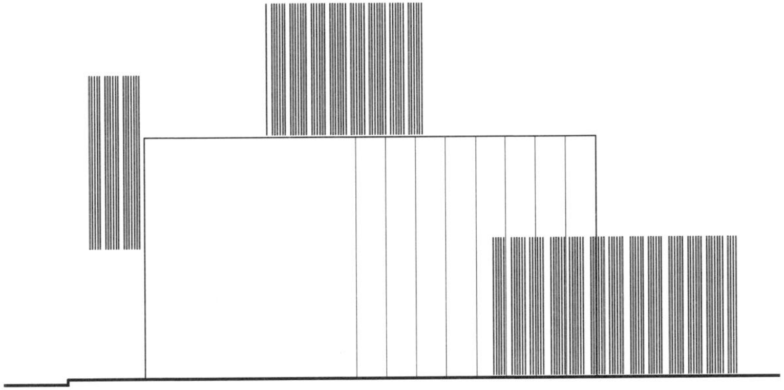

South elevation
Alzado sur

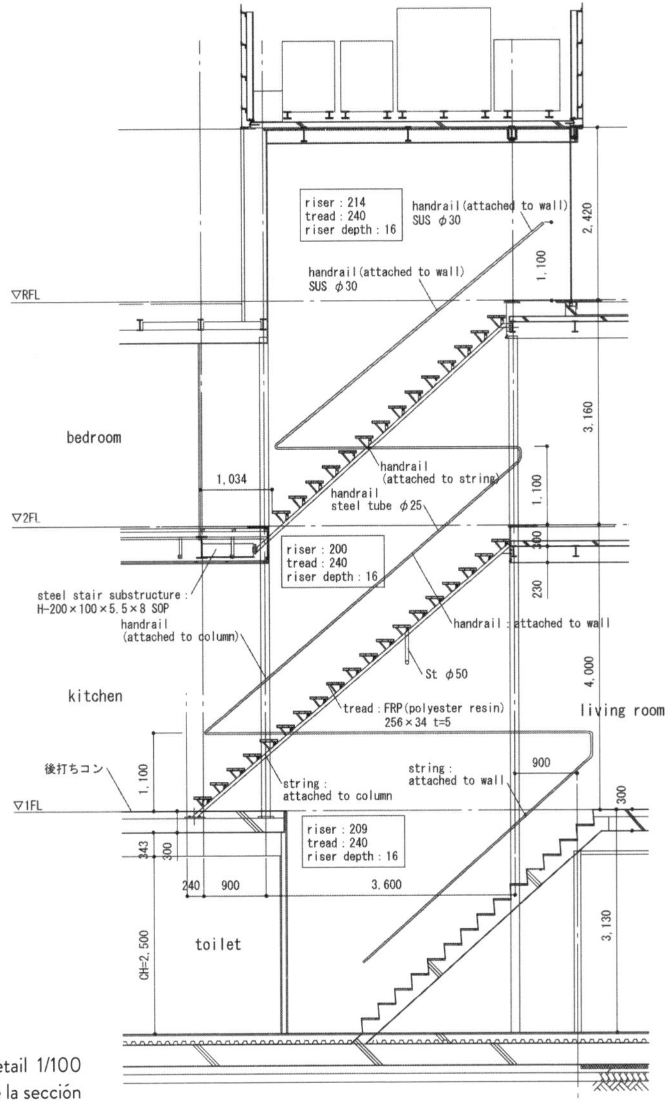

Section detail 1/100
Detalle de la sección

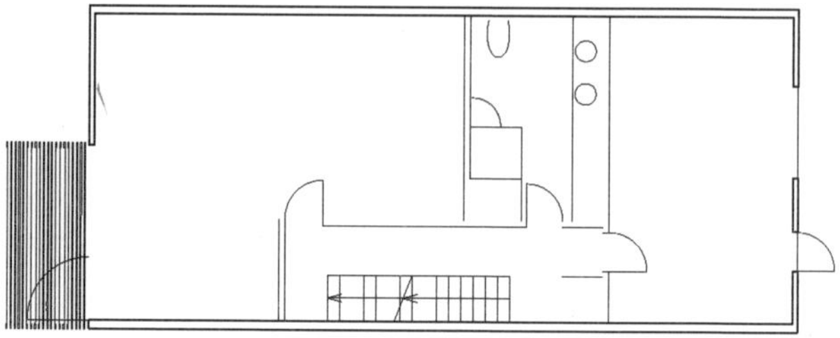

First floor plan
Primera planta

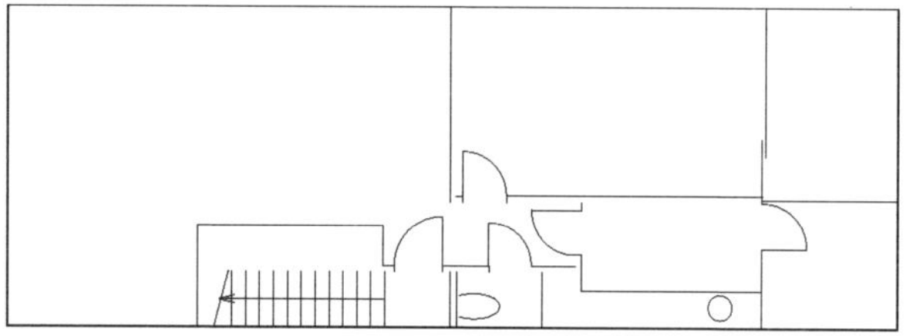

Basement floor plan
Sótano

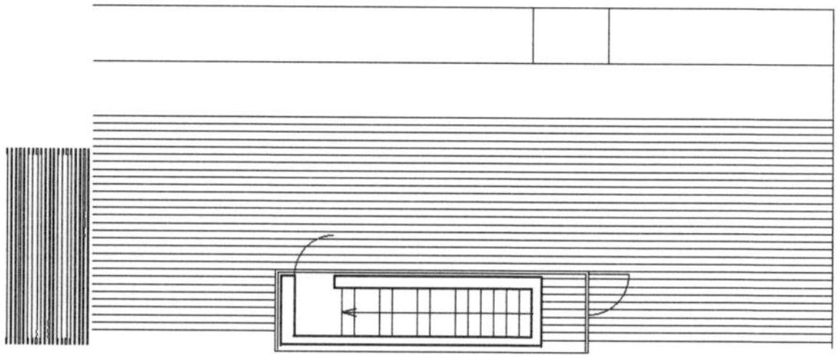

Second floor plan
Segunda planta

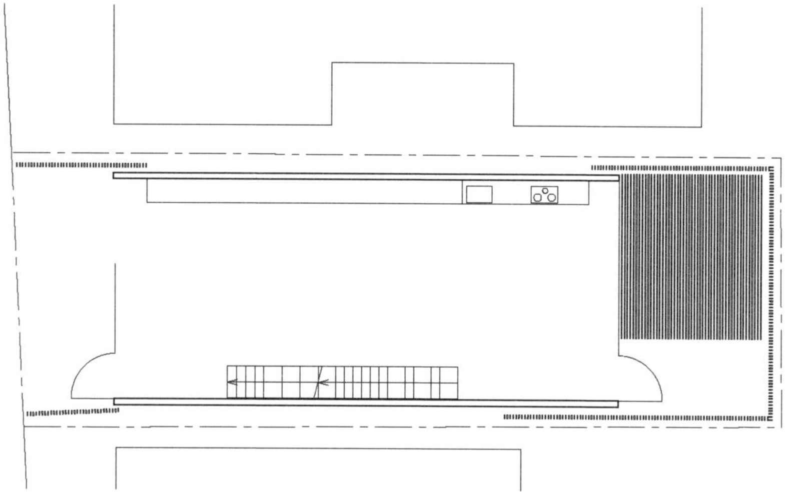

Ground floor plan
Planta baja

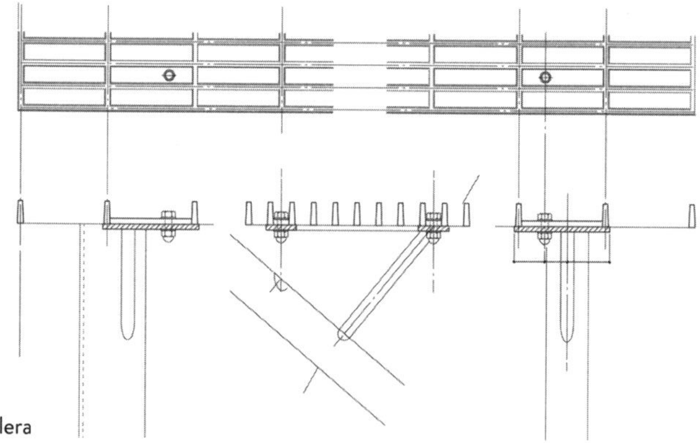

Staircase detail
Detalle de la escalera

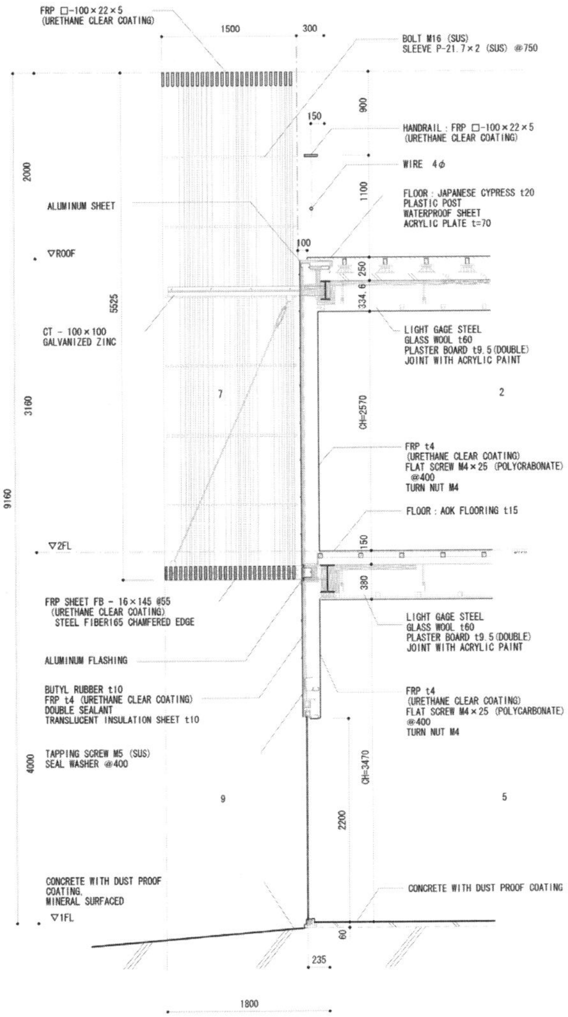

Section detail 1/50
Detalle de la sección

1. Gallery
2. Bedroom
3. Bathroom
4. Areaway
5. LDK / studio
6. Outdoor space
7. Terrace
8. Storage
9. Garage

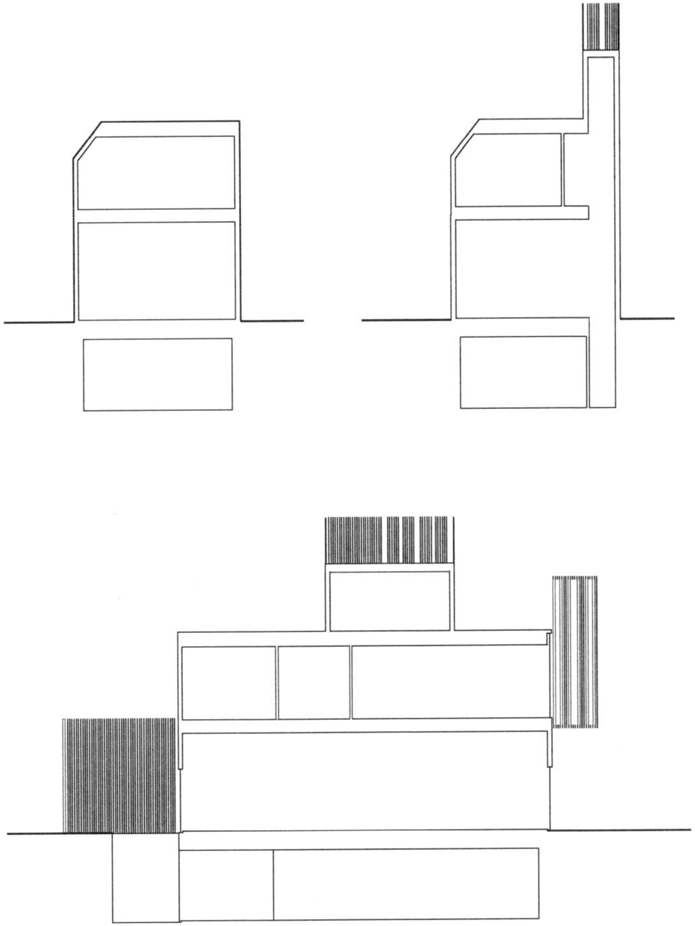

Schematic sections
Secciones esquemáticas

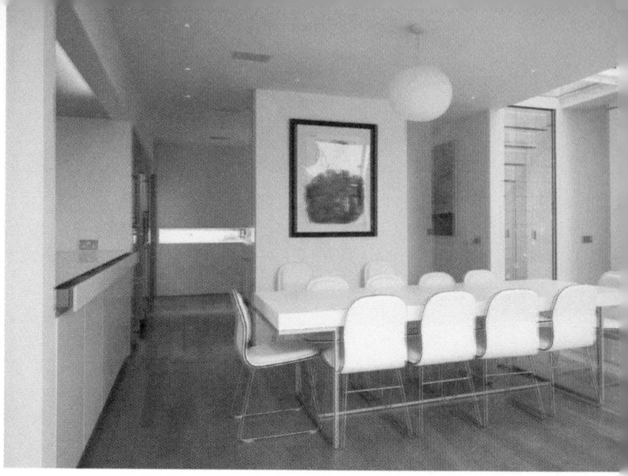

50 Pilgrim's Lane

Eldridge Smerin
London, United Kingdom
Photos © Lyndon Douglas

Front elevation
Alzado frontal

Longitudinal section
Sección longitudinal

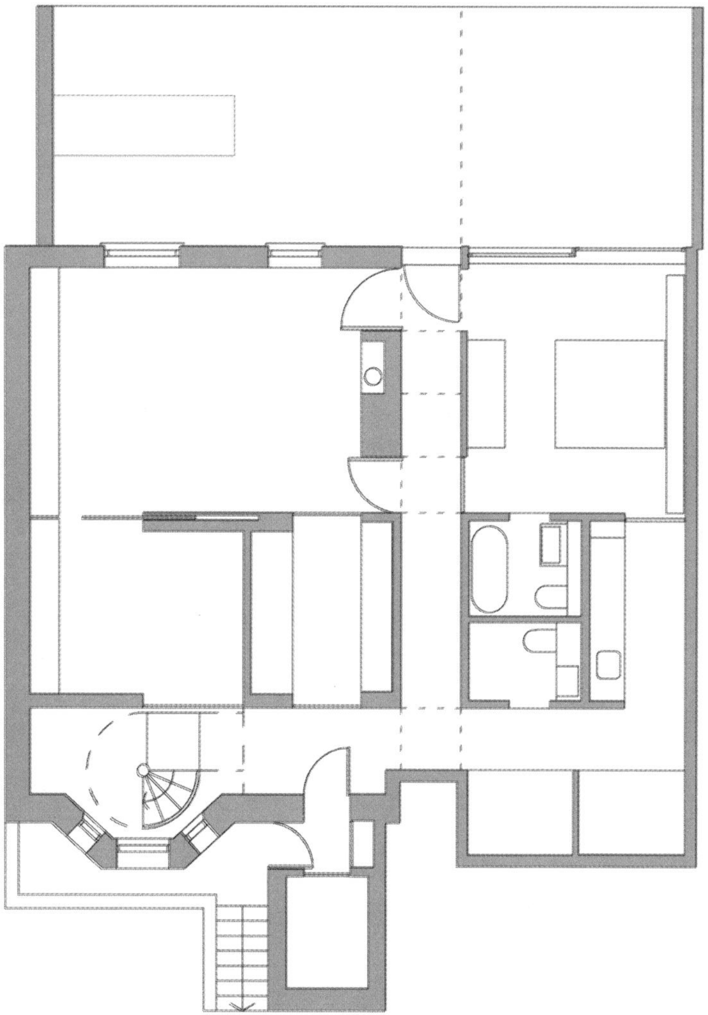

Basement floor plan
Sótano

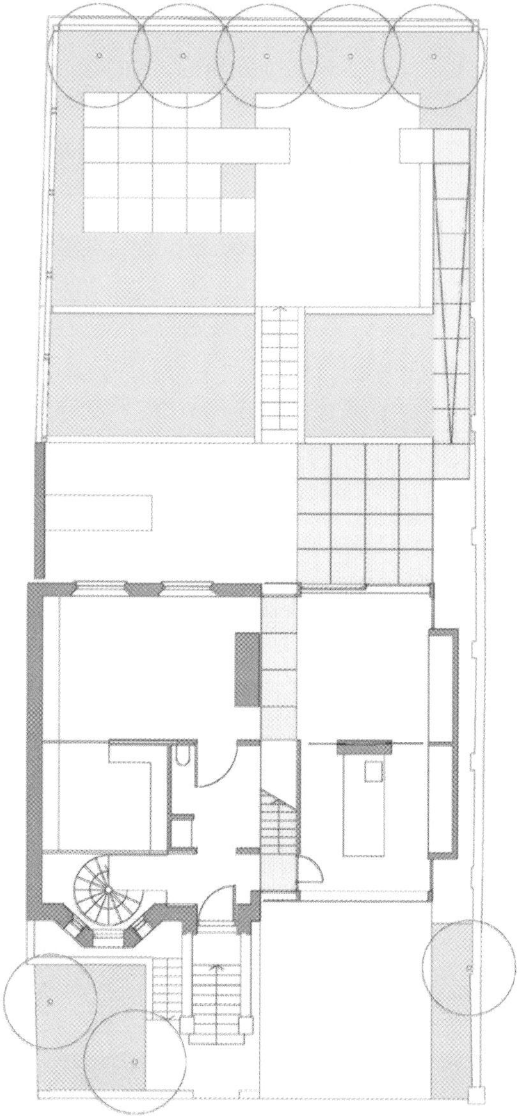

Ground floor plan
Planta baja

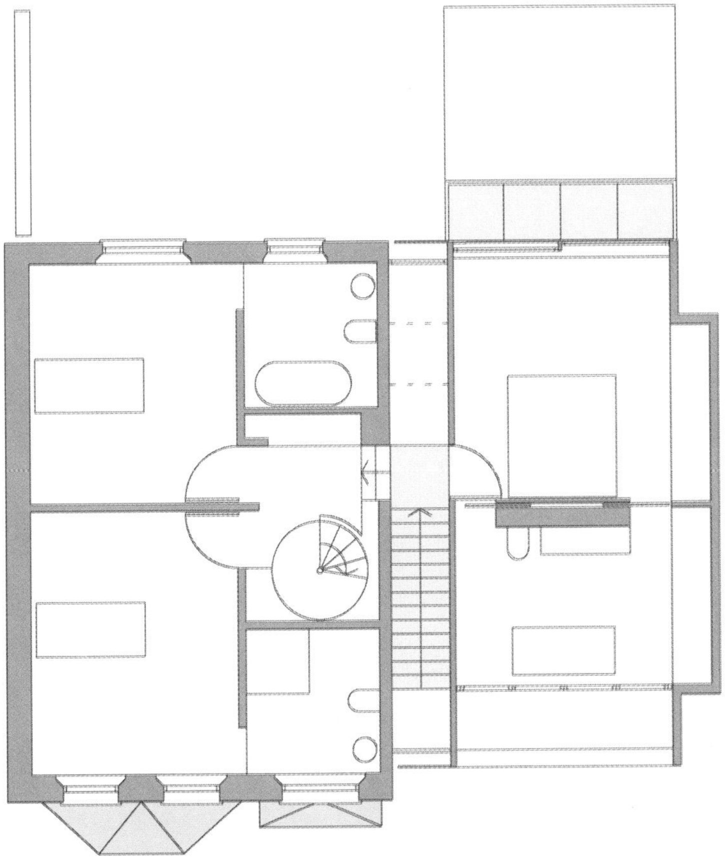

First floor plan
Primera planta

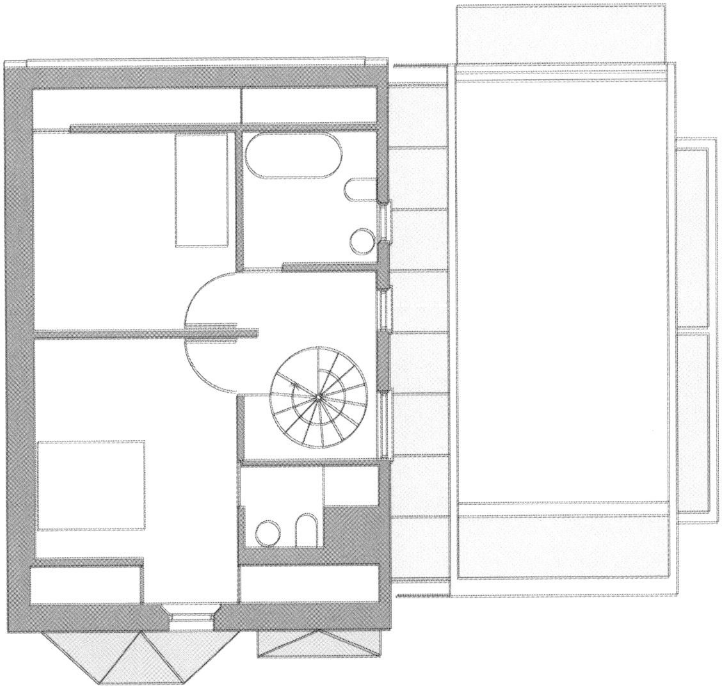

Second floor plan
Segunda planta

Flag House

Satoshi Kurosaki / APOLLO Architects & Associates
Tokyo, Japan
Photos © Masao Nishikawa

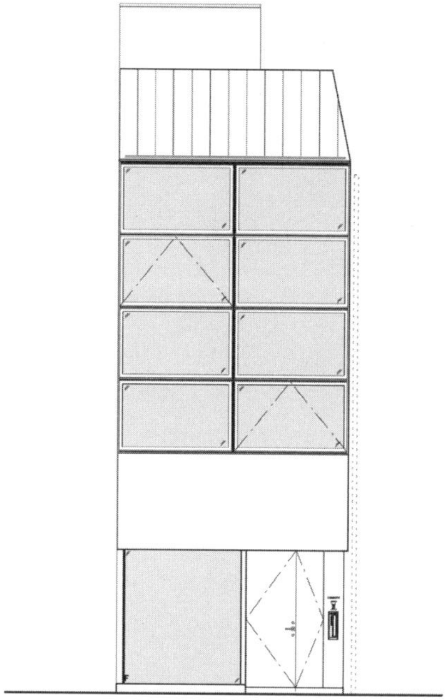

East elevation
Alzado este

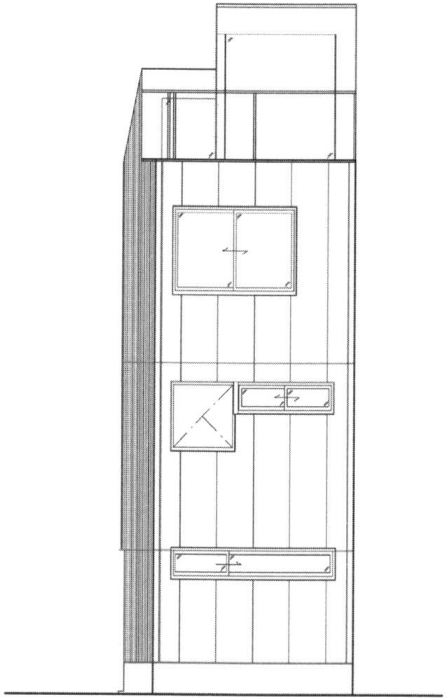

West elevation
Alzado Oeste

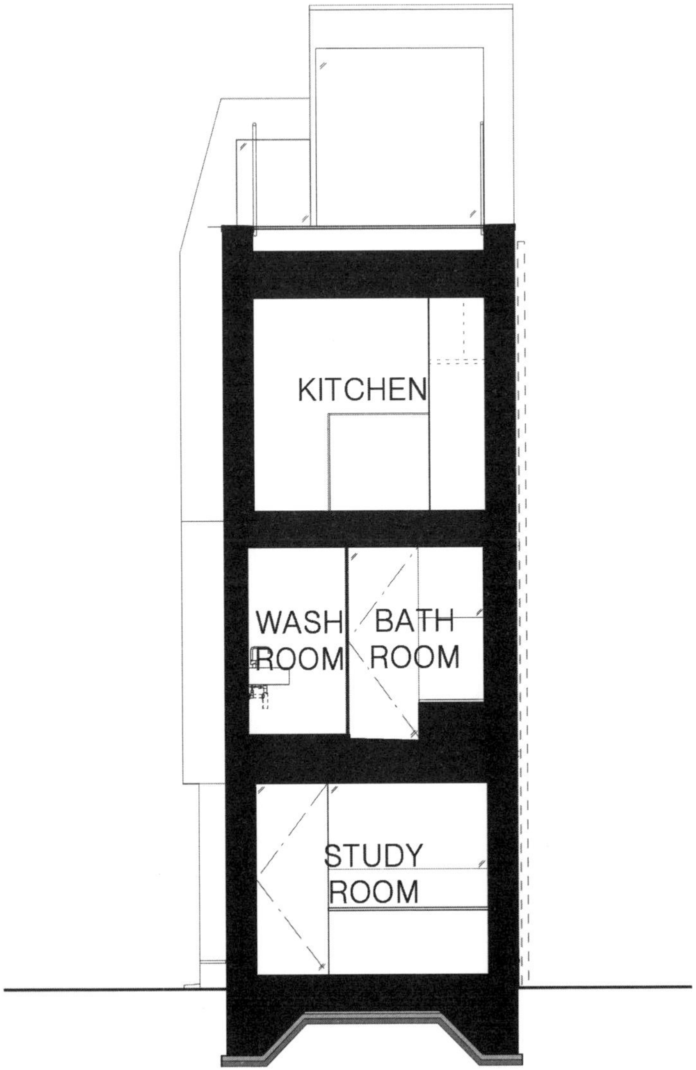

Section
Sección

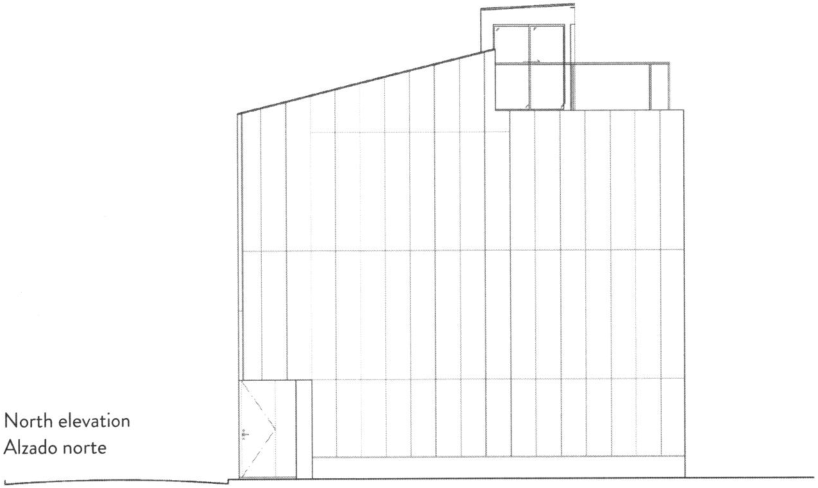

North elevation
Alzado norte

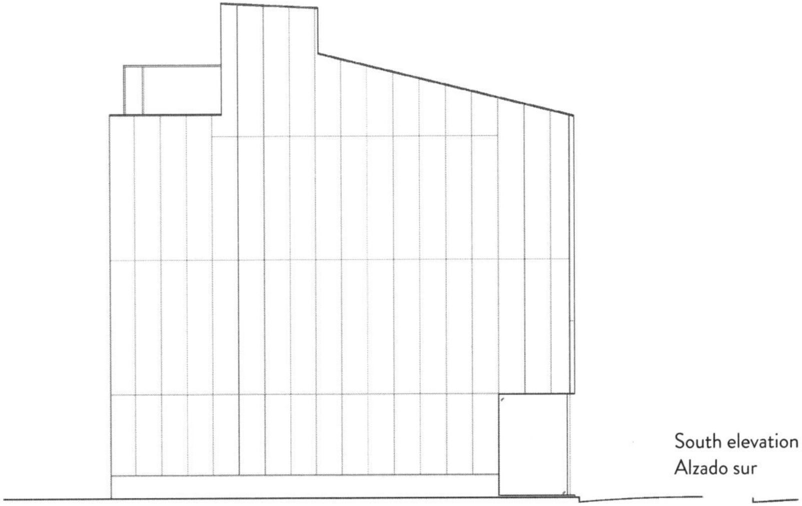

South elevation
Alzado sur

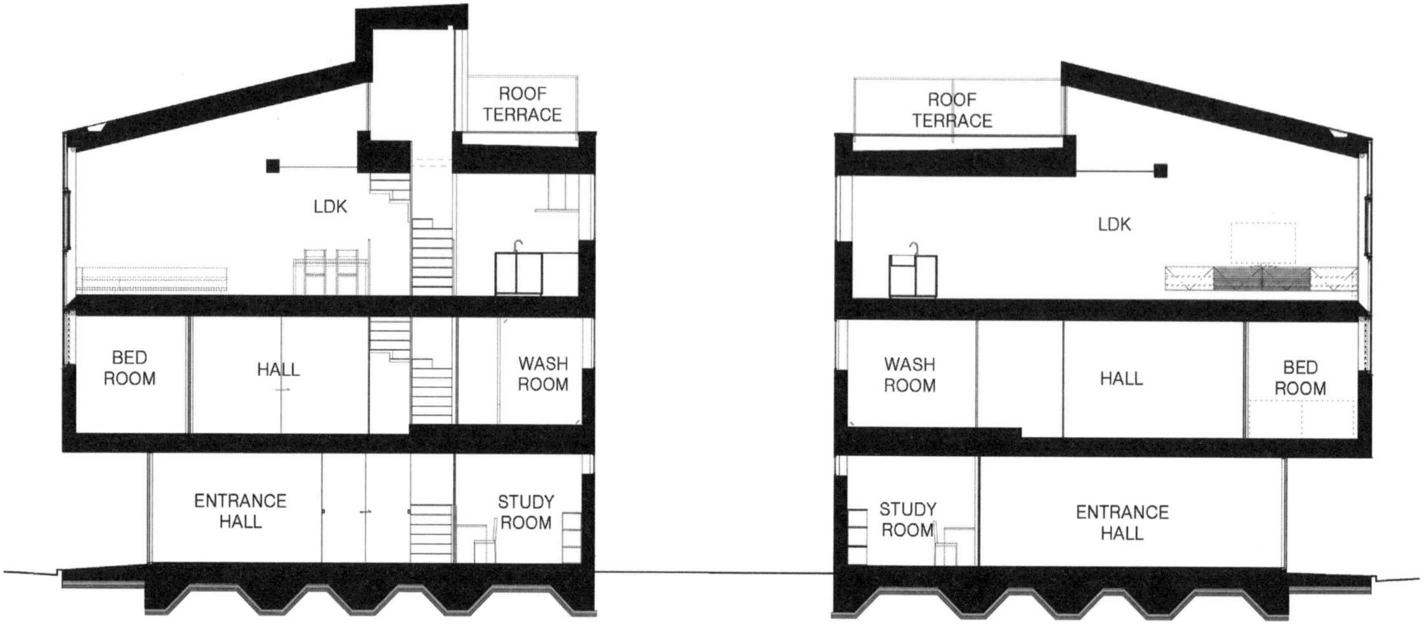

Section
Sección

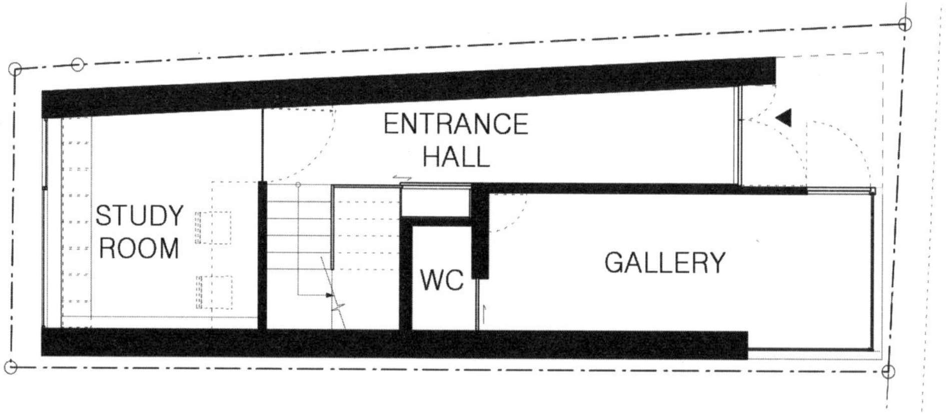

First floor plan
Primera planta

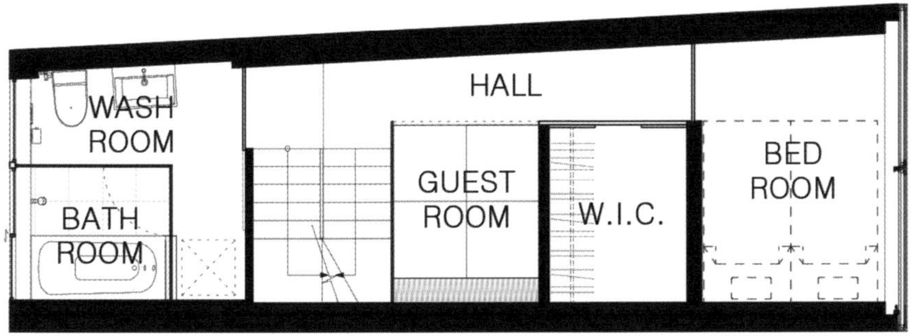

Second floor plan
Segunda planta

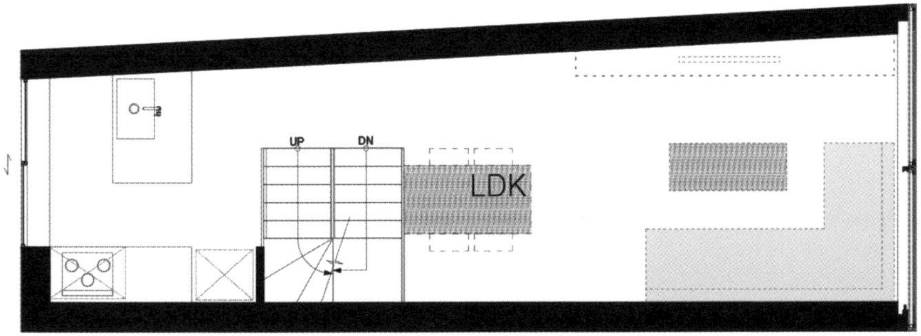

Third floor plan
Tercera planta

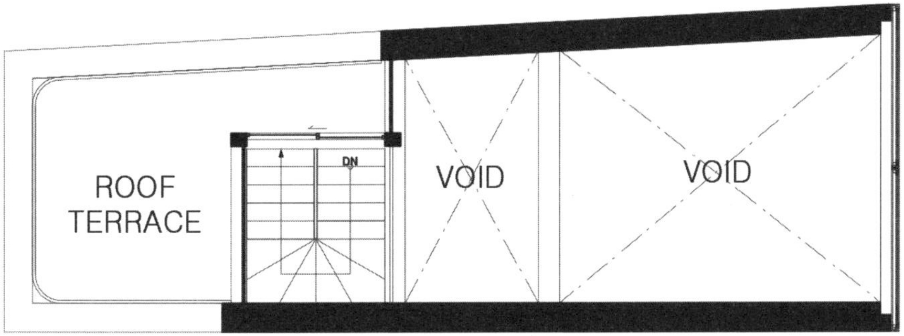

Rooftop
Azotea

Jyu-Bako

Yasuhiro Yamashita / Atelier Tekuto
Tokio, Japan
Photos © Makoto Yoshida

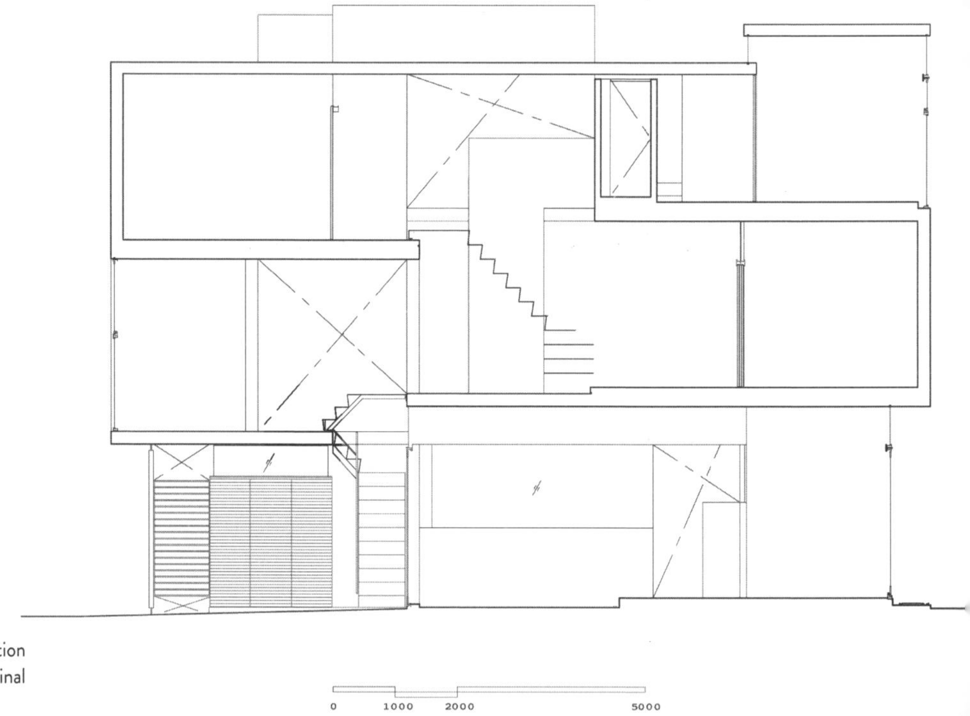

Longitudinal section
Sección longitudinal

Street elevation
Alzado calle

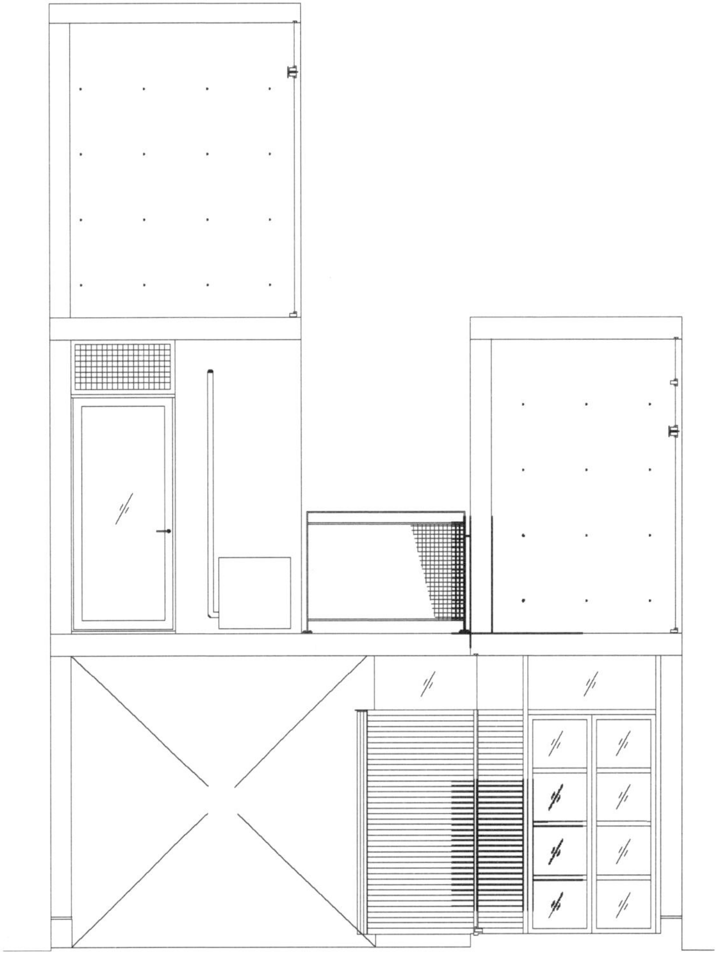

Southern section
Sección sur

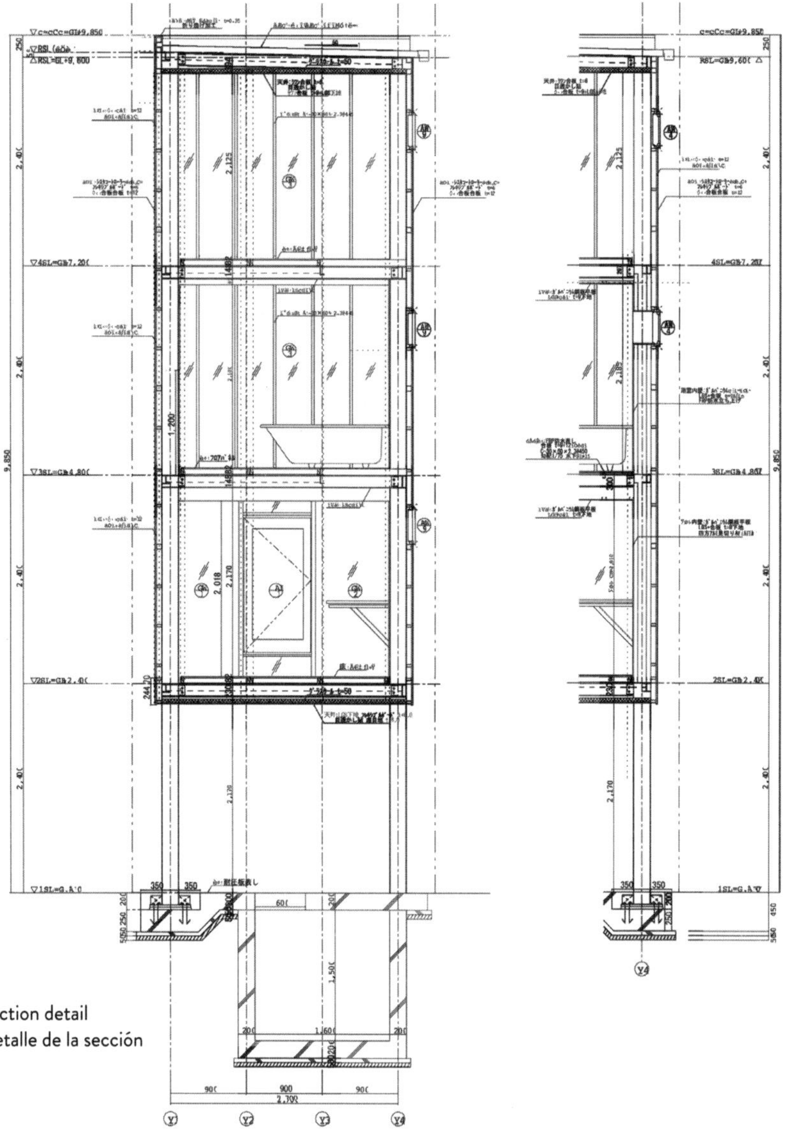

Section detail
Detalle de la sección

Site plan
Plano de situación

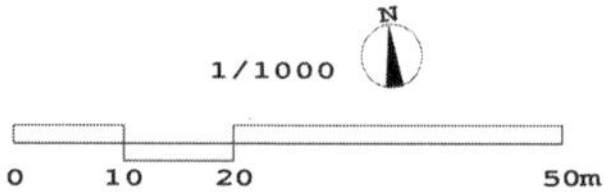

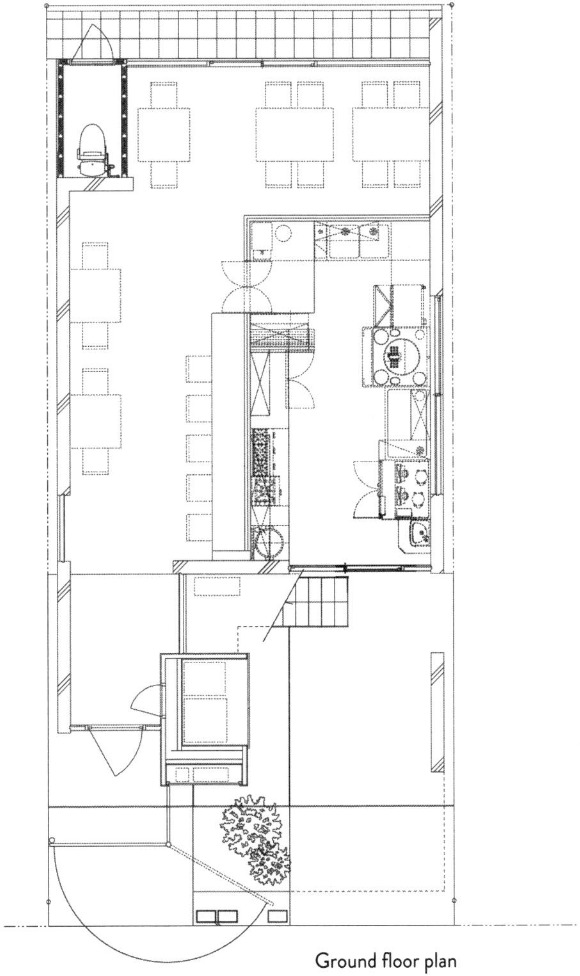

Ground floor plan
Planta baja

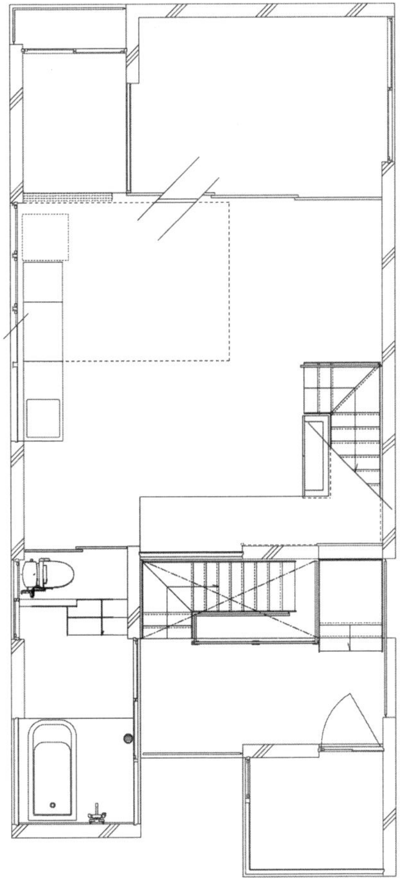

First floor plan
Primera planta

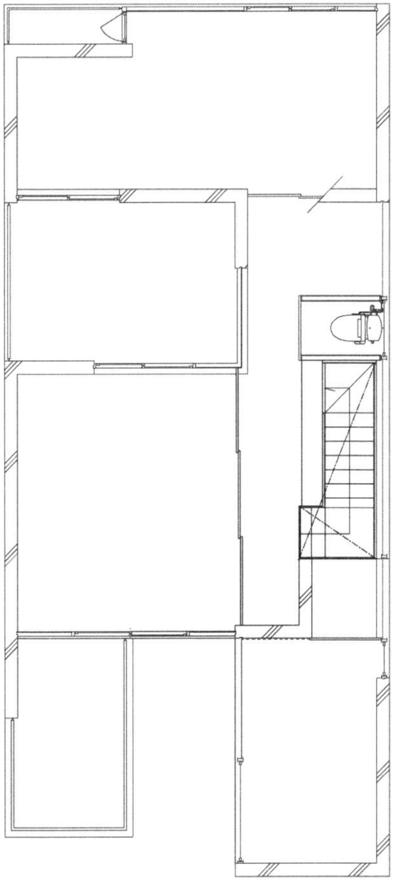

Second floor plan
Segunda planta

House in Uehonmachi

Junya Toda Architect & Associates
Osaka, Japan
Photos © Miyogi Ueda

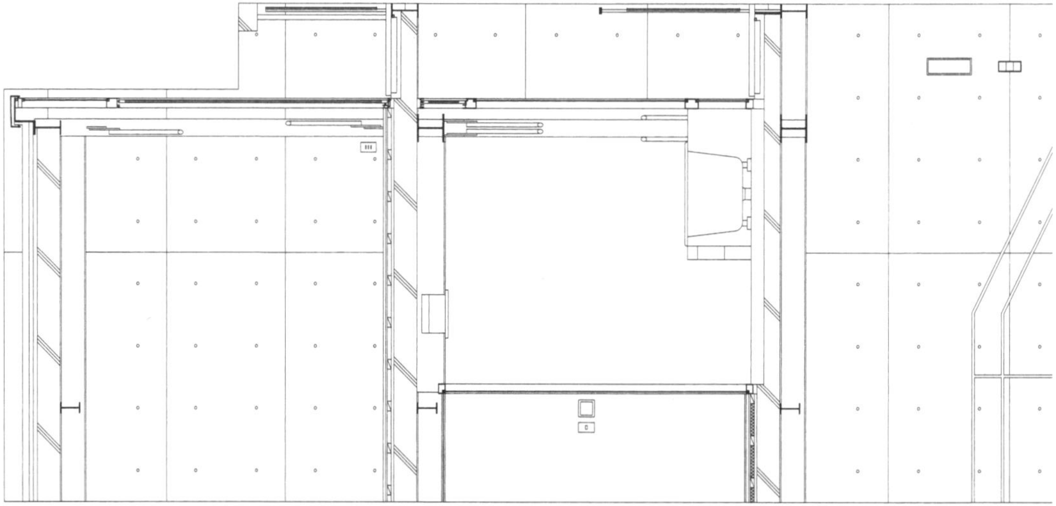

Longitudinal section detail
Detalle sección longitudinal

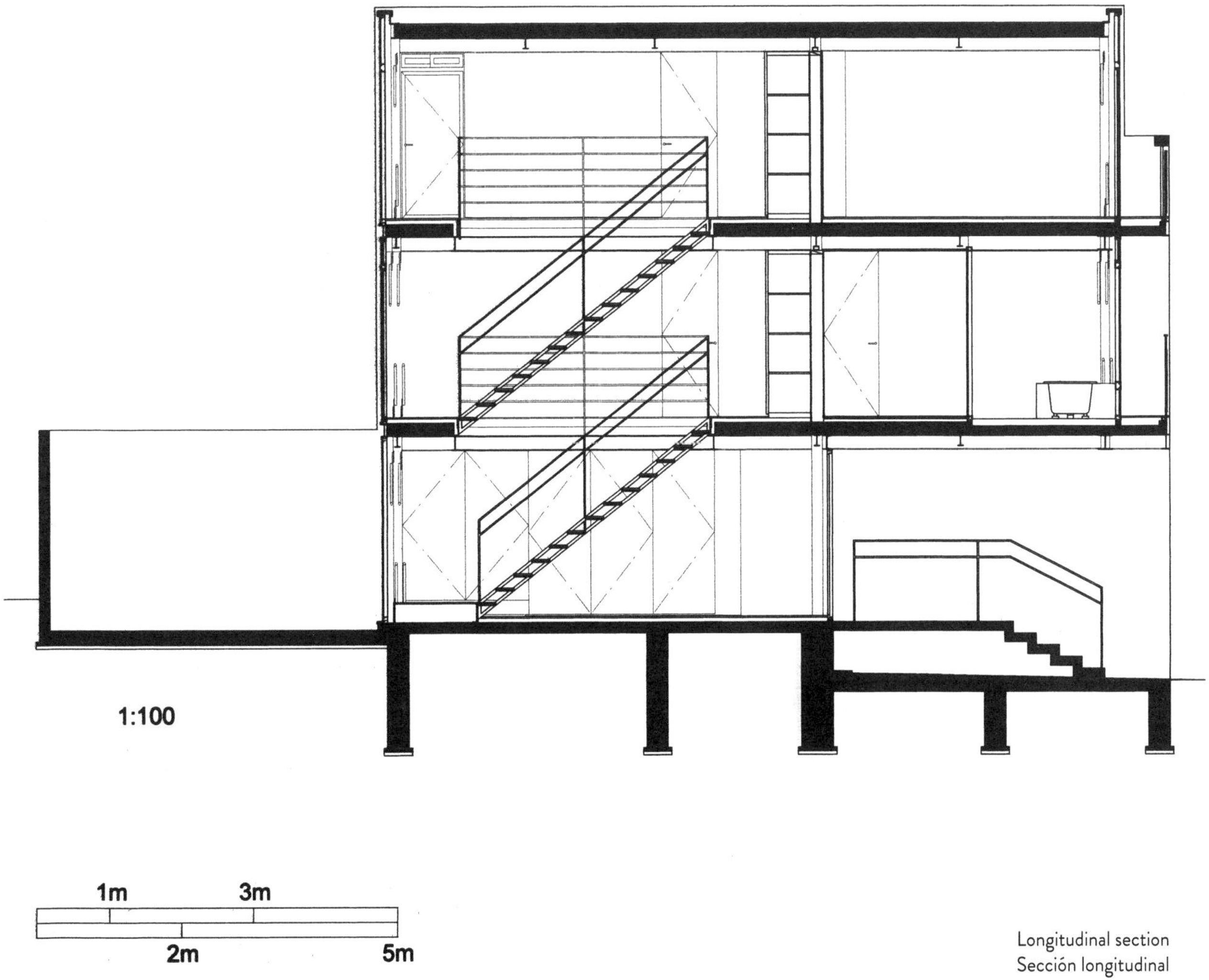

Longitudinal section
Sección longitudinal

Ground floor plan
Planta baja

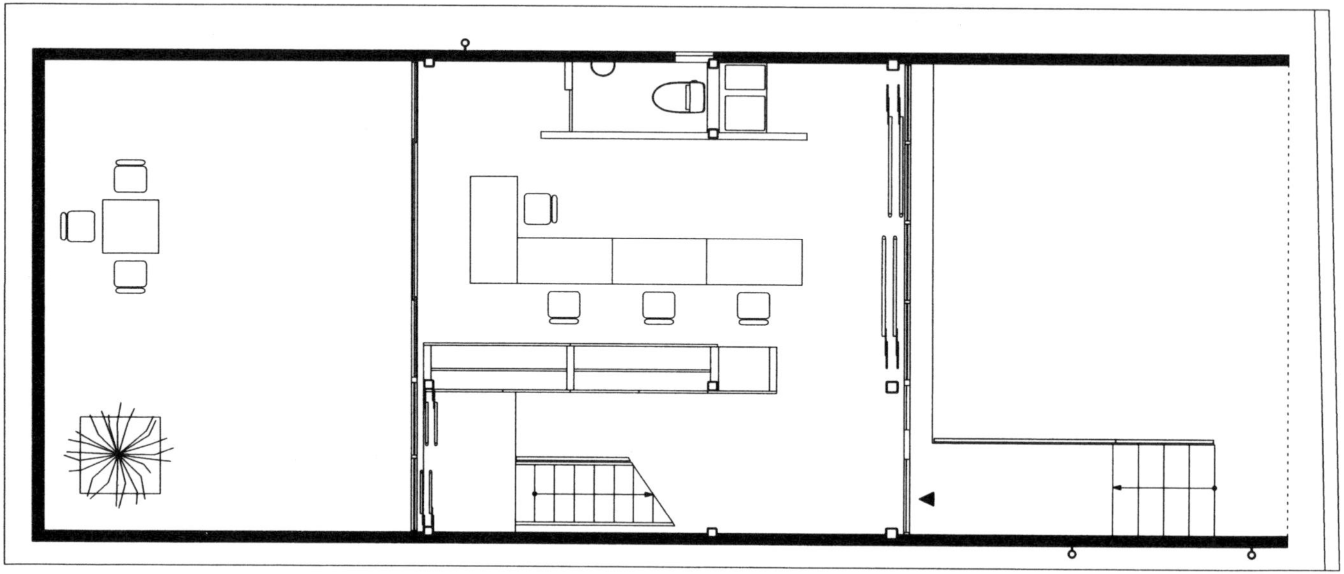

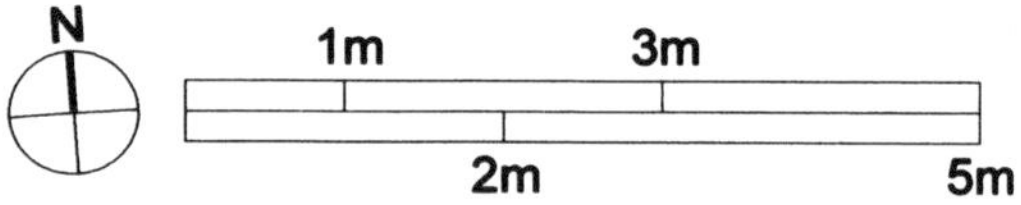

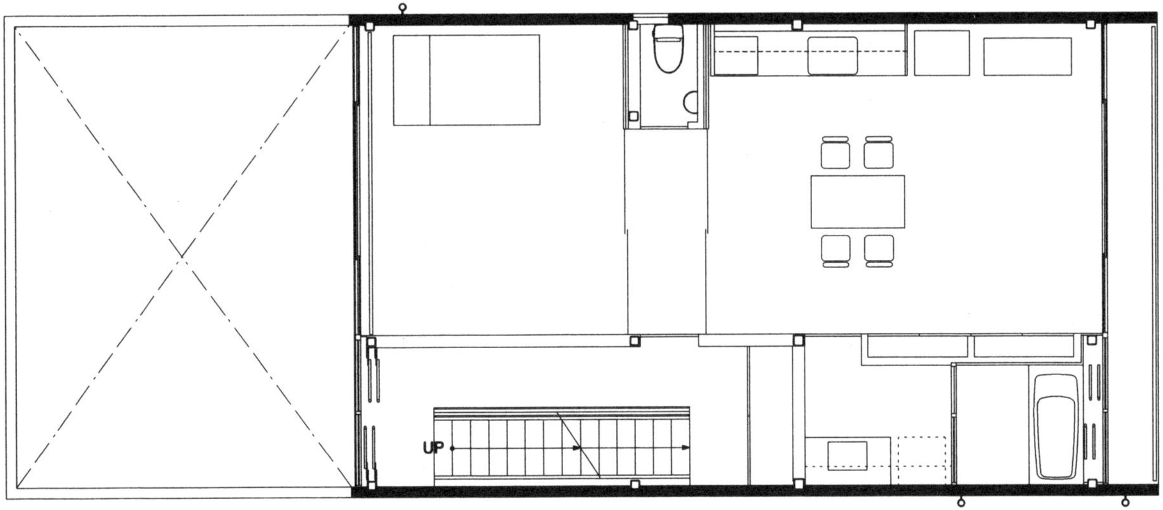

First floor plan
Primera planta

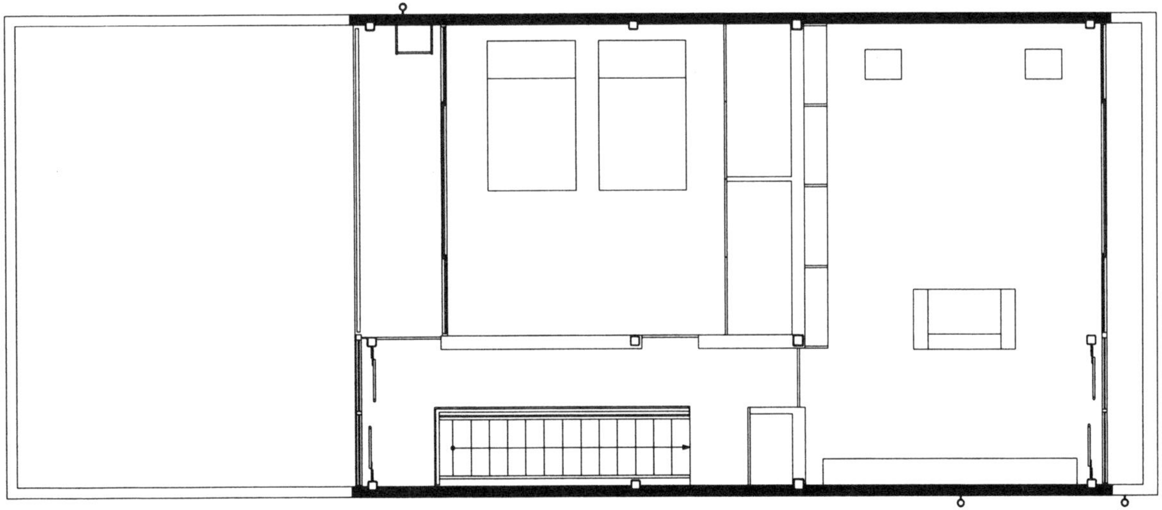

Second floor plan
Segunda planta

Weiss House

Jörg Ziolkowski / Ziolkowski.ws
Colonia, Alemania
Photos © Frank Struck, Ziolkowski.ws

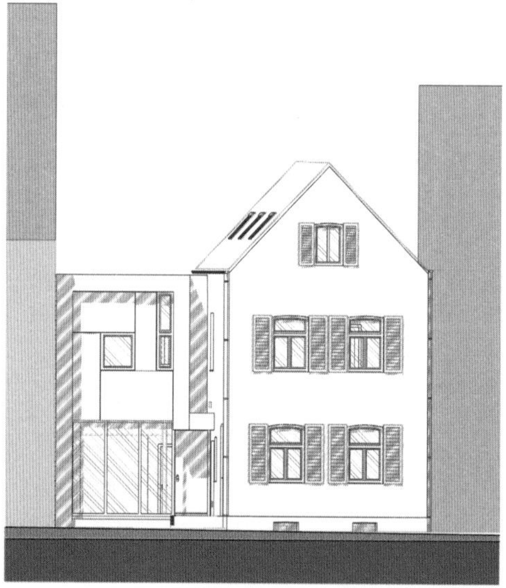

Front elevation
Alzado frontal

Rear elevation
Alzado posterior

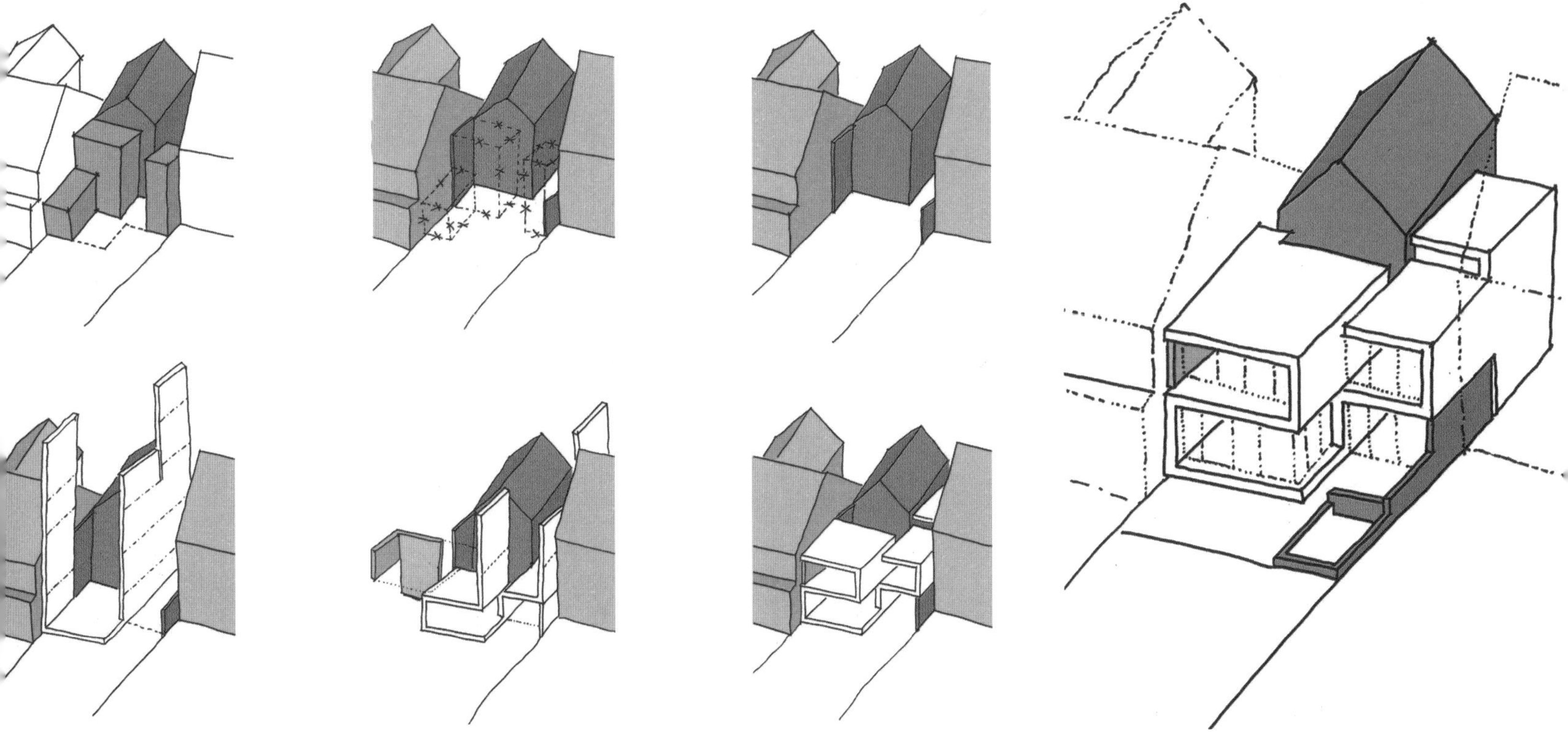

Volume diagram
Diagrama de volumen

Ground floor plan
Planta baja

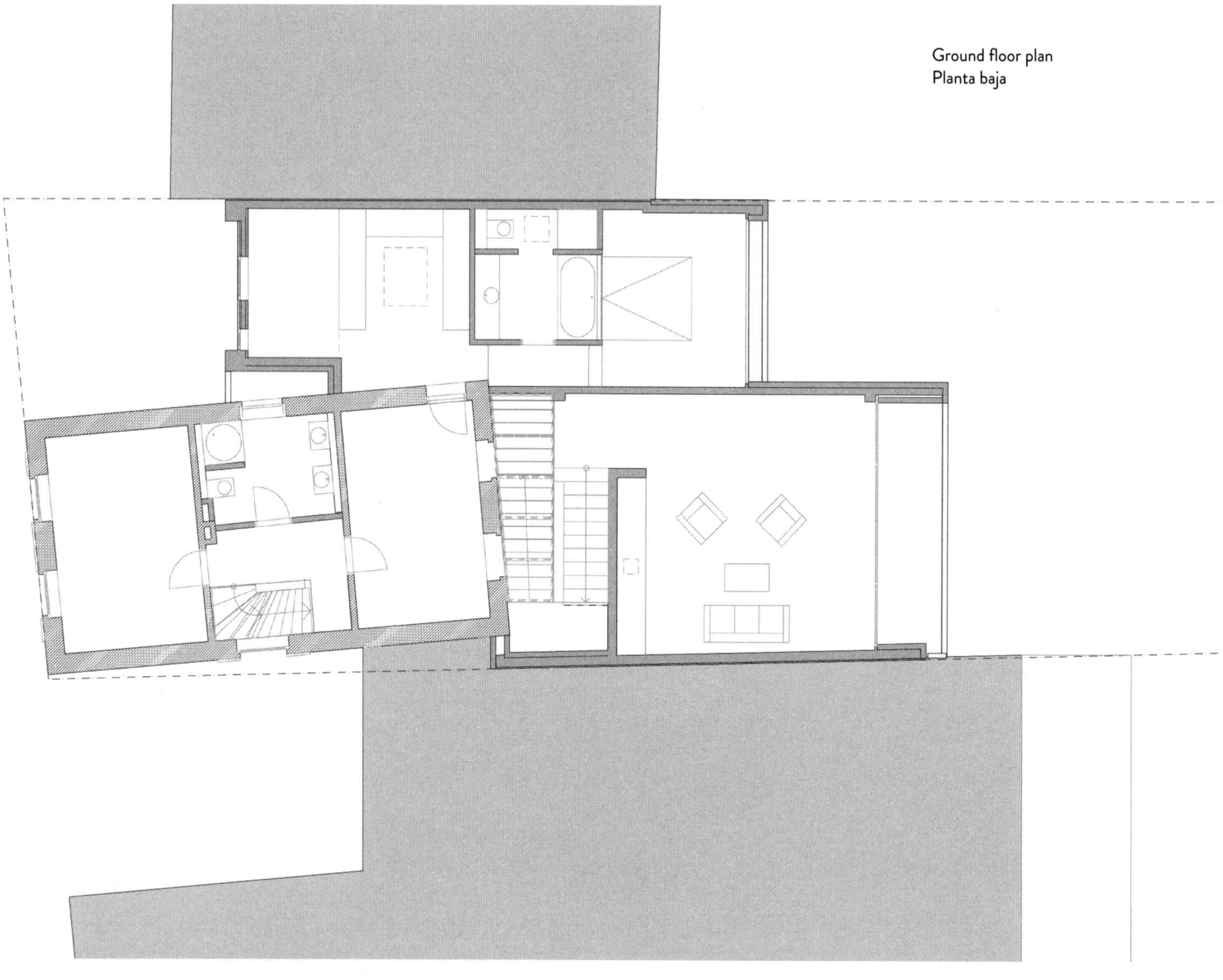

First floor plan
Primera planta

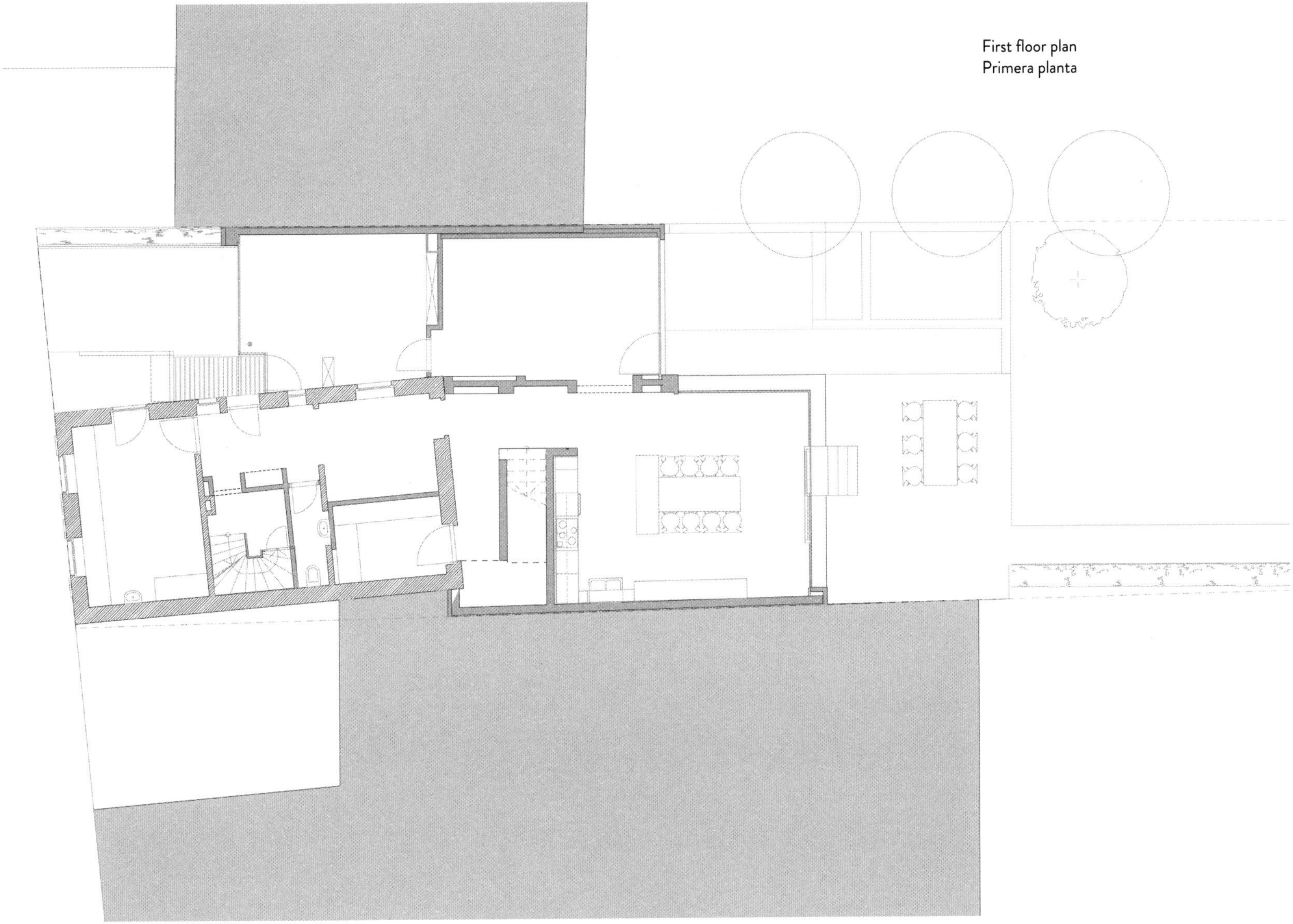

AYM House

Manuel Cerdá Pérez / MCP Architectura
Valencia, Spain
Photos © Joan Roig

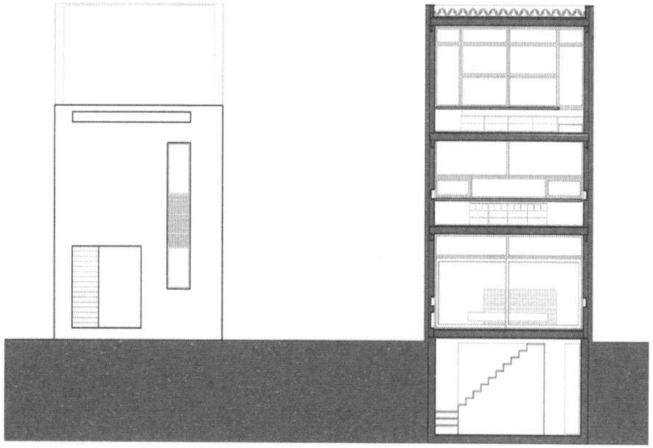

Front elevation
Alzado frontal

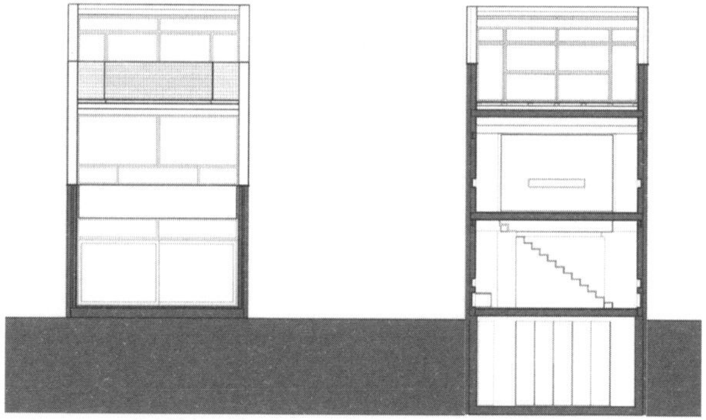

Rear elevation
Alzado posterior

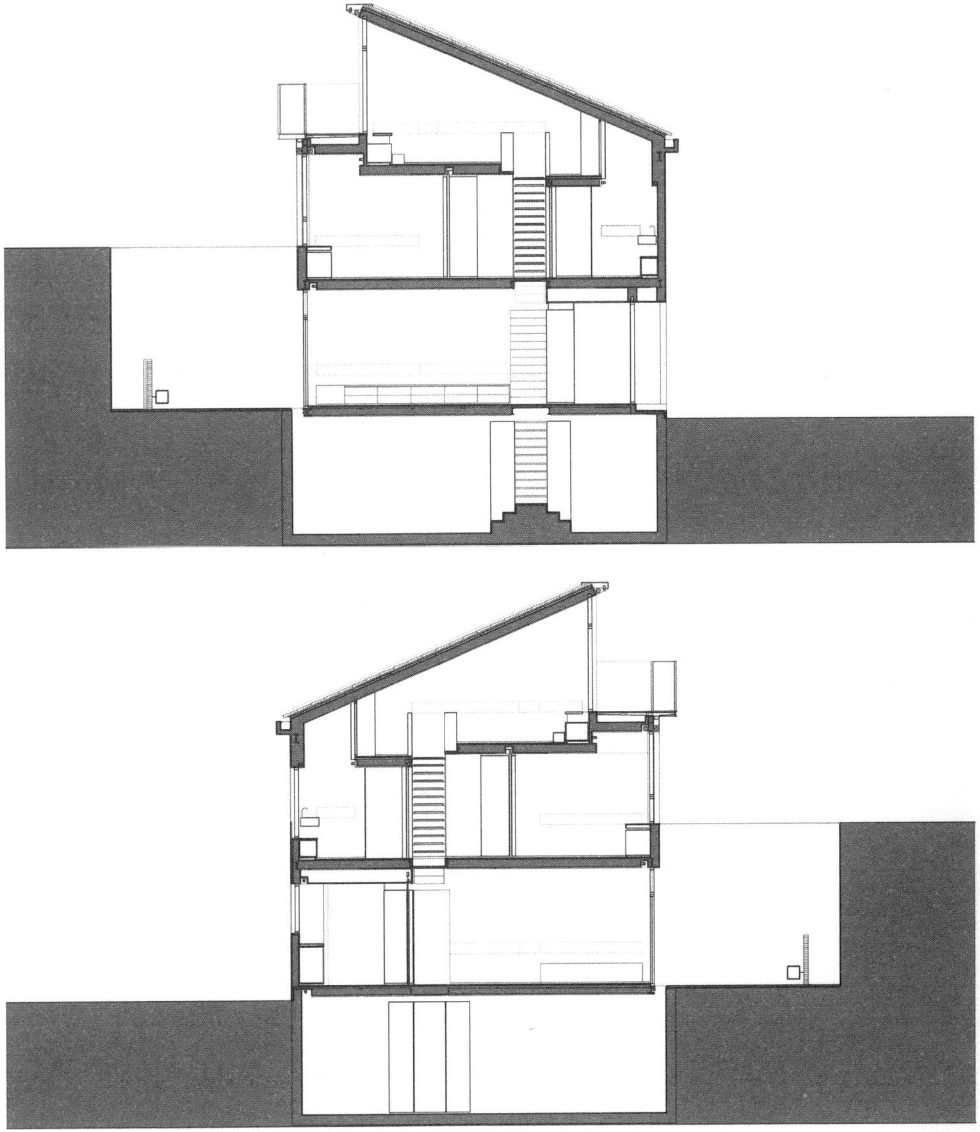

Longitudinal section detail
Detalle sección longitudinal

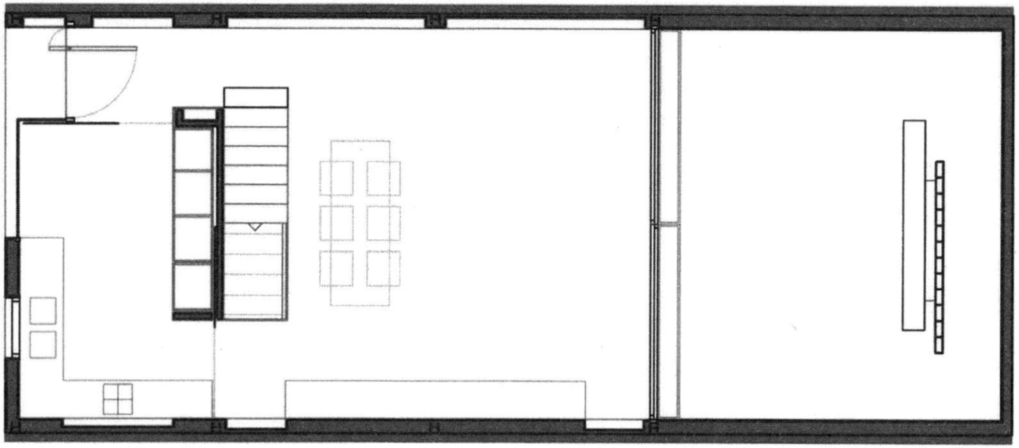

Ground floor plan
Planta baja

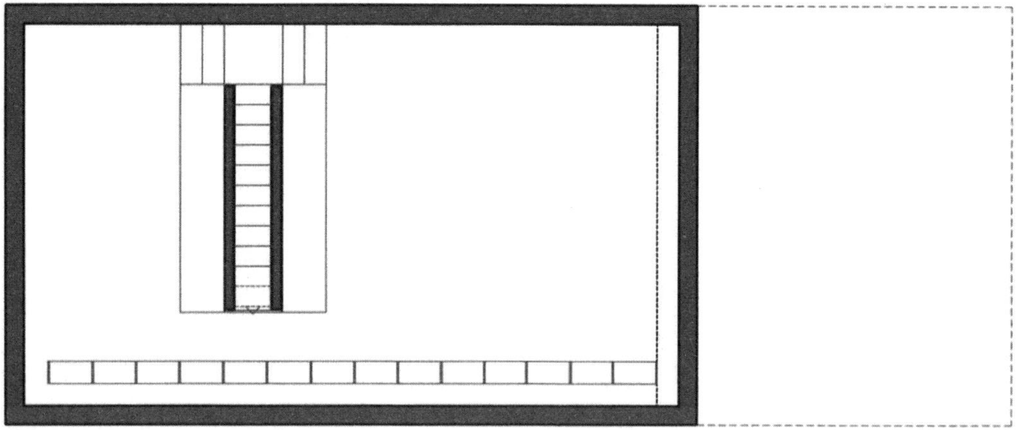

Basement
Sótano

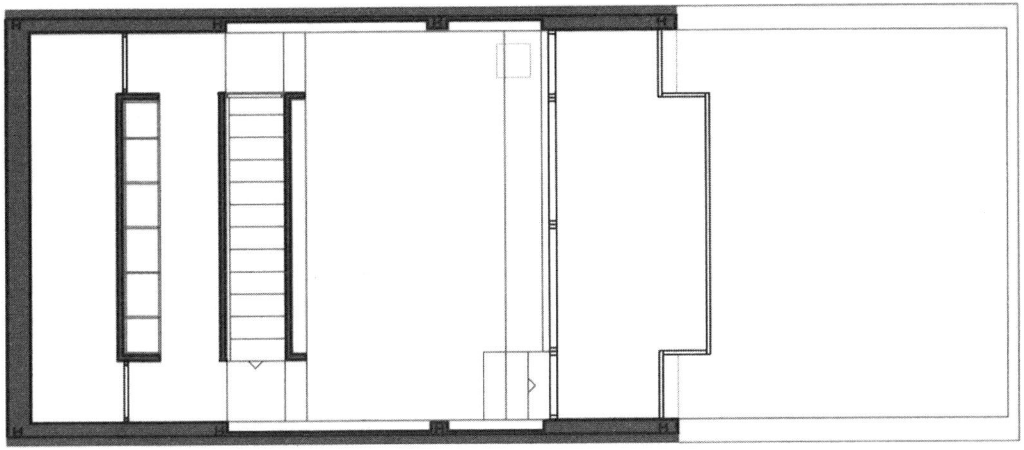

First floor plan
Primera planta

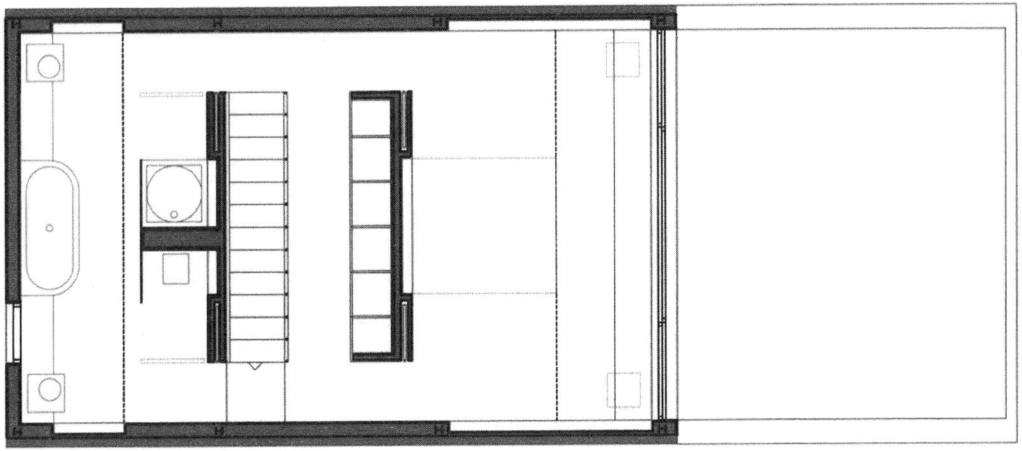

Second floor plan
Segunda planta

Fong House

Craig Steely Architecture
San Francisco (California), USA
Photos © Roger Casas

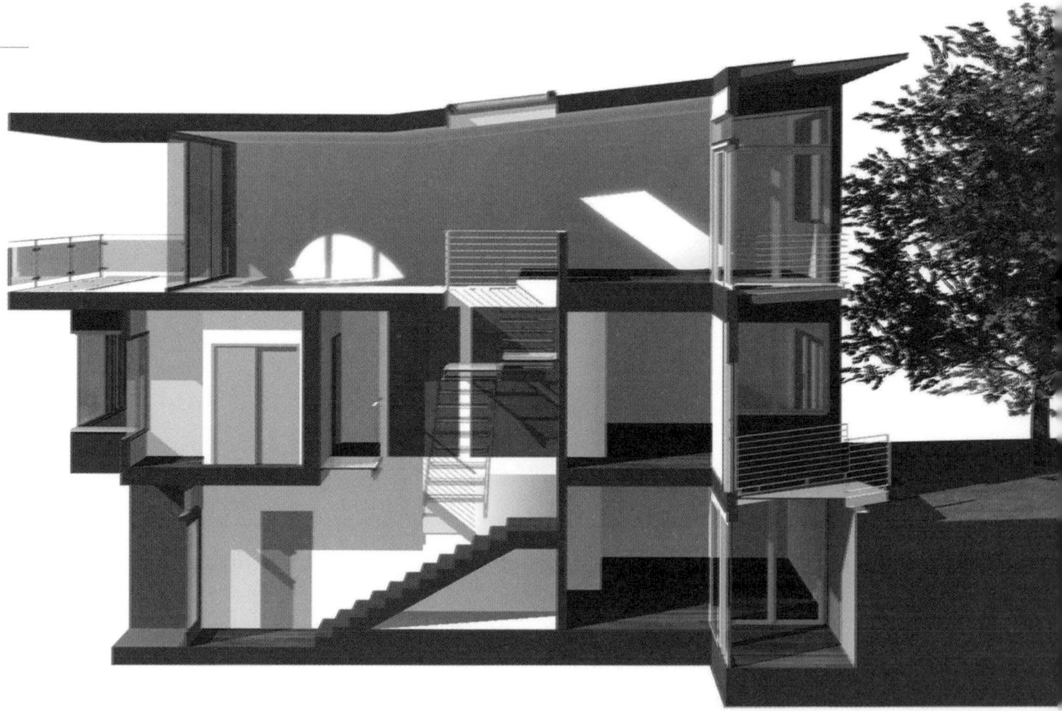

Three dimensional section
Sección tridimensional

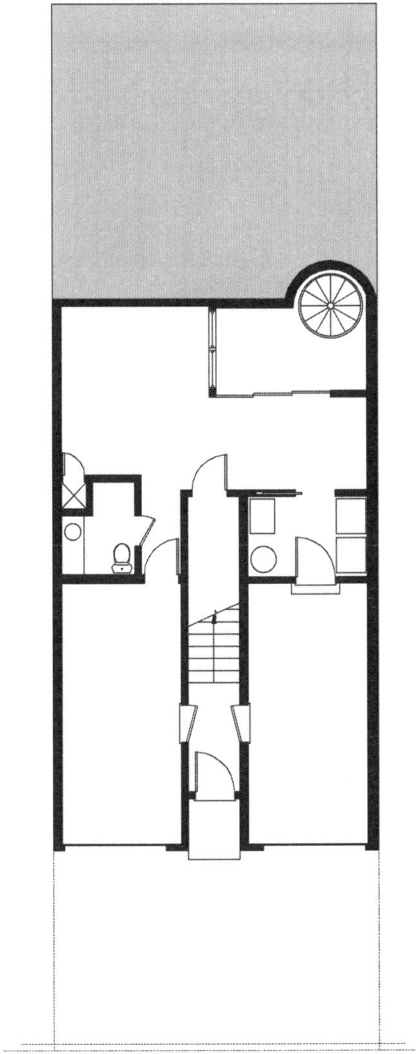

Ground floor plan
Planta baja

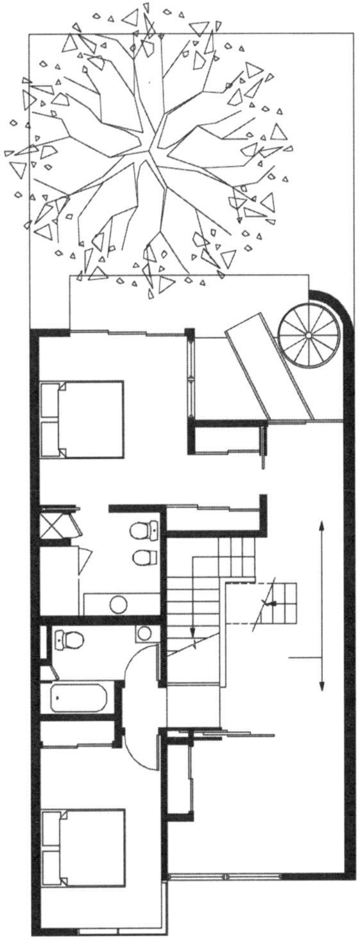

First floor plan
Primera planta

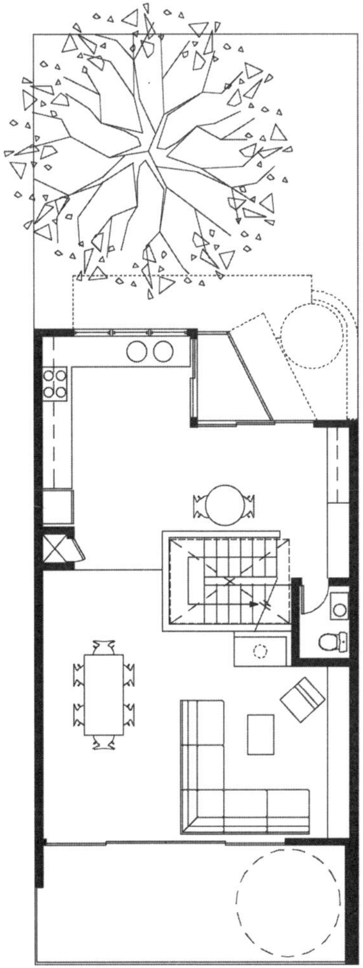

Second floor plan
Segunda planta

PML House

Manuel Cerdá Pérez / Julio Vila Liante
Valencia, Spain
Photos © Joan Roig

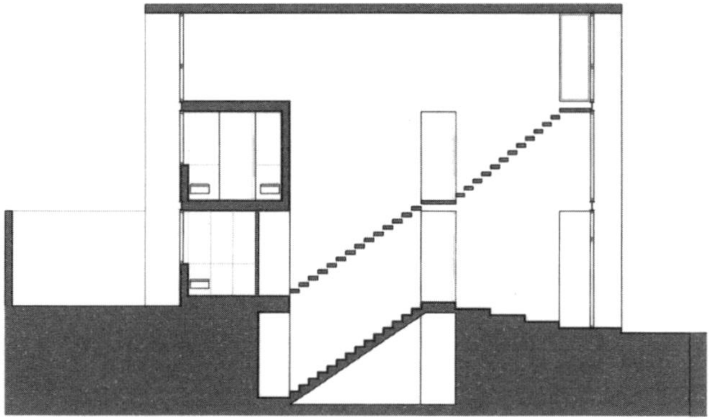
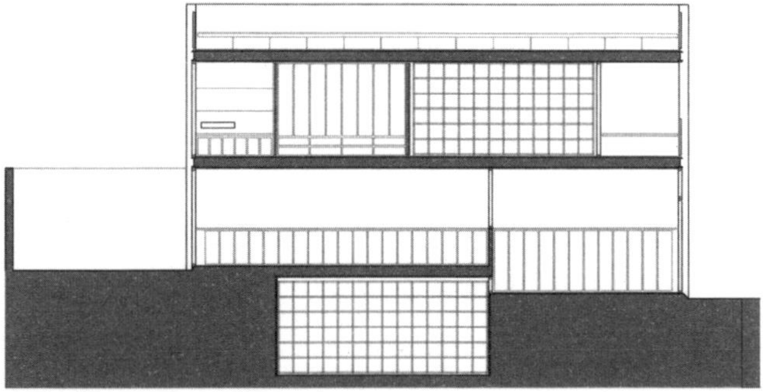

Longitudinal section
Sección longitudinal

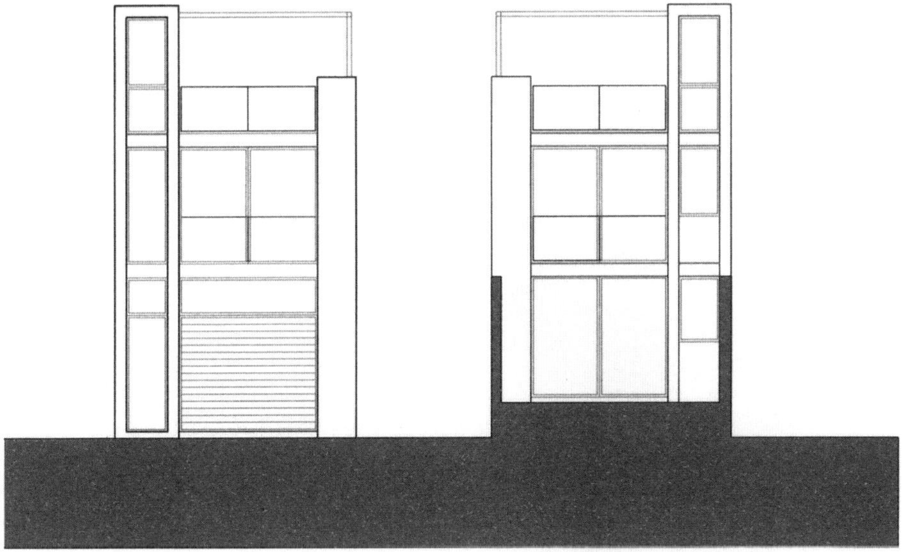

Raised
Alzado

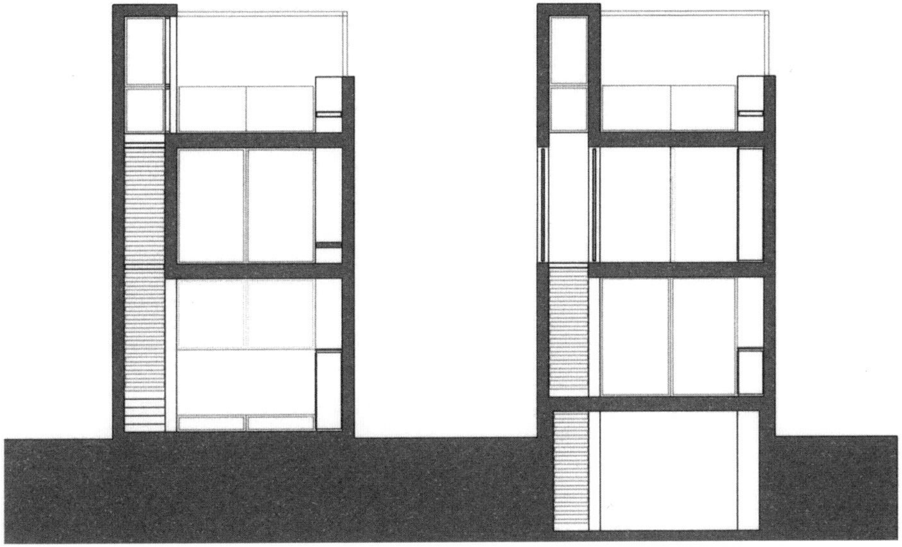

Cross sections
Secciones transversales

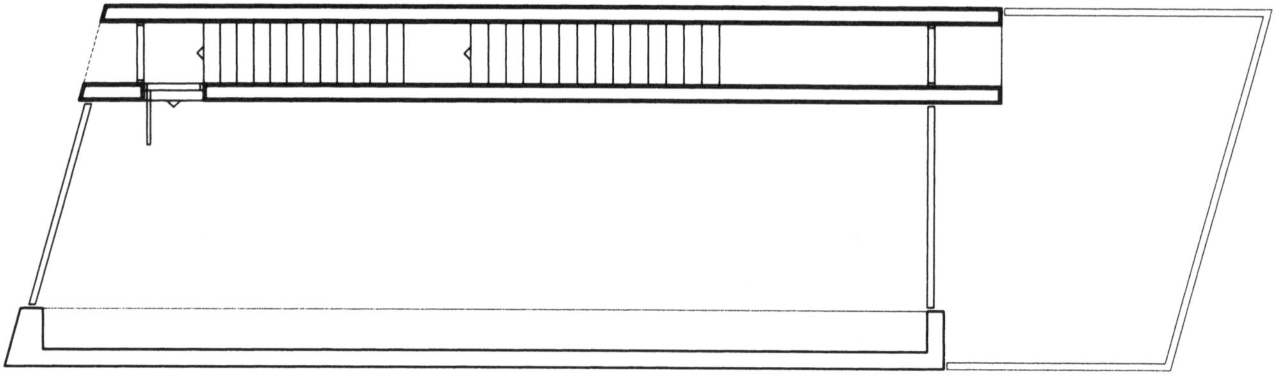

Second floor plan
Segunda planta

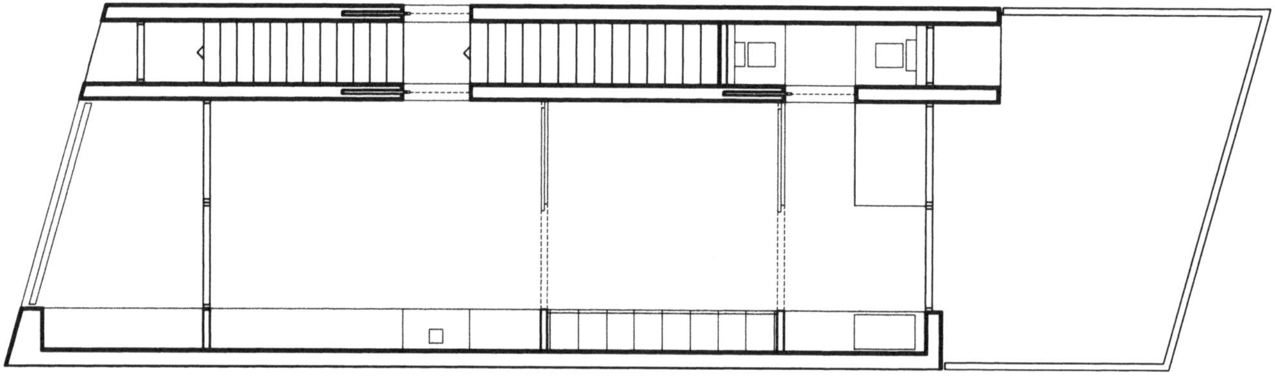

First floor plan
Primera planta

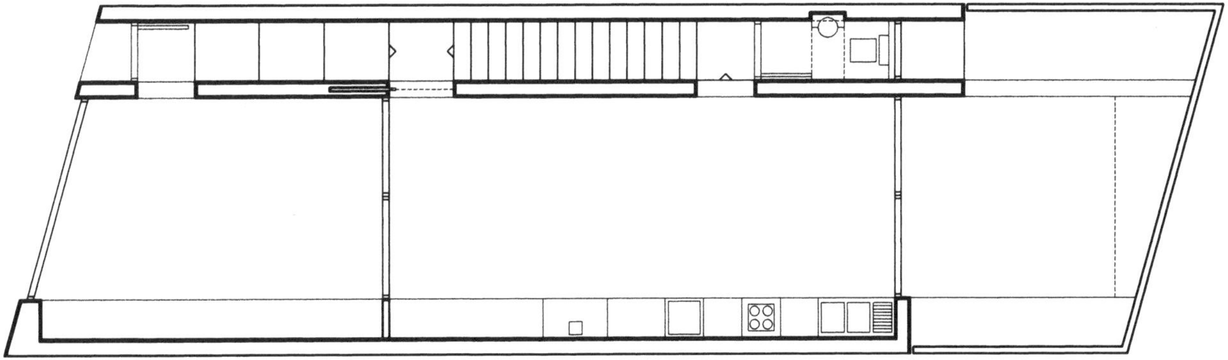

Ground floor plan
Planta baja

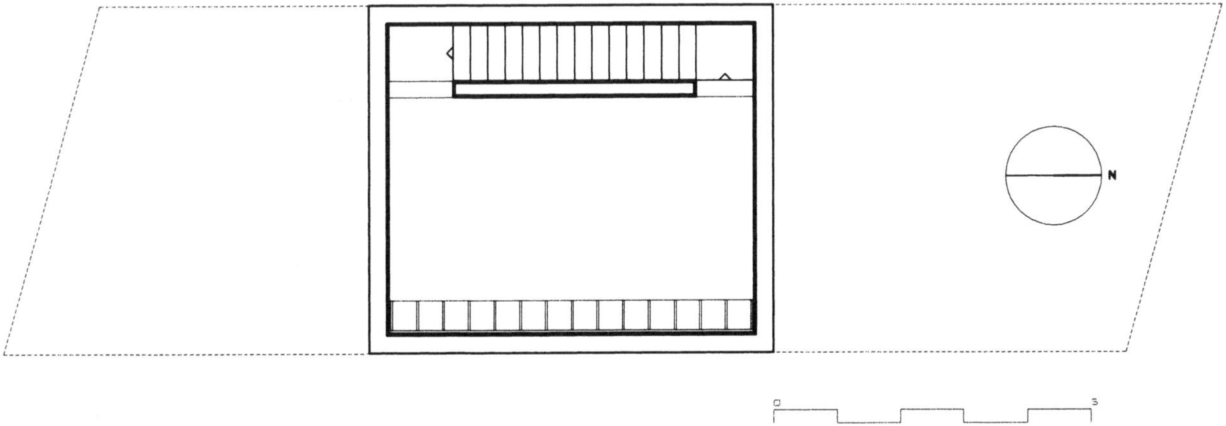

Basement
Sótano

Katendrecht House

René Heijne / Jacques Vink / Ruimtelab
Rotterdam, The Netherland
Photos © Mels Van Zutphen / Van Deventer

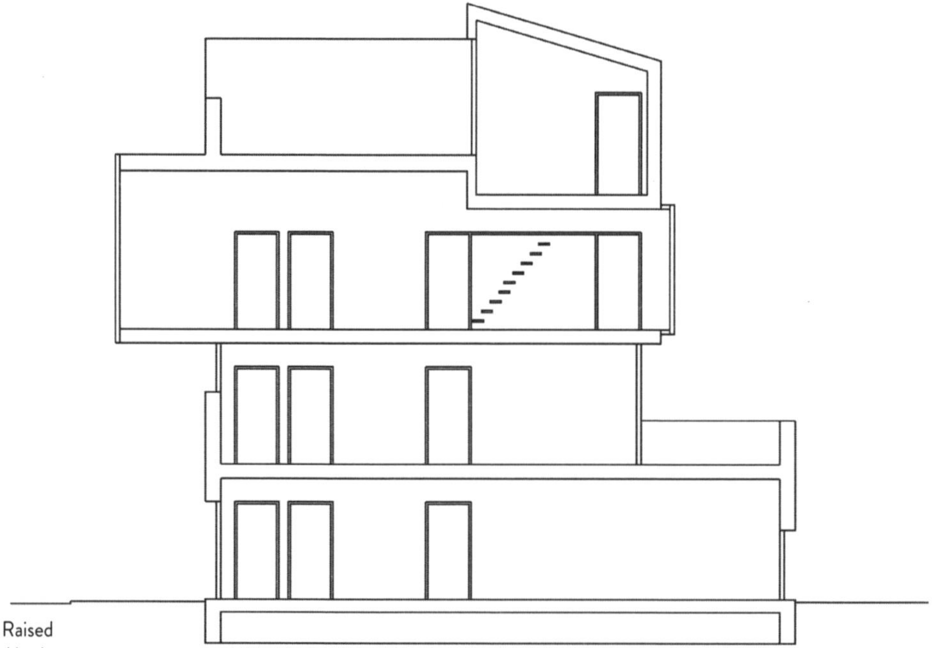

Raised
Alzado

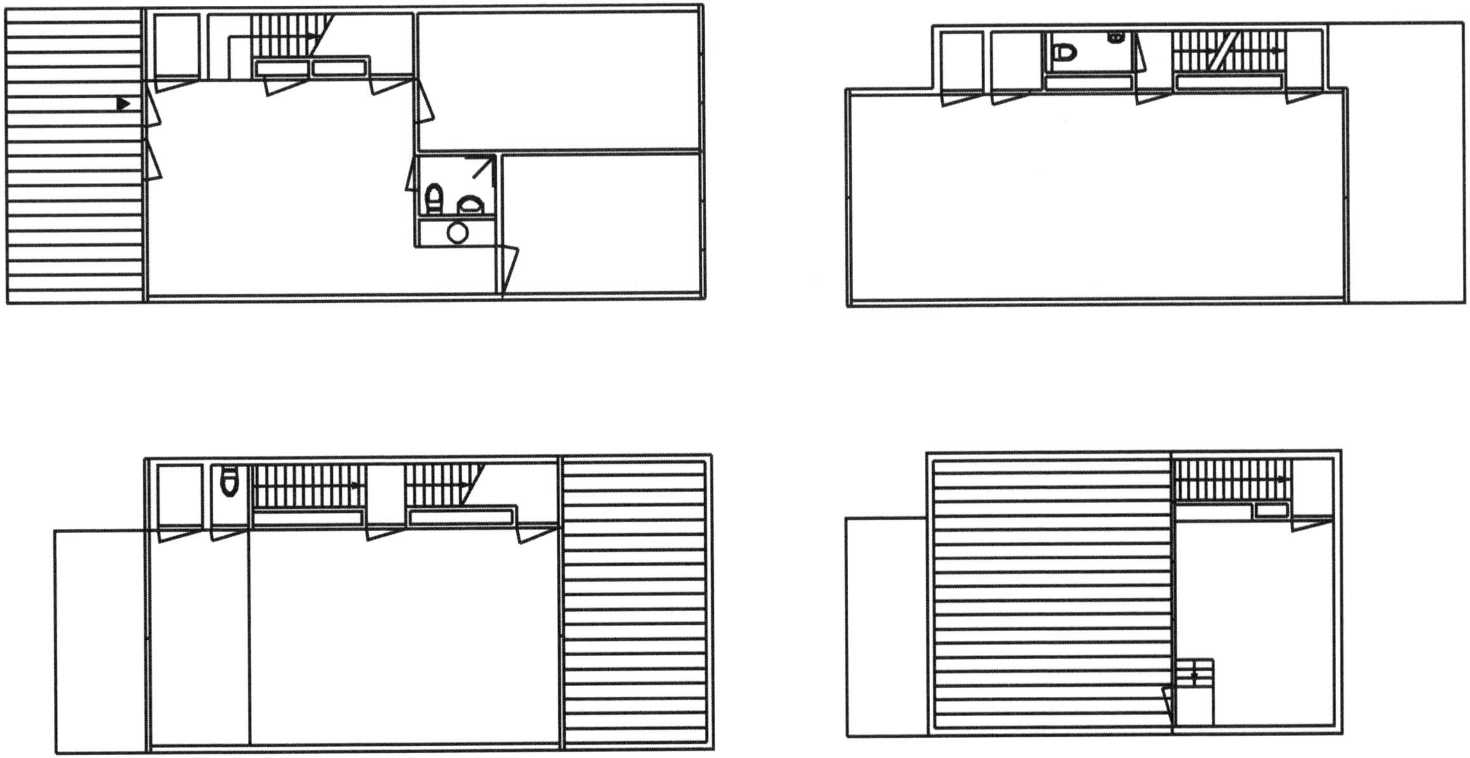

Floors plans
Plantas

To Catch a Breeze

Hyla Architects
Singapore, Singapore
Photos © Derek Swalwell

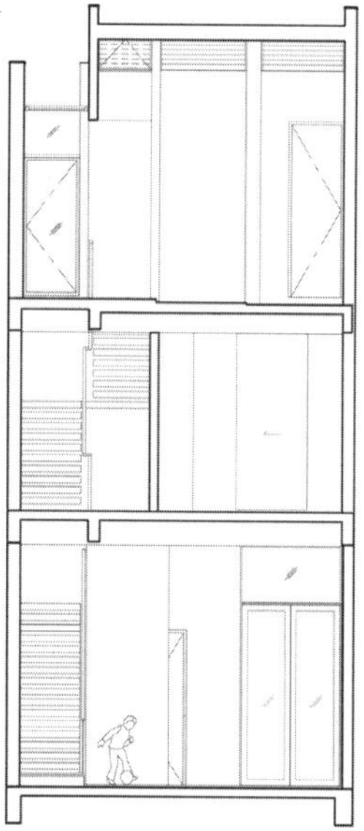

Section across staircase
Sección a través de la escalera

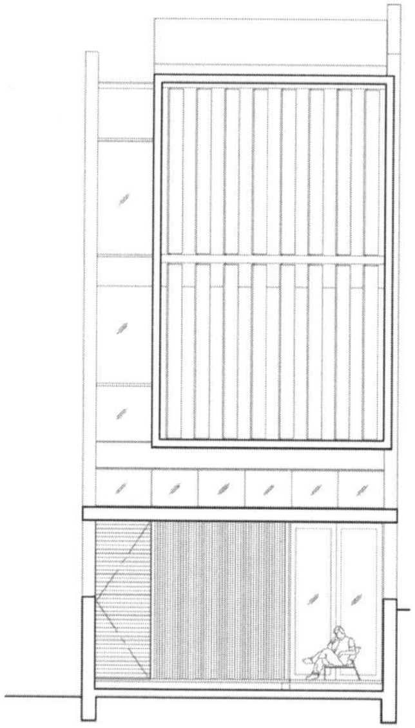

Front elevation
Alzado frontal

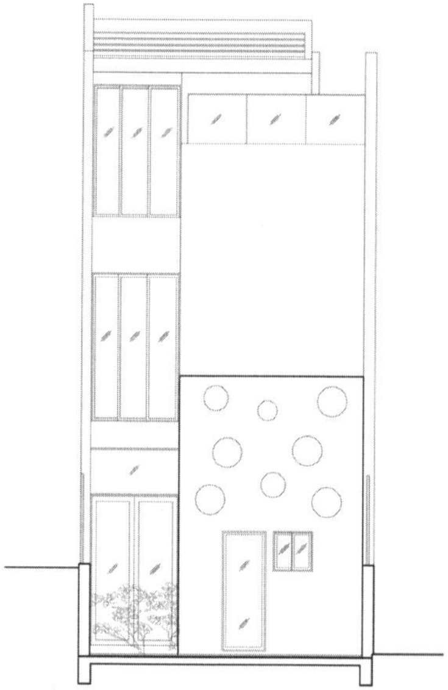

Rear elevation
Alzado posterior

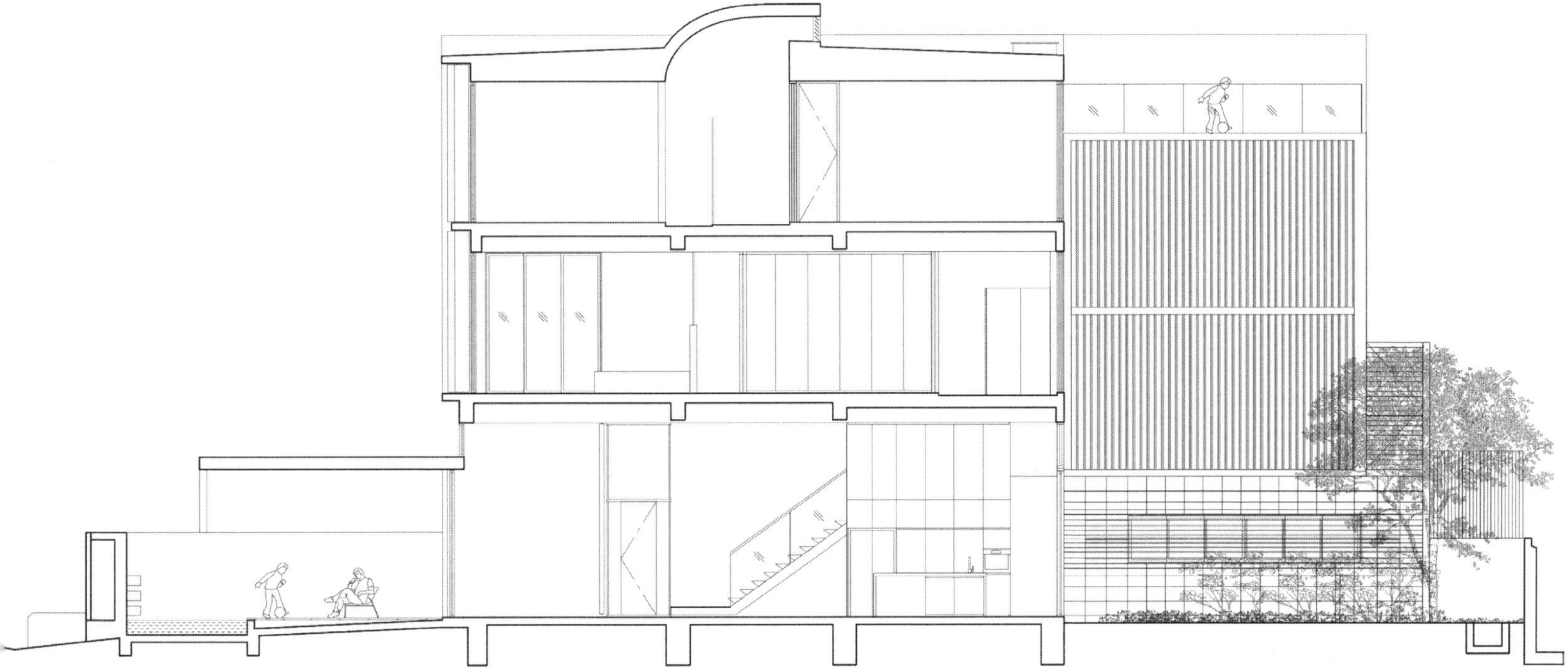

Section across garden
Sección a través del jardín

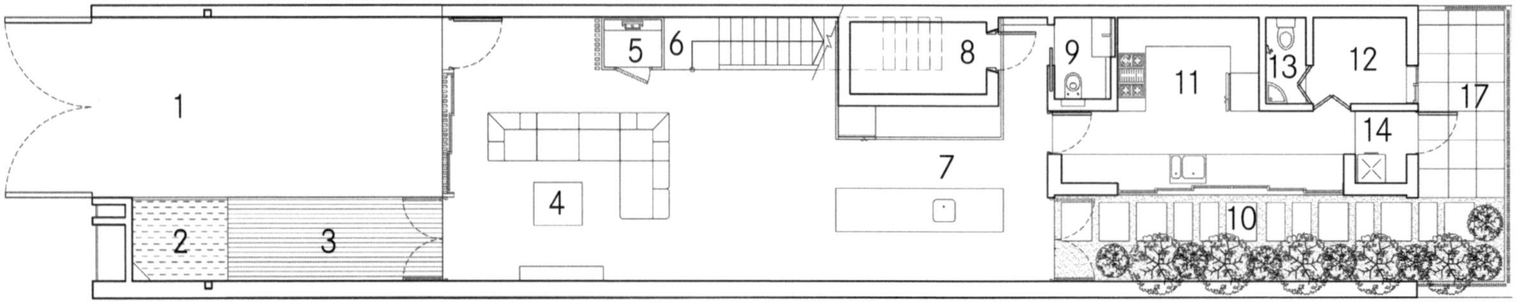

Main floor
Piso principal

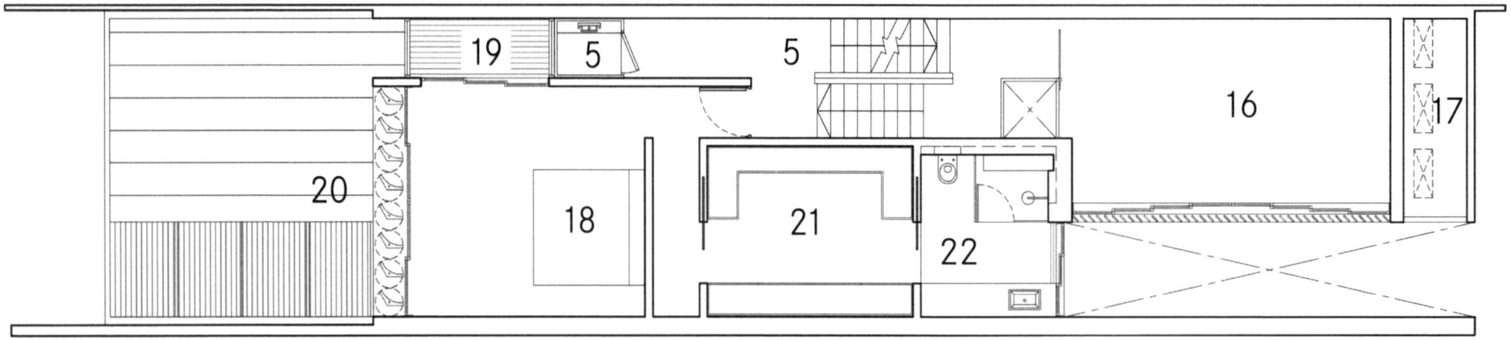

Second floor
Segundo piso

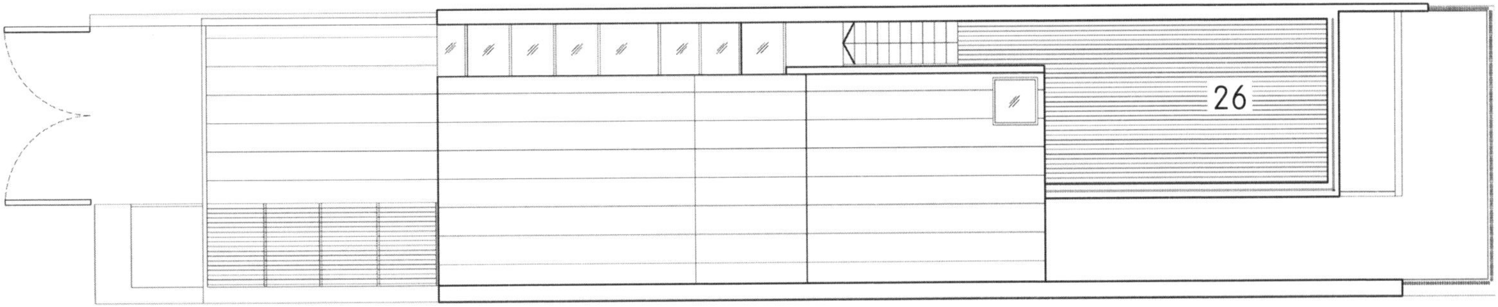

Rooftop
Azotea

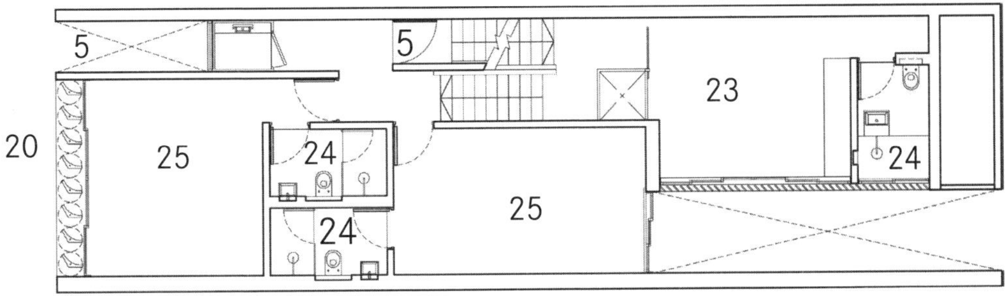

Third floor
Tercer piso

1. Carport
2. Pond
3. Deck
4. Living
5. Elevator
6. Stair
7. Dry kitchen
8. Household shelter
9. Powder room
10. Garden
11. Wet kitchen
12. Maid's quarters
13. Powder room
14. Laundry
15. Yard
16. Family room
17. Air conditioning
18. Master bedroom
19. Covered terrace
20. Screen
21. Wardrobe
22. Master bathroom
23. Study room
24. Bathroom
25. Kid's bedroom
26. Roof terrace

1. Garaje abierto
2. Estanque
3. Cubierta
4. Sala de estar
5. Ascensor
6. Escalera
7. Cocina en seco
8. Refugio de la casa
9. Aseo
10. Jardín
11. Cocina en húmedo
12. Cuarto de servicio
13. Aseo
14. Lavandería
15. Patio
16. Sala de estar
17. Aire acondicionado
18. Dormitorio principal
19. Terraza cubierta
20. Rejilla
21. Armario
22. Baño principal
23. Sala de estudio
24. Baño
25. Dormitorio infantil
26. Terraza de la azotea

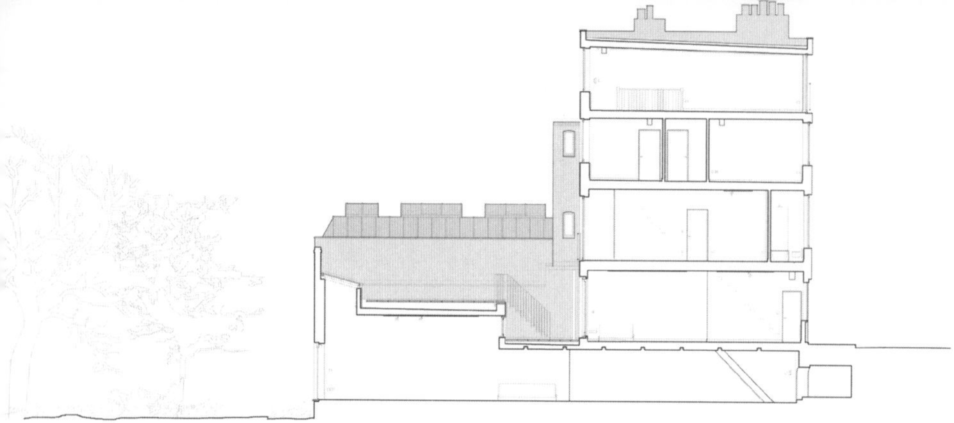

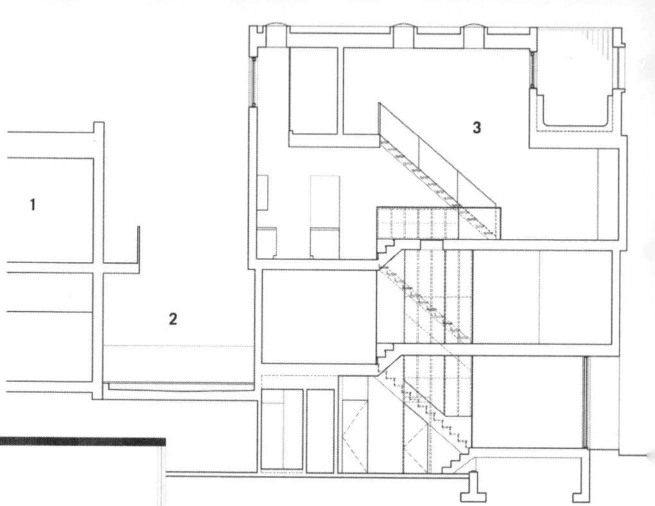
1
2
3

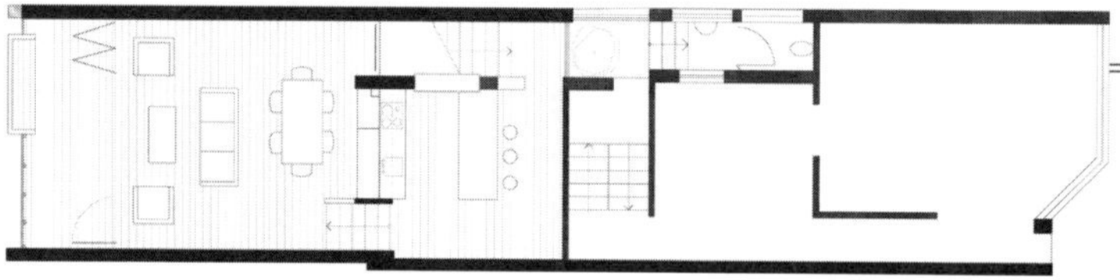

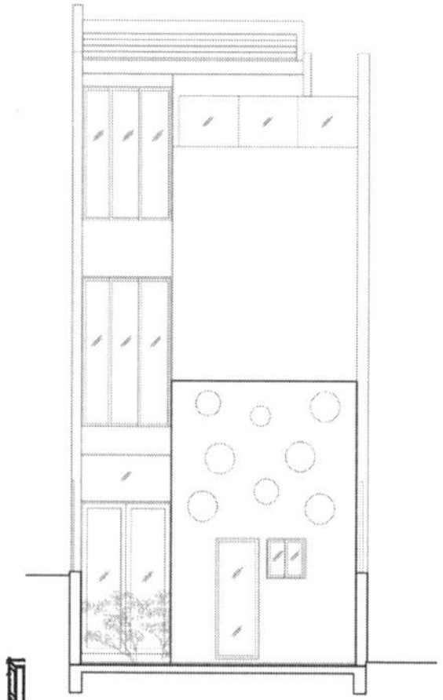

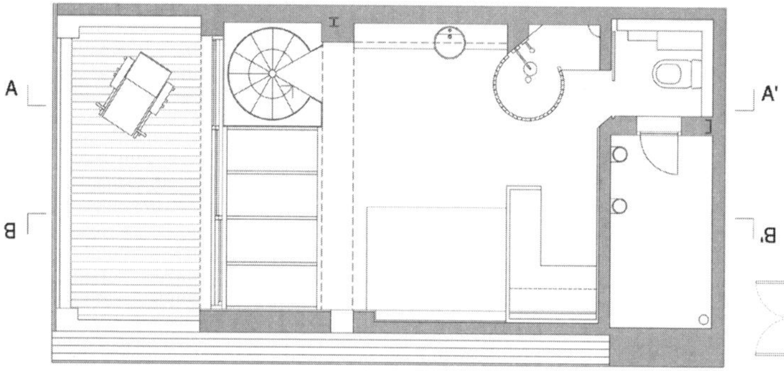
A
A'
B
B'

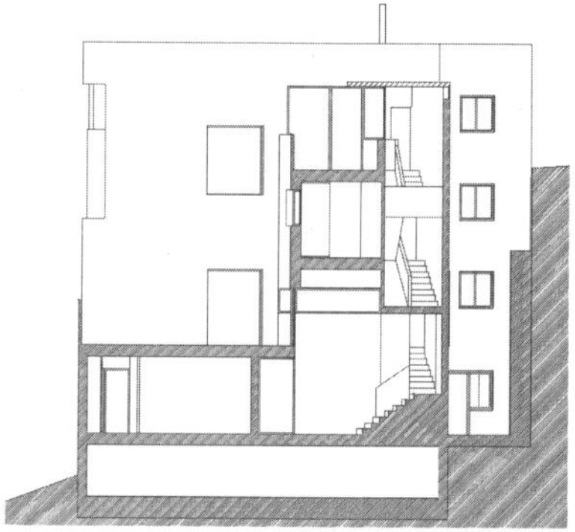

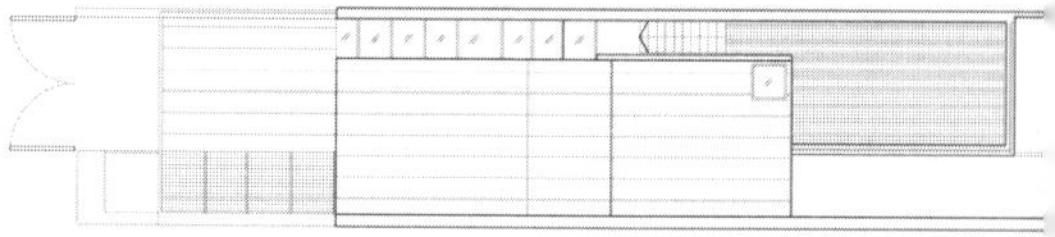

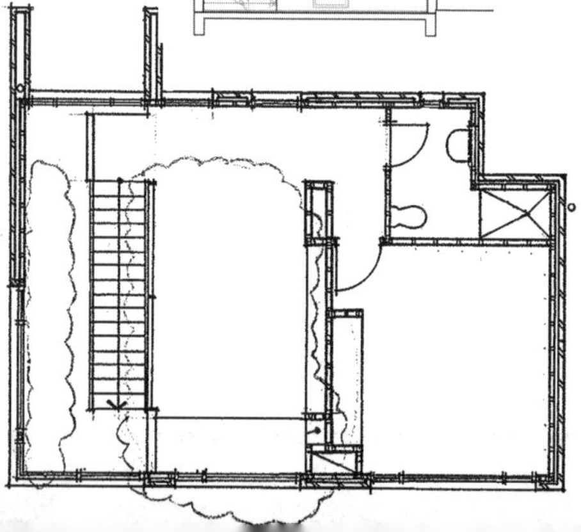

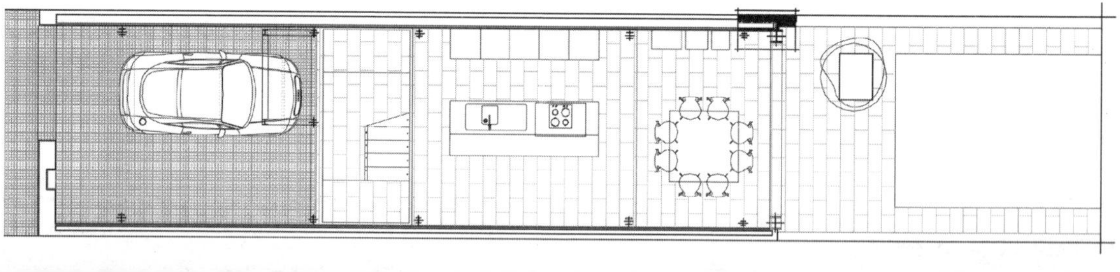